Demystifying EDI

A Practical Guide to Electronic Data Interchange Implementation, Transactions, and Systems

Russell A. Stultz

D1568132

Wordware Publishing, Inc.

Library of Congress Cataloging-in-Publication Data

Stultz, Russell Allen
    Demystifying EDI / by Russell A. Stultz.
      p. cm.
    ISBN 1-55622-708-6 (pb)
      1. Electronic data interchange. 2. Computer networks. I. Title.

    HF5548.33.S78   2000
    658'.0546--dc21   00-063311
                                              CIP

© 2001, Wordware Publishing, Inc.

All Rights Reserved

2320 Los Rios Boulevard
Plano, Texas 75074

Printed in the United States of America

ISBN 1-55622-708-6
10 9 8 7 6 5 4 3 2 1
0009

All inquiries for volume purchases of this book should be addressed to Wordware Publishing, Inc., at the above
address. Telephone inquiries may be made by calling:

(972) 423-0090

Contents

Part 2—Using EDI Software (Trading Partner Desktop)

Chapter 6   Setting Up Trading Partner Desktop **63**

Chapter 7   Installing Trading Partner Desktop (TPD) **67**

Chapter 8   Configuring Communications and Adding a
Trading Partner **83**

Chapter 9   Configuring a Trading Partner and Adding
Transaction Sets **97**

Part 3—Appendixes

Acknowledgments

Wordware Publishing, Inc. and the author wish to express their deep appreciation for the assistance and contributions made by the knowledgeable people at Mercator Software, Inc. and by Ken Sigler, instructor of computers and information systems at the University of Detroit Mercy. Mercator Software, Inc. provided the Trading Partner Desktop EDI software, on-line documentation, and transaction sets found on the companion CD to give readers the opportunity to experience a robust, fully functional EDI software system. Ken, who teaches EDI classes, provided extensive reviews of the text, made many valuable suggestions, and contributed review questions to ensure that this book is suitable for both the commercial and academic environment. This book would not be complete without your help. You have my eternal gratitude.

Russell A. Stultz
Wordware Publishing, Inc.

Part 1

Introduction to EDI

- About This Book
- Compelling Reasons for EDI
- EDI Standards and Legal Issues
- Selecting EDI Software
- Data Communications, VANs, and Security

Chapter 1

About This Book

Introduction

Electronic Data Interchange, or EDI as it is referred to by most people who use it, is a highly structured data communications system that is used to exchange commercial documents. Some people think that every commercial electronic data exchange is an EDI transaction. For example, when you swipe your credit card at a retail outlet or a gas pump, it could be considered an EDI transaction. Your name, credit card number, and expiration date is being sent to the credit card clearinghouse in a prescribed format. There, it is validated and an authorization number is returned to the merchant. In the case of a gasoline purchase, the pump is enabled and the transaction proceeds until completed. This all happens while you're standing at a gas pump or checkout counter. Within the credit card clearance system, the amount of the transaction is automatically billed to your account. User identification, accuracy, and information security are all issues that must be accommodated in these simple, fast events.

Is it an EDI event when the cashier scans a product barcode at the supermarket's checkout counter? Electronic data is sent to the store's point-of-sale and inventory control system. The scanned stock-keeping unit (SKU) number searches a database, and a price and description are returned to the cashier's terminal. Both the credit card and barcode scanner examples show the benefits of speed, accuracy, and convenience offered by EDI. However, the electronic document formats used to send and receive the data do not comply with sanctioned EDI standards. Simply put, the magnetic strip reader and barcode scanner are part of the same system. These devices are simple data entry units that are faster and more accurate than a manually operated keyboard. While benefits of speed and accuracy are similar to those that occur in EDI, these examples are not EDI transactions, per se.

This book focuses on those transactions that relate to the exchange of commercial documents between trading business and governmental enterprises. The document formats and interior data elements comply with strict EDI standards that have been established by a sanctioning body. In the United States, almost all EDI transactions comply with the American National Standards Institute (ANSI). In Europe, many organizations have adopted the United Nations' EDI for Administration Commerce and Trade (EDIFACT) convention. Both of these standards are discussed in Chapter 3. You should know that there are other sanctioning bodies that issue EDI standards for specific industries. You may run into Automotive Industry Action Group (AIAG), Voluntary Interindustry Commerce Standards (VICS), and other standards, depending on where you live. For example, the AIAG standard is used by European automakers.

EDI documents that are exchanged include purchase orders, invoices, functional acknowledgements (which are like a postal return receipt), electronic catalogs, requests for quotation, bid documents, and more. Millions of business, governmental, and business-to-governmental transactions involving EDI documents occur every day over dozens of public and private networks, point-to-point connections, and even the Internet. These exchanges occur throughout the world. Many of the public networks used by EDI are designed specifically to process these transactions. These networks, called *value-added networks*, or VANs, employ security and guarantee data integrity using a variety of technologies.

The enterprises that send and receive (or exchange) EDI data are commonly referred to as *trading partners*. The EDI documents that are exchanged, whether orders or invoices for goods or services, contracts, requests for quotation, or financial instruments, are all referred to as *EDI mail*. Notice the words in italics. These are EDI terms that are defined and used throughout this book.

Organization

This book is organized into two parts for two distinct audiences. Part 1 includes chapters that provide a layman's overview of EDI. It tells you the way EDI works by examining system components and common EDI terminology. You should also refer to the glossary at the back of the book for EDI terms and acronyms, and their definitions. Therefore, Part 1 provides an executive overview and introduction to EDI.

If you plan to specialize in the EDI field, or if you want to examine the many features offered by a state-of-the-art Microsoft Windows-based EDI application, then you should definitely read both Parts 1 and 2 of this book.

Part 2 is for EDI practitioners and those who are entering the EDI commerce field. It provides practical, hands-on experience with a working EDI system by stepping you through the setup, configuration, and operation of Trading Partner

Desktop (TPD). TPD is a full-featured Windows-based EDI application. It works in exactly the same way as Trading Partner Work Group, which is a network version of the program. A trial version of TPD is included on the companion CD-ROM located at the back of the book. This program demonstrates real-world transactions and encourages you to look at transaction set maps and the actual content of an EDI document, often referred to as EDI mail.

TPD is a full-featured EDI processing system that includes several communications programs and most of the standard EDI transaction sets that you will need. When you complete the activities in Part 2, you will definitely be ready to enter the EDI field. And hopefully, the experience will be as enjoyable as it is rewarding.

Part 2 also shows you how to examine and interpret the information found in an EDI mail document (or *transaction set*) specification. The hands-on experience with transaction set files helps you understand how information is organized and what it means. In Part 2, you walk through the specification analysis and transaction set mapping operations that are required to exchange purchase orders and invoices between trading partners.

This book also explains how common in-house programs, such as inventory control, order processing, and purchasing systems, must interface an EDI system to automate the exchange of data. While Part 1 points out the need to export to and import from external systems and explains the derived benefits, Part 2 steps more technically astute readers through some approaches to the development of export and import utilities. Note that these utilities can be written in almost any programming or database applications development language such as BASIC, Visual Basic, C, C++, Delphi, dBASE, MS Access, or Paradox.

In addition to Parts 1 and 2, the book includes two appendixes: EDI transaction set guidelines and a glossary of EDI terminology. These are located in Part 3. The transaction set guidelines are used with the hands-on EDI activities contained in Part 2.

The CD-ROM

The CD-ROM included at the back of this book includes the trial version of TPD. This is a full-featured 32-bit Microsoft Windows-based EDI application from Mercator Software, Inc., an international leader in EDI and e-commerce software. The CD also includes on-line references, EDI transaction set specifications, several transaction set layouts, or *maps*, and a number of files that serve as a basis for the import and export process that is required when your order processing system must exchange information with your EDI application.

Getting Started

Now proceed to the next chapter. There, you encounter a number of compelling reasons for the adoption of EDI. If you are either an EDI advocate or already involved in the EDI field, you can use examples like those described in Chapter 2 to both rationalize and cost justify the implementation of an EDI system in your enterprise.

Chapter 2

Compelling Reasons for EDI

Introduction

A simple EDI definition is:

> The transfer of structured data by agreed message standards from computer to computer by electronic means.

This is indeed simple and there is certainly much more to EDI than this. When you exchange documents using EDI, it is faster, more reliable, more accurate, and in the long run, much cheaper. In this chapter we examine a few scenarios that illustrate these points.

EDI Mail

The generic term for EDI exchanges, including credit card transactions, purchase orders, invoices, catalogs, and acknowledgements are called *EDI mail*. In the following discussion, both old-fashioned paper trading transactions and EDI mail transactions are contrasted.

Manual Trading

Continental Distribution, Inc. (CDI) is a large automotive parts distributor with warehouses located in major cities across the United States and Canada. National Auto Accessories (NAA) is one of CDI's key suppliers, or *trading partners*. CDI's inventory levels have reached the reorder level for several different stock-keeping units (SKUs).

The Purchase Order CDI's buyer who is responsible for the NAA account runs a reorder report and notices that the inventory levels for several SKUs are at or below the recommended reorder points. Each SKU has a unique NAA part number, description, carton quantity price, weight (which is important for calculating freight), and distributor discount. Using traditional methods, the buyer prepares a paper-based purchase requisition and submits it to the purchasing department, which is responsible for preparing and sending purchase orders to CDI's suppliers.

Once the requisition is approved, the information, including SKU numbers, quantities, and item descriptions, is entered into the distributor's purchasing system and paper purchase orders are printed on multipart paper. Due to the large size of the order, the documents are put into a large packing envelope and mailed to the manufacturer using express mail. Small orders are frequently sent to suppliers by facsimile, while large orders consisting of dozens of printed pages are unwieldy to transmit by facsimile.

The Invoice When CDI's purchase order package arrives at NAA, it is given to the order processing department. A data entry operator spends nearly a full day typing the purchase order information into the company's order processing system. Invoices and packing slips are printed. The system also adjusts inventory balances and adds freight based on the part numbers and quantities entered by the order processing department.

Cycle Time The packing slips are given to the shipping department and the invoices are mailed to CDI. The entire cycle from purchase order to receipt of invoice takes more than one week. By the time the ordered accessories arrive, several SKUs are completely depleted. The late arrival forces several automotive store chains that are normally served by CDI to seek alternate sources for the parts. They have a responsibility to their customers, and do not want to lose them to their competition. Maintaining the good will of consumers is vital in an extremely competitive business. Therefore, second sources are sought for those parts normally supplied by CDI. This is a serious problem for both CDI and NAA, as the automotive store chains' confidence in CDI and NAA is eroded by what is construed as both poor and sloppy service.

Errors Other problems exacerbate this situation. Because of the high potential for human error that is caused by the manual entry of purchasing and invoice information, document handling, misrouted and/or delayed mail, some of the wrong parts are delivered. CDI's out-of-stock situation worsens, and NAA must pay the round-trip freight bill for the wrong parts that were sent in error. This is the way it used to be, and still is, for many companies that are using paper-based transactions.

The Impact on Accounts Receivable and Billings Every sophisticated company monitors its sales terms, accounts receivable aging documents, and collections. Well-managed companies do everything possible to establish and then achieve their sales goals. And since time and money are integral, billing and collections must be given priority. In other words, once an order is billed, collection should be made as soon as possible in keeping with established payment terms. Using manually produced ordering and invoicing documents can extend the billing cycle by several days and even weeks. Errors can extend transactions still further. This means that a company may miss the current month's sales goals because of delayed invoices and postponed collections. A company that uses a revolving line of credit may be required to make additional draws to meet current obligations. This increases the company's debt service and ultimately decreases the company's profitability.

There's More The errors and document processing delays experienced in the distributor-to-manufacturer part of the supply chain only represents an incremental part of the problem. The same issues exist between the automotive stores and CDI when exchanges depend on manually prepared paper-based transactions. The identical problems occur when the automotive retailers order parts from their distributors. It also exists between NAA's purchasing unit and the suppliers of the raw materials used in the parts fabrication processes. The following diagram illustrates the transactions that exist in the entire supply chain.

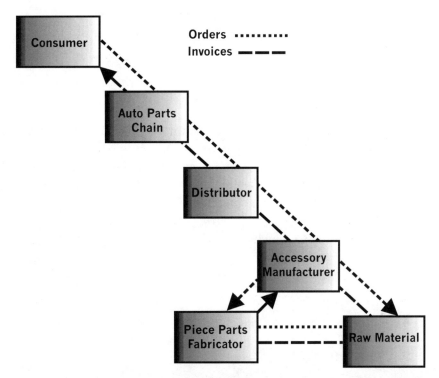

The EDI Transaction

Now consider the same transactions described between CDI and NAA using EDI. First, CDI accepts electronic catalogs from NAA to assure that all part numbers, prices, and stock status codes are current and accurate. In addition, both companies have data links between their inventory control, purchasing, and EDI systems.

Ordering CDI's inventory system automatically produces a purchase requisition report. This report suggests what should be ordered based on current stock balances and sales volumes (or *stock turnover*). The buyer examines the orders and makes adjustments based on any additional information that might require a change. For example, if a new model is being released that supersedes an existing SKU, then the buyer may want to order the new item and cancel the order for the old one. If a retail buyer has indicated his or her need to increase the order quantity for a certain SKU, then the buyer should increase CDI's order quantity based on that knowledge. Therefore, humans are in charge of the system, because they have information that cannot be anticipated by the system.

The EDI Mail Exchange Once the buyer releases the order, an electronic purchase order is produced as EDI mail and put in NAA's electronic mailbox. When NAA checks their EDI inbox, they download CDI's EDI mail along with any other EDI mail that may be present. The mail is sorted into different folders that are used to store each of NAA's trading partner's mail. When the EDI mail from CDI is processed, at least four distinct things are produced:

- A functional acknowledgement
- An electronic invoice
- Picking tickets and packing slips for the shipping department
- Inventory records for NAA's accounts receivable system

How Long Did It Take? Within minutes, NAA sends a functional acknowledgement (FA997) and an invoice (IN810) to CDI by putting these documents in their VAN's outbox. The VAN automatically relays CDI's EDI mail to CDI's inbox, where it waits for the retrieval of the mail. The entire transaction, from purchase order to invoice, can happen in minutes depending, of course, on how often each trading partner checks their EDI mailbox. The final step in the process is when CDI picks up and processes the IN810 from NAA. When this is done, CDI sends a functional acknowledgement back to NAA to verify the receipt of the invoice.

How Many Errors Were Made? It is unlikely that any errors occurred, as long as the original information was accurate. When information is flawed in an EDI exchange, it is almost always caught in an initial transaction. If flawed data originates in the buying company's PO, the error will be flagged because it will not match the data that exists in the vendor's database. This is especially true if the buyer's purchasing system includes data that is derived from a vendor-generated electronic catalog. These electronic catalogs are typically derived from the vendor's inventory database. Therefore, it will accurately match the vendor's information. Furthermore, the computer-generated data is isolated from manual data entry errors, assuring a high degree of reliability.

How Many People Were Involved? In the case of system-generated EDI mail, one person in each of the trading partner's companies can typically accomplish most of the exchange. Of course, barring an automated warehouse, the shipping and receiving departments must still use manual labor to pick, pack, ship, receive, unpack, and stock orders.

Stepping Up to EDI

When considering EDI, you must understand much more than the benefits just described in the preceding simple examples. A substantial amount of preparation is required—you can't just decide to enter the EDI arena without a thorough analysis and enlisting the help of qualified people.

Getting Started If you decide to install and administer the total EDI system process in house, then you or someone in your employ must understand the entire EDI process and each of the component parts that constitute a reliable information exchange. You also need a person who can develop a software interface between your current in-house systems and your EDI solution. This is typically a systems-level programmer.

Transaction Sets More than a thousand different EDI document types, or *transaction sets*, exist in support of commercial and governmental exchanges in virtually all industries. Because purchase orders and invoices were among the earliest EDI documents and are still the dominant document types exchanged through EDI, this book focuses on these. However, bear in mind that hundreds of other transaction categories exist.

When you consider EDI and the people who must work with EDI, pick personnel who are familiar with computer technology, software, and database management systems. Your EDI staff must know how to interpret standard guidelines, be able to map and extract the data that is sent by your trading partner, and respond with properly formatted invoices. Often, purchase order acknowledgements and electronic catalogs are also required. These documents (purchase orders, invoices, functional acknowledgements, electronic catalogs, etc.) are called transaction sets.

Value-Added Networks In addition to understanding the precise entries required in the transaction documents themselves, you must also agree upon and establish a suitable method of exchange. Here, you and your trading partners must decide on how you are going to send EDI mail to each other. This typically involves one of the many *value-added networks* (or VANs) that are available throughout the world. Even this arena is changing, as some network communications companies that specialize in EDI communications are beginning to evaluate and use the Internet as a communications backbone. One company, Internet Commerce Corporation (ICC), already offers such services. Trading partners can even use different VANs which can perform a network *interconnect*, that is, one network can connect and exchange EDI mail with another, so that EDI mail reaches the proper destination. More information about VANs is presented in Chapter 5.

Some trading partners that do a large volume of EDI mail have direct (*point-to-point*) connections with one another. This approach, called *interactive transactions* by some, is not as prominent as the other methods, but it does occur between major companies with sufficient resources to maintain a fully staffed and equipped information technology organization.

Consultants There are also EDI consulting companies that can help you. A good EDI consultant should be able to design a turnkey system and even write import and export software that exchanges EDI information with your order processing and inventory control systems. However, beware. Many consultants have a predisposition toward a particular brand of EDI software and VAN. Be sure that they have a variety of solutions and aren't just selling you their own brand of goods.

Service Bureaus EDI service bureaus typically exchange EDI mail for you for a nominal fee. However, to truly do the job, the service bureau must understand your in-house order processing and invoicing system and help you develop a working interface between your system and theirs. If they do not provide this interface service, then you may not realize the benefits afforded an in-house system. If you are simply receiving paper copies of purchase orders and sending back paper copies of invoices, then you will not have received the benefits offered by EDI. You've only pacified a customer that insists on EDI to keep their business. The manual data entry tasks and propensity for errors associated with manual data entry and paper documents will still exist.

In summary, if you want to:

- Grow your business by trading with major accounts
- Reduce your data entry costs
- Reduce your transaction errors

then you should give serious consideration to an in-house EDI system. If you want to concede business to your competitors, or if you simply want to stay small (which isn't necessarily bad), then don't install EDI in your enterprise.

Conclusions

It should be fairly obvious that EDI can greatly accelerate the trading process. Consumers encounter fewer "out-of-stocks," trading costs are reduced, errors are essentially eliminated, and each trading partner's accounts receivable ledger is made stronger by the fast turnaround of purchase orders and invoices.

The next chapter delves even deeper into the component parts of EDI. There, EDI exchanges are examined in more detail. The information there may give you some ideas about how you might approach the implementation of EDI.

Review Questions

1. Speed and accuracy are two benefits of using EDI over manual trading. Compare and contrast the two methods to generate a list of other EDI benefits, and give an explanation for each.

2. What are transaction sets, and what are they equivalent to in manual trading?

3. Describe three ways of sending EDI mail to a trading partner. In your answer, determine when you might use one approach over another.

Chapter 3

EDI Standards and Legal Issues

Introduction

In the beginning of Chapter 2, a simple EDI definition was presented. Then a comparison between conventional, paper-based trading and EDI trading was presented. You should now have a grasp of the benefits in cycle time, quality, and reliability that EDI offers over the old-fashioned manual methods. You were also introduced to some options available to you relative to how your enterprise, whether commercial or governmental, might enter the EDI arena. This chapter takes you a step further into concepts and issues that should be considered prior to and during EDI implementation.

Standards

There are numerous EDI standards that are used to serve a broad range of business and governmental enterprises. EDI transactions are dominated by two different standards: X12 and EDIFACT. For an exchange to be considered valid EDI, it must comply with a standard that is governed by a sanctioning body. The AIAG and VICS standards, mentioned in Chapter 1, are among others that are sanctioned by their respective governing bodies.

A Brief History

EDI was developed when trading organizations realized a need to improve responsiveness in order to remain competitive. They needed to exchange information faster and more accurately. Rapid advances in electronic data processing and communications provided the tools required to put electronic trading in place.

Some Background

In the early 1970s, large merchants such as Sears, Roebuck & Company and Kmart Corporation began developing electronic business communications. With thousands of stores and suppliers, these companies were producing and exchanging mountains of paper with their suppliers.

To support electronic exchanges with these companies, thousands of suppliers had to develop and maintain unique systems and file formats for each of their key accounts. Imagine the cost and confusion faced by a small company trading with several large customers. By the late 1970s, the problems and chaos that existed in the industry gave rise to the establishment of a committee made up of representatives from the transportation, governmental, and computer manufacturing sectors. Committee members discussed ways to improve electronic business communications through standardization. In 1978, the United States Electronic Data Interchange (EDI) Standard known as Xl2 was issued.

The Standards

Transaction sets were established by the American National Standards Institute (ANSI)/Accredited Standards Committee (ASC) X12. Another set of internationally approved message sets were established by the EDI For Administration, Commerce, and Transport (EDIFACT) standards group. ANSI/ASC X12 and EDIFACT are both public data standards that were developed to provide a common format for data interchange. ANSI/ASC X12 and EDIFACT standards are constantly reviewed and refined by the interested industry groups. New transaction sets are approved and included in updates when new releases of the X12 and EDIFACT standards occur.

Changes and Updates

Trade associations are primarily responsible for changes and updates to the interchange standards. For example, the National Wholesale Druggists Association established message format standards for orders transmitted to pharmaceutical manufacturers. The transportation industry developed message standards through the Transportation Data Coordinating Committee. Committee standards apply to carrier-to-carrier and shipper-to-carrier EDI.

Message Content

The Transportation Data Coordinating Committee system focuses on how to format message content rather than how to transmit the message. It uses a transaction set structure for defining different message types. Each transaction set corresponds to a business form used to conduct a particular transaction. The transaction set contains structured data segments that are used to present specific types of information. For example, the ship-to address, quantity, identifying number, and price are just a few of the included elements.

Data segments contain a defined sequence of data elements. Data elements are designated by their position within each data segment. The standard defines the format and length of each data element. For example, a date element in YYMMDD 6/6 format that reads 011021 represents October 21, 2001 (or 21 October 2001 outside the U.S.). The 6/6 specifies that the minimum/maximum length is 6. A value of 1/22 specifies a length of from 1 to 22 digits. Other format information specifies a date value (DT), alphanumeric (AN), etc. More information on actual transaction set guidelines is presented in Chapter 10.

More Adoptions

While the grocery industry was adopting Transaction Data Coordinating Committee standards, another group comprised of the Transportation Data Coordinating Committee, the National Association of Credit Management, and interested corporations formed an ANSI working group. They focused on general EDI between buyers and sellers of durable goods. This group now makes up the Accredited Standards Committee X12 on Electronic Data Interchange. With few exceptions, the ANSI X12 standards use the transaction set structures created by the Transportation Data Coordinating Committee.

In the late 1970s, the National Retail Merchants Association also developed a set of purchase order message standards for EDI. Retailers and suppliers didn't use these standards because they were poorly defined and ambiguous. Therefore, the National Retail Merchants Association decided to adopt the ANSI X12 standards.

New Applications

Originally, most EDI systems dealt with the exchange of purchase orders and invoices. However, status information has increased in importance and is now being exchanged in substantial volume. Today, most companies use database systems to manage their goods. Using today's technology, trading partners use EDI to update each other on the status of inventory, shipments, and more.

Aligning the ANSI ASC X12 and UN/EDIFACT Standards

Today, there is a movement toward aligning the X12 and EDIFACT standards. Following is the text of a statement delivered by ASC X12 Chair R.T. (Bob) Crowley to delegates attending the UN/ECE WP.4 meeting March 20-24, 2000, in Geneva, Switzerland. The group requested that Mr. Crowley keep them informed about the United States' plan for alignment between the ASC X12 and UN/EDIFACT standards for EDI.

The EDI community of the United States of America remains fully committed to a process alignment between its domestic EDI Standard, X12, and the international EDI Standard, UN/EDIFACT. I said this before in my last address to this body six months ago, and I say it again today. This commitment was made clear by vote of the membership of Accredited Standards Committee (ASC) X12 in November of 1992, and remains clear. We are now implementing a plan for this alignment and will see the effort through to a finish.

The membership of ASC X12 has approved a plan for administrative alignment with, and technical migration to, UN/EDIFACT. This Alignment Plan is not unlike the one that was outlined in general terms at the time of the last meeting of this body. It provides for an orderly path that can be followed to move the EDI community of the United States into the world of UN/EDIFACT, and includes the filing of UN/EDIFACT as an American National Standard with the American National Standards Institute (ANSI), confirming our commitment to the effort.

Watching ASC X12 work, however, can produce some misreading of what is actually happening regarding Alignment and other issues. There is no need for any confusion. It is only necessary to understand the procedures of ASC X12 to know that specific issues affecting the internal needs of the United States can sometimes appear to overshadow the larger matters with which we are concerned here. There should be no less than a complete belief that Alignment will take place.

The procedures of ASC X12 require an open discussion of all issues regarding any decision and provide that any discussion can be ongoing. The discussion of Alignment will go on for a long time to come, and it is right and proper that it should. It should be borne in mind that we have a plan and not a law. Plans are always open to discussion and modification based on changing circumstances. So it will be as we move forward into Alignment with UN/EDIFACT.

Since it was passed by the membership of ASC X12, the Alignment Plan has already been amended once, and I have no doubts that it will be further amended as we move onward with the process. The Father of EDI, Edward A. Guilbert, once said, "To be involved in EDI is to be passionately in love with change!" Change is to be expected as the result of what we do, and we should expect that the way we do things will change as well. The ASC X12 Alignment Plan will be a fluid document as we move toward its full implementation. This should not, however, detract from the fact that it is being implemented.

In summary, the countries of the world need not have any doubts about the commitment of the EDI community of the United States of America regarding the use of UN/EDIFACT or our intent to continue the implementation of our Alignment Plan. This process will take place, and in a timeframe and manner that will ensure that the needs of all, both domestic and foreign, are met as well as possible.

Current Status

As of this writing, the ANSI ASC X12 standards group agreed "...unequivocally that ASC X12 allow continued dual track development as long as recognized industry groups support both ASC X12 and EDIFACT standards." A summary of the group's conclusion is that "the domestic (U.S.) EDI user community believes that the migration from X12 to EDIFACT standards should be based on user preference, market forces, and business needs." This would lead U.S. EDI practitioners to believe that the ASC X12 standard will be in use for many years to come within the U.S. because of the effort and expense of changing to different formats. The adage, "If it ain't broke, don't fix it" certainly may apply here. Do you remember when the U.S. government decided to convert to metric measure? You can probably draw your own conclusions about what will happen.

Proprietary Standards

Proprietary exchange guidelines that govern the format of transactions that are exchanged between two or more trading entities also exist. However, there is some dispute as to whether proprietary guidelines, which are augmented by the trading entities themselves, are actually EDI. Some EDI purists maintain that for an exchange to qualify as EDI, it must be in compliance with a standard that is sanctioned by a recognized governing body.

ANSI X12

The X12 standard uses American National Standards Institute (ANSI) sanctioned transaction sets. Each transaction set, and there are well over a thousand, has a unique document and version number and contains data segments and interior elements that accommodate the industry being served. The transaction set number is always specified by the procuring trading partner, which is typically a large distributor, retail chain, or governmental agency. Hence, the data segments and interior data elements contained in the different transaction sets vary so that one industry can purchase bulk items such as wood pulp or cotton, another may purchase linear feet or meters of wire or steel rods, and still another may purchase books or medical supplies. The transaction sets used by the pharmaceutical industry are different than those used by the book publishing and automotive industries.

EDIFACT

The EDIFACT (EDI For Administration, Commerce, and Trade) standard achieved recognition when adopted by the United Nations and then the International Organization for Standardization (ISO) in September 1987. This standard was derived from two widely used standards: the American JEDI standard and the United Nations standard for Europe. Technical Committee 154 of the ISO combined what they considered the best features of both standards into the EDIFACT international standard. Both X12 and EDIFACT can be used with any order processing or purchasing application in which values are either generated or can be exported in character format for the purpose of exchanging data.

Both the X12 and EDIFACT standards are intended to be:

- Application independent
- Communication medium independent
- Machine independent

Both standards provide users with:

- Quicker delivery
- Greater accuracy in ordering and invoicing
- Faster fulfillment
- Reduced inventory levels
- Lower warehousing costs

Once an EDI standard and transaction set is agreed upon between trading partners, the internal data is easily formatted and exchanged using simple reformatting utilities. These can be written in practically any language including, but certainly not limited to, Visual Basic, C++, Delphi, and even dBASE or Paradox.

The transaction sets used in both standards begin with a header segment that includes, among other things, the identities of the sending and receiving trading partners, the date and time sent, a unique control number, and the transaction set type and version. The transaction sets also include trailer segments to designate the end of the set. The segment beginning with the interchange control header and ending with the interchange control trailer is often called an envelope. Several different segments exist between the interchange control header and trailer. Look at the following two examples that diagram both an ANSI X12 and an EDIFACT EDI document.

ISA Interchange Control Header ———————

GS Functional Group Header ———————

ST Transaction Set Header ———————

PO #1 (Segments)

SE Transaction Set Trailer ———————

ST Transaction Set Header ———————

PO #2 (Segments)

SE Transaction Set Trailer ———————

GE Functional Group Trailer ———————

GS Functional Group Header ———————

ST Transaction Set Header ———————

INV #1 (Segments)

SE Transaction Set Trailer ———————

ST Transaction Set Header ———————

INV #2 (Segments)

SE Transaction Set Trailer ———————

ST Transaction Set Header ———————

INV #3 (Segments)

SE Transaction Set Trailer ———————

GE Functional Group Trailer ———————

IEA Interchange Control Trailer ———————

ANSI X12 Transaction Set Structure

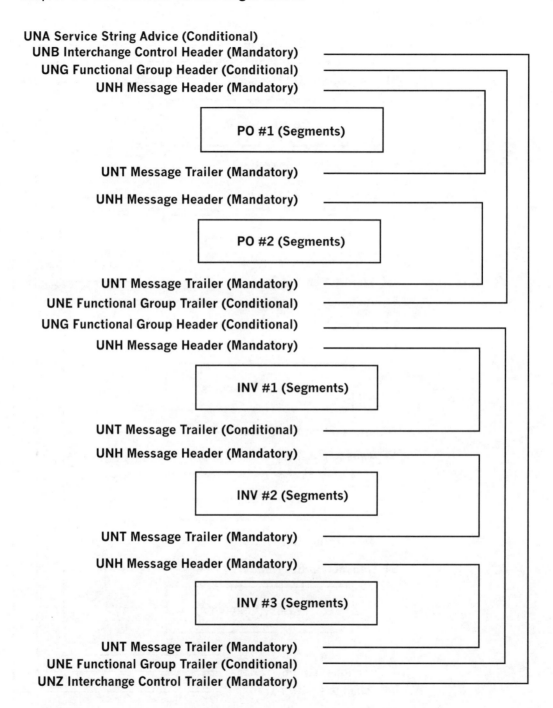

UNA Service String Advice (Conditional)
UNB Interchange Control Header (Mandatory)
UNG Functional Group Header (Conditional)
UNH Message Header (Mandatory)

PO #1 (Segments)

UNT Message Trailer (Mandatory)

UNH Message Header (Mandatory)

PO #2 (Segments)

UNT Message Trailer (Mandatory)
UNE Functional Group Trailer (Conditional)
UNG Functional Group Header (Conditional)
UNH Message Header (Mandatory)

INV #1 (Segments)

UNT Message Trailer (Conditional)

UNH Message Header (Mandatory)

INV #2 (Segments)

UNT Message Trailer (Mandatory)

UNH Message Header (Mandatory)

INV #3 (Segments)

UNT Message Trailer (Mandatory)
UNE Functional Group Trailer (Conditional)
UNZ Interchange Control Trailer (Mandatory)

EDIFACT Transaction Set Structure

EDI Mail Small and Large

An order or invoice for a single item with a single destination may only contain a single set of interior segments. This is the simplest kind of EDI mail document. The elements within a data segment include such information as the bill-to and ship-to destinations, quantity, unit of measure, suggested retail price, discount, and the discounted net price. When multiple purchase order numbers and destinations are included in an EDI mail document, hundreds and even thousands of separate segments are included.

Now consider a large retail chain with several thousand outlets across the country. Thousands of different purchase order numbers are used to designate each of the more than a thousand ship-to destinations. Each destination may include dozens of data segments for each destination representing different products, or *line items*. Similarly, the responding invoice EDI mail document must respond to each of the purchase orders received in the purchase order transaction set. The response must indicate which units will ship and which items are placed on backorder status or have been discontinued and are out of stock. The standard provides for status codes and other data elements that tell the entire story. Also included is the total billing amount for all available items.

Digging Deeper

If you want to dig even deeper, you can examine some of the elements contained in a typical ANSI X12 and EDIFACT document. Note that these documents are in ASCII format and can be viewed with any standard text editor including WordPad, the Windows Notepad, and even the MS-DOS Edit.com program. Note that the ISA and GS segments are always found at the top of the file. Matching GE and IEA trailer segments are found at the end of the file. In between are transaction sets that correspond to the type of information that is being exchanged. Each set begins with an ST header element and ends with an SE trailer element. You can think of these as an ST-SE pair. Now let's look at the first three segments of an EDI file.

The ANSI X12 Format

```
;Receipt Tag=960717,1601
ISA*00*0000000000*00*0000000000*ZZ*7083179000    123122721850
9607171113*U*00304*00000001*0*T*>
GS*PO*7083179000*3132721850*960717*1113*1*X*003040
ST*850*000000001
```

ISA marks the beginning of the ISA segment. Find the elements contained within the ISA segments. These are presented in order and described in the following list.

ISA Element	Description
*	The asterisk (*) is an example of an ANSI ASC X12 data element separator character. You will see this character throughout the ISA segment used for separating the fields.
00	ISA01, Authorization information qualifier. This qualifies the next element. In the example, 00 means ignore the next element.
0000000000	ISA02, Authorization information. This is the sender's password.
00	ISA03, Security information qualifier. This qualifies the next element. In the example, 00 means ignore the next element.
0000000000	ISA04, Security information. This is the receiver's password.
ZZ	ISA05, Interchange ID qualifier. This qualifies the next element.
7083179000	ISA06, Interchange sender ID. This is the sender's EDI address.
12	ISA07, Interchange ID qualifier. This qualifies the next element.
3122721850	ISA08, Interchange receiver's ID. This is the receiver's EDI address.
960717	ISA09, Interchange date. This is the date of the interchange in YYMMDD format.
1113	ISA10, Interchange time. This is the time of the interchange. Time is expressed in a 24-hour format.
U	ISA11, Interchange standard ID. This identifies the standard for this interchange. The "U" is the ANSI ASC X12 standard identifier code.
00304	ISA12, Interchange version ID. This identifies the standard version/release for this interchange.
00000001	ISA13, Interchange control number. A unique number used to track interchanges.
0	ISA14, Functional acknowledgement request flag. The "0" signifies that your trading partner does not need to receive an interchange acknowledgement (TA1) segment.
T	ISA15, Test indicator. The "T" signifies this interchange is test data, as opposed to "P" for production.
>	ISA16, Subelement separator.

GS Element	Description
*	The asterisk (*) is an example of an ANSI ASC X12 data element separator character. You will see this character throughout the GS segment used for separating the fields.
PO	GS01, Functional ID code. Indicates the transaction set type for the transaction sets in this functional group. In the example, the code is PO for a purchase order.
7083179000	GS02, Application sender's code.

GS Element	Description
3132721850	GS03, Application receiver's code.
960717	GS04, Group date. The date this functional group was sent in YYMMDD format.
1113	GS05, Group time. The time this functional group was sent. Time is expressed in a 24-hour format.
1	GS06, Group control number. A number that is different for each functional group enveloped by an ISA segment.
X	GS07, Responsible agency code. The agency responsible for this functional group. This code for ANSI ASC X12 is X.
003040	GS08, Version/Release indicator. The agency version/release of the transaction sets in this functional group.

ST Element	Description
850	Message reference number, where 850 is a purchase order. Other common numbers are 810 (invoice), 997 (functional acknowledgement) 832 (catalog), and 855 (purchase order acknowledgement).
000000001	Transaction set control number; a unique sequence number is assigned for each data segment. If five data segments exist, the last ST number is 000000005. Recall that for every ST (Set Top) element there is a matching SE (Set End) element. The SE element includes the transaction set control number. Detailed information elements exist between the ST and SE elements. Therefore, every separate transaction set within the EDI file that relates to a different purchase order, invoice, catalog, functional acknowledgement, etc., always begins with an ST segment and ends with a companion SE element.

The EDIFACT Format

The fields found in the EDIFACT UNA and UNB segments resembles the following example.

```
UNA:+
UNB+UNOA:1+TSI12013:01+TSITEST+921216:1000+5
UNG+CUSDEC+TSIINTL+TP+921216:1000+5+UN+2:912+12345PASS
UNH+45+CUSDEC+2+912+UN
BGM+AB+111+++TN:800000052
```

Find UNA (first line, far left). This marks the beginning of the UNA segment. Find the fields contained within the UNA listed in order and described in the following table.

UNA Element	Description
:	Component data element separator used in this interchange.
+	Element separator used in this interchange.

UNA Element	Description
,	Decimal notation. A comma (,) or period (.) is used.
?	Release indicator. A symbol that allows you to use the character delimiter as data.
Blank	Reserved symbol. Place reserved for future use.
'	Segment terminator.

Find UNB (second line down, far left). This marks the beginning of the UNB segment. Find the fields contained within the UNB listed in order and described in the following table.

UNB Element	Description
UNOA	Syntax identifier.
1	Syntax version.
TSI12013	Sender ID. Your trading partner's EDI address.
01	Sender ID code qualifier. This qualifies the element.
TSITEST	Recipient ID. Your EDI address.
921216	Date of preparation. The date this interchange was prepared.
1000	Time of preparation. The time this interchange was prepared.
5	Recipient's ref./pass. Your password.

UNG Element	Description
CUSDEC	Functional ID code. Indicates the message type for the messages in this functional group. In the example above, the code is CUSDEC for a Customs Declaration message.
TSIINTL	Application sender's ID.
TP	Application receiver's ID.
921216	Date of preparation. The date this functional group was prepared in YYMMDD format.
1000	Time of preparation. The time this functional group was prepared. Time is expressed in a 24-hour format.
5	Functional group reference number.
UN	Controlling agency. The agency responsible for this functional group. The EDIFACT controlling agency code is "UN" for the United Nations.
2	Message type version number.
912	Message type release number. The UN/EDIFACT standards release number for this functional group.
12345PASS	Application password. Your trading partner's password.

UNH Element	Description
45	Message reference number.
CUSDEC	Message type ID. Identifies the type of this message. For example, CUSDEC is for a Customs Declaration message.
2	Message type version.
912	Message type release number.
UN	Controlling agency. The controlling agency responsible for this message. The UN/EDIFACT controlling agency code is "UN" for the United Nations.

Legal Issues

Is EDI trading different from other forms of trading? For the most part, there is no difference between EDI trading and traditional, paper-based trading. The actual trade is a contract between the trading partners. It is nothing less than a contract of sale, regardless of the involved products. Simply put, the trade is not affected by the way in which you exchange information about it or any other related issues. In most jurisdictions contracts are made in both verbal and written form, or even just by each party's actions. These contract expressions can be just as binding as if an attorney had drafted them. Of course, the written agreement is superior, and can substantiate the deal, particularly when conflicting testimony of the involved parties becomes an issue.

There are some interesting issues to consider when contracts are implied by EDI exchanges. First, not all implied or verbal contracts are enforceable through the courts, especially when the involved amounts exceed statutory amounts. Therefore, the overwhelming reason for written contracts, even when not required by law, is to substantiate the deal and to satisfy the statutes of the involved jurisdictions. Even more, written contracts define and clarify each party's understanding of the specific terms of the agreement.

EDI trading often involves more than a single contractual relationship. It is common for a trade to impact relationships between each of the primary trading partners in addition to one or more network service suppliers. Also, by its very nature, EDI trading often occurs in long chains between vertically related trading partners. Trades can encompass extremely long, diverse chains. A problem at one end of the trade can impact a large number of separate contractual relationships.

Hence, the legal aspects of EDI may not be as simple as they initially seem. Remember, much depends on jurisdictions and the amounts. However, prudent trading partners should ensure that established interchange agreements clearly define each of their positions in case legal issues are encountered.

Trading Partner Agreements

Given the uncertainty of EDI and the law, users should exercise care in developing and entering into trading partner and third-party agreements. Comprehensive trading partner and third-party agreements should certainly be considered when engaging in EDI trade. In addition to conventional "standard terms and conditions," which (with some variability) are used to define conventional trading relationships, such as the terms and conditions typically appearing on purchase orders, users should consider what impact data communications and computer systems have on their business correspondence and trading relationships. The agreements should also include provisions for the manner of customarily doing business, such as use of responses, acknowledgement 997s, and other provisions that are appropriate for EDI trading.

Many EDI users enter into special agreements with their trading partners to govern EDI. Provisions that are included in these agreements can vary from user to user. Following are typical issues that are addressed in trading partner agreements.

- The specification of the type of EDI format the parties will use.
- The specification of the third-party network (if any) each partner will use.
- The division of the costs of conducting EDI.
- The confidentiality of messages.
- The authentication of messages.
- The records trading partners must keep.
- An affirmation of the legal enforceability of the transactions entered under the agreement.
- The procedures for requesting and communicating legal offers, acknowledgements and acceptances and amendments thereto.
- The specification of the time when messages become effective.
- The interpretation of EDI codes.
- The specification of the substantive terms and conditions that will govern underlying transactions communicated through EDI.
- The allocation of responsibility (including liability for any resulting damages) for any EDI error or fraud or for the occurrence of uncontrollable disasters.

Similar considerations are required for financial institutions and clearinghouses used in the transmission of the Payment Order/Remittance Advice (transaction set 820).

Third-Party Agreements

If one or more trading partners employ a value-added network (VAN), the VAN will probably require that the user enter into a data communications agreement. Among the issues the user should take into account when considering such agreements are:

- A description of the services to be provided.
- The warranty by the VAN of its services.
- The liability of the VAN for a breach of the agreement or any damages resulting from the mistakes of the VAN or its employees.
- The security, confidentiality, and integrity of messages handled by the VAN.
- The responsibility of the VAN in the event of a system failure or disaster.
- The disposal of data stored by the VAN in the event of a disagreement or an interruption or termination of services.
- A description of the applicable pricing structure.
- The termination of the agreement.
- An assumption of an independent third-party review of the third-party vendor.

Laws, Rules, and Regulations

There is no adequate or comprehensive source of "EDI law." Therefore, no attempt is made to list any. When implementing EDI, trading partners and their attorneys should consider whether any special laws, rules, or governmental regulations apply to the type of transaction being performed or to the people involved in the completion of EDI transactions. Regulations may restrict and can even prevent the implementation of EDI. How can this be? It is common for governmental regulations to require (or at least be interpreted to require) that legal documents be written on paper and ink with original signatures. The American Bar Association (ABA) has developed a *Model Electronic Data Interchange Trading Partner Agreement and Commentary*. Copies of this document can be obtained by contacting the ABA directly.

Review Questions

1. Compare and contrast the EDI standards presented in this chapter. In particular, identify situations where one would be preferred or necessary over another.

2. Describe each of the three layers of control envelopes in a typical ASC X12 transmission.

3. Identify and explain three issues that need to be addressed in an EDI trading partner agreement.

Chapter 4

Selecting EDI Software

Introduction

This chapter provides a number of suggestions for those who are looking for an EDI package for their organization, whether it is a commercial enterprise or a governmental agency. Before you automate any process, it is important to conduct a detailed analysis of your current system, staffing, industry, and certainly whether or not your investment is worthwhile. These and other key issues described below must be considered.

- Trading practices used in your industry
- Systems that you currently use (manual and computerized)
- Experience, qualifications, and potential of your staff
- Benefits that your organization can derive from EDI (operational and financial)
- How EDI is being used by similar organizations and trading partners
- Costs associated with converting from your current systems to an EDI system
- Ability to interface your current ordering system with the EDI system
- Available EDI applications
- EDI alternatives

Analyzing Your Business

The list of issues is essentially an analysis of your industry and the way that your company trades within that industry. It is vital that you start with a clear understanding of the ways things are presently being done, your current systems and staff, and just as important, how your industry fits into the industry you serve.

Specifically, what is happening in your industry? What systems are being used to successfully trade? If you are on the supply side of your industry, then you need diagram your order entry, invoicing, and inventory control systems. You may also need to examine your manufacturing control systems to determine how it interacts with your ordering and inventory systems. Retail companies use EDI to purchase finished goods and in conjunction with stocking and point-of-sale systems. Manufacturing companies use EDI to purchase piece parts and raw materials. EDI systems can also be linked to the company's manufacturing control systems. The balance of this chapter examines the issues listed above, in addition to exploring a few different system scenarios.

Trading Practices

EDI often becomes an issue when a major trading partner strongly suggests, or even demands, that you and your peers install EDI systems. The trading partner will often suggest sources for EDI software as well as the preferred *value-added network*, or VAN. If the trading partner represents a major amount of business, you may find yourself without a choice. This is particularly true if your competitors are using EDI to exchange orders, and are ready and willing to take your share of the business away from you.

Even if your industry is not required to use EDI, you should find out if it is being used by others in the industry. If so, then begin an evaluation process as soon as practical. It may only be a matter of time before EDI becomes the standard of exchange. In fact, being early may present new opportunities with major accounts.

Current Systems

It is important to diagram your current order processing system so that you understand how an EDI module can be integrated into it. Look at the following diagram.

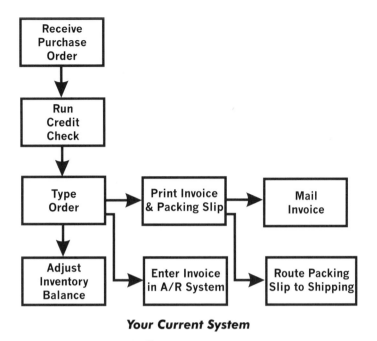

Your Current System

The Your Current System diagram represents the receipt of a paper invoice. After it is examined and the credit is approved, the order must be typed by an order entry operator. The order processing system adjusts the inventory balance and provides an invoice register for the accounts receivable system. It also prints a paper invoice and packing slip. The paper invoice is mailed to the customer. The packing slip is routed to the shipping department, where the ordered items are picked and packed for shipment to the customer.

The paper purchase order transit time, internal routing, credit check, and order entry process can take several hours in a busy environment. Addressing (or folding invoices so that the address shows through a window envelope), stuffing, and finally mailing paper invoices can also take many hours or even days depending on the volume of business.

Now look at the same processes using an EDI system.

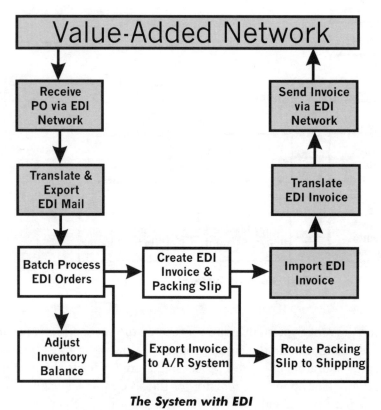

The System with EDI

The shaded blocks represent tasks performed by the EDI system. This diagram illustrates how an electronic invoice is received from a value-added network. The invoice file is translated into a format used by the EDI software. From there, it is reformatted into a file that can be read by the in-house order processing system. Once in this format, the electronic order records are read into the order processing system in the same way as being typed. The difference is that the electronic order entry process takes seconds, while the manual entry process can take hours and days.

When properly programmed, almost any reasonable order processing system can produce files that are compatible with the installed EDI system. These files are imported back into the EDI system, where they are translated to a valid EDI exchange format that complies with the governing ANSI X12 or EDIFACT standard. The EDI mail (or invoice and functional acknowledgement files) generated by the EDI system are sent to the trading partner's inbox using the agreed upon value-added network. The entire cycle from purchase order receipt to invoice output takes a matter of minutes.

Once both systems are diagrammed, it is a good idea to put down times associated with each of the tasks. Add the task times of both systems and then compare them to determine the time savings. Apply the average labor rates and you should have an estimate of your labor savings. Labor savings should usually include benefits and overhead. The exception would be if your staff were static, would remain on the payroll regardless of the workload, and would not be used to perform other work during slack time.

Staff Qualifications and Potential

People comprise a vital part of every system. You should look at the people who presently work in your manual order entry unit. What skills do they presently have? Are they using computers and a variety of computer applications? Are they able to adapt quickly to the automated system and involved technologies? Will they appreciate the benefits of the new system or resist it as something that threatens their job security? The answers are usually favorable. However, it is important that you know up front if the people you currently have will be able to adapt to the new systems. You will have to invest some on-the-job training time, as they will have to learn the terminology and the new steps involved in creating, receiving, processing, and sending EDI documents.

EDI Benefits

Before considering the direct benefits that your company may realize from the installation and use of an EDI system, you will usually consider the necessity of such a system. If you are on the supply side of your industry and your major customers are encouraging suppliers to use EDI, then you must look at an EDI alternative. Otherwise, you may lose business to your competitors. If your business achieves a reasonable inventory turnover, then EDI will reduce your *cost-to-sale*, which is the cost associated with marketing, order processing, invoicing, and product delivery. If you are on the procurement side of your industry, EDI will reduce your purchasing costs. The labor, speed, accuracy, and system costs, including maintenance, that EDI provides in both the order and invoice processing functions can be quantified. The simplest approach is to measure the labor, cycle time, and error reduction. Then compare the added cost of your system investment, training, and technical support. Once you look at all of the factors, you can derive a fairly accurate comparison. Following is a monthly cost comparison table.

Description	Manual Cost	EDI Cost	Savings/Loss	Rate	Amount
Sort Purchase Orders	4.2 hr	0.0	4.2 hr	$14.00	$58.80
Order Entry	90.0 hr	2.0	88.0 hr	$14.00	$1232.00
Print Invoices/Packing Slips	15.0 hr	7.5	7.5 hr	$14.00	$105.00
Separate/Mail Invoices	10.0 hr	0.0	10.0 hr	$14.00	$140.00
Enter Invoices into Accounting	54.0 hr	1.0	53.0 hr	$14.00	$742.00
Error Corrections	3.0 hr	0.00	3.0 hr	$14.00	$42.00
Postage (Invoice mailings)	$335.00	0.00	$335.00		$335.00
System Cost (5-yr depreciation)	$0.00	$100.00	-$100.00		-$100.00
Monthly VAN charges	0.0 hr	$300.0	-$300.00		-$300.00
Technical Support	$100.00	$150.00	-$50.00		-$50.00
Monthly Savings or (Loss)					$2,204.80

The above comparison shows a $2,204.80 monthly savings, which amounts to $26,475.60 per year. The cost of EDI training, which should be a one-time setup fee, is not included. The total savings shown would only be garnered if you use the time saved in the performance of other work. Of course, there is also the possibility of losing business revenue because of your inability to trade electronically with a major customer—this could threaten your company's survival. Setting aside this possibility along with your labor and expense factors, there are certainly other considerations. These were discussed in Chapter 2. Recall that EDI gives you the ability to shorten your order to billing cycle. If you grant your customers 30-day payment terms, the billing terms begin much sooner when you can receive, process, and invoice an order in a single day rather than taking a week to ten days with an old paper-based, manual system.

EDI Use by Others

It is always a good idea to find others, either in your industry or one that is similar to yours, who have been trading with EDI for a period of time. Find companies that are using computer systems like yours, i.e., Windows-based PCs, AS400s, etc. Explain that you are preparing to implement EDI and that you'd like to see what a few other people are doing. See if you can visit their facility for a tour and a frank discussion. Consider buying your hosts lunch over which you can delve into their overall impression of EDI including the benefits, problems, and hidden costs. If your technical background and grasp of the jargon is limited, consider bringing along someone who works for your company who will have a better grasp of a technical dialog. Be sure to take notes and record individual and product names and contact information for future reference.

Also try to determine what types of systems they are using for exchanging EDI documents. Ask about the ways that they communicate, their experience with value-added networks, Internet links, and direct point-to-point or FTP (file transfer protocol) links. See if they are willing to show you a few transaction sets so that you can see what they actually look like. Finally, be sure to see how they interface their EDI system to their order processing, inventory control, and accounting systems. This is a vital link in the process, and it's important to determine what is required to integrate EDI into your own in-house systems. If your host's system is similar to yours, find out how they developed the system interfaces. Did they use internal IT professionals or enlist the help of a software service company? More information about this vital link is presented later in this chapter and then again at a much more technical level in Chapter 11.

Finally, when you finish your tour with the first EDI user, see if you can set up visits with at least two additional users in your industry. You will likely discover a variety of approaches and diverse systems used to exchange EDI mail documents. When you finish your investigation, you should have some definite ideas about how you want to proceed.

Conversion Costs

Conversion costs can vary greatly, depending on the systems that you currently use. If you are presently using a totally manual system, then your costs as well as your learning curve may be extensive. Of course it is also possible that your current computerized order processing, inventory control, and accounting systems are old and incompatible with a new, state-of-the art EDI system. If so, then you may have to start from scratch by obtaining all new system hardware and software. This can be a daunting prospect. In this situation, it's best to look at EDI, order processing, inventory control, and accounting systems in concert. Be sure that they run on the same systems or network and can readily exchange data. This can be a tall order, and may require some custom software development. Be sure to have a firm plan that allows you to integrate your EDI system with your order processing, inventory control, and accounting systems.

If you have a modern order processing system that can easily import and export order information, then the conversion costs can be minimized. In this case, you must find an EDI system that can export and import EDI documents. Since this feature is a common requirement, it is not uncommon to find this feature in "off-the-shelf" EDI software packages. If you are using an internally produced order processing system, you may need someone to prepare custom exchange utilities. If you have a programmer on staff or if one is available through a local service company, have them examine the system's ability to exchange information. Request an estimate of the time required to develop utilities that can read and write compatible files between the systems.

Interface Issues

The ability to interface an EDI system with your other in-house systems is critical if you are to truly reap the benefits of automation. Otherwise, you will still be required to print purchase orders from your EDI system and type the order information into your order processing system. Once paper invoices are printed, the invoice information must be manually entered into the EDI system. Instead of reducing work, you may have doubled it.

To avoid this unwanted situation, be sure that your EDI software and your order processing system either use easily parsed file formats or have built-in import/export utilities. This permits you to exchange order and invoice documents between your systems. If you have a programmer on staff, then he or she should be able to write utilities that read and write order information. In addition, the same utility that reads the order information should also be able to batch process the data to automatically create an invoice file that can read into and be processed by the EDI system.

Once data is being interchanged between your systems, the processing tasks take minutes instead of hours, and as you know from the available benefits, you also eliminate manual data entry errors. The following diagram shows a typical interface between an order processing and an EDI system. Note the PO850 and IN810 document types. EDI practitioners refer to EDI mail documents using numbers. An 850 is always a purchase order, an 810 is an invoice, and a 997 is a functional acknowledgement.

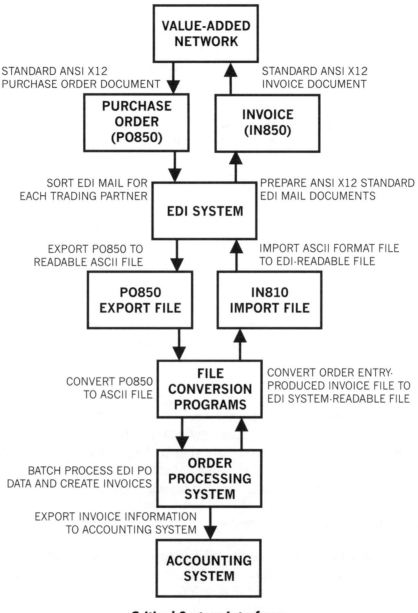

Critical System Interfaces

Available EDI Applications

There are several suppliers of EDI software. Some can be found by searching the World Wide Web. A few provide evaluation versions of their software, while others will supply you with information packages that describe their products. Whichever system you decide on, be sure that the supplier has a fully staffed technical support team, as you will likely require support during the first several months of system use. You may also want to check into formal training programs.

The companion CD contains an evaluation version of Trading Partner Desktop (TPD) from Mercator Software, Inc. The evaluation program runs for 60 days, which gives you ample time to examine the entire program. Part 2 of this book guides you through the setup and operation of TPD. You can view Mercator's Web site at www.mercator.com.

EDI System Alternatives

It is not always necessary to install your own EDI system. You may also want to consider EDI service bureaus. Service bureaus exchange the EDI mail documents for their clients. They typically supply a copy of the EDI mail documents in a plaintext format that you can read. You use the documents to process the information in the normal manner and give the resulting information, such as an invoice, back to the service bureau. The bureau, in turn, converts your document into a standard EDI document and then transmits it back to your trading partner. Although you can satisfy your trading partner's EDI requirements by using a service bureau, it is unlikely that you will achieve the cost reduction and other benefits that accrue from having your own in-house system.

Inflexible and Flexible Systems

The first EDI system used by the author was extremely inflexible. Although it featured import and export utilities, it was designed to satisfy a limited group of trading partners in the publishing industry. A major trading partner encouraged the company to begin exchanging commercial transactions using EDI and suggested the system. Thanks to fairly rudimentary import/export requirements, I was able to write the data conversion programs that permitted our order processing and EDI systems to exchange data.

However, when the system was originally installed, I didn't know enough about EDI to ask very many questions, particularly the right ones. For example, what if one of my trading partners changes their transaction set standard, like moving from the current ANSI X12 3010 standard to 4010? What if they request an additional EDI document type, such as a PO acknowledgement (855) or an electronic catalog (832)? The answers to these questions would have been, "Sorry, our system doesn't support that. It is designed to handle a specific set of transactions and trading partners."

During the first several years, our company was not called upon to add any new trading partners to our inflexible system. Fortunately, it was several years before our trading partners began to ask for new transaction set types. The old inflexible system did work for several years with very few problems. However, when we finally realized how inflexible the system was, we also recognized that we had been lucky.

When we discovered that the old system was not Y2K compliant, we began looking at new, more flexible systems. This meant that we would have to find and install a completely new EDI system solution, rewrite the system interface utilities, and then test the new system with each of several trading partners. Over the years, the business had experienced substantial growth, and we wanted to begin trading with several new large customers using EDI.

TPD was one of the systems that we evaluated. Not only was it a modern, 32-bit Windows application (in contrast to our old MS-DOS system), it was extremely flexible. It came with a full set of ANSI ASC X12 standard data maps for virtually all industries. These maps could be added to accommodate the requirements of virtually any trading partner. It also came with a variety of communications interfaces that supported most of the popular value-added networks.

It took about four months to write the interfaces. Once written, another month was spent testing EDI mail documents with our trading partners. We exchanged the last EDI mail using the old system on a Friday. TPD was put into production on the following Monday and has worked perfectly ever since.

What's Next

In this chapter you read information about EDI system evaluation. Hopefully, it provoked you to think about ways to evaluate an EDI system and to determine how you can use EDI in concert with your current in-house systems. In addition, you should now understand some of the differences between an inflexible system that can limit your compliance with future requirements and one that is flexible and can be reconfigured to meet new requirements. In the next chapter you explore data communications, value-added networks, and security issues—all key issues in the success of every EDI system.

Review Questions

1. List five key issues to consider when contemplating the installation of an EDI system.

2. What are some conversion costs that are typically encountered when an enterprise moves from a manual trading system to an EDI trading system?

3. What might you consider as an alternative to an in-house EDI system?

4. What might be two limitations of an inflexible EDI system?

Chapter 5

Data Communications, VANs, and Security

Introduction

Data communications is constantly changing, and special terminology and new acronyms abound. It can be overwhelming when you add the terminology and acronyms found in EDI to those found in data communications. Here, some definitions and descriptions are provided to help avoid some of the confusion.

Data Communications

Data communications is a vital link in the process of exchanging information between two trading partners. In the context of EDI, communications is a separate system that is used to transfer encoded EDI documents between your computer and your trading partner's computer. EDI systems produce, read, and process EDI documents. However, the EDI system does not send and receive documents—that's left to the data communications system.

The overall process is described and diagramed here, again using the purchase order and invoice metaphor.

1. The consuming trading partner prepares a purchase order in EDI standard format (using an agreed-upon transaction set and document format).

2. The issuing trading partner uses his communications program to send the EDI purchase order (form PO850) to a secure data mailbox, where it can be retrieved by the supplying trading partner.

3. The supplying trading partner launches a data communications session, which checks the secure data mailbox for EDI documents.

4. The document is found and then retrieved and stored in the supplier's computer for processing.

5. The supplier uses his EDI system to process the document, which is translated into human-readable format.

6. The PO is exported to the supplier's order processing system, where it is interpreted and used to generate the corresponding stock picking information and an invoice.

7. The invoice is converted into a format that is readable by the EDI system. The invoice file is then imported back into the EDI system, which generates a valid invoice document.

8. The supplier next launches his data communications system and sends the EDI invoice (IN810) to a secure data mailbox where it can be retrieved by the consuming trading partner.

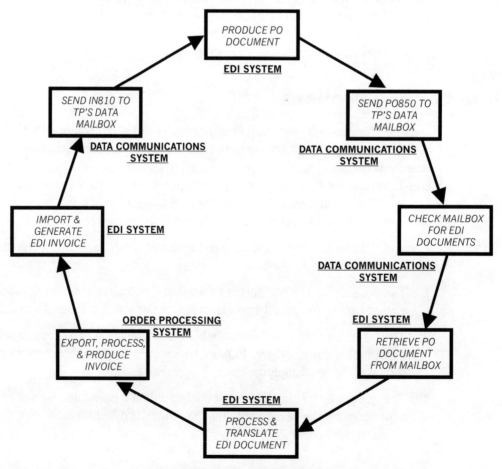

The Data Communications and EDI Cycle

A trading partner may require a data communications method and value-added network for EDI transfers. The requirement is often based on an established commitment that has been made by the consuming trading partner and a value-added network. However, sanctioned EDI standards do not define the communications method that moves the data between the trading partners' computers.

The full version of the EDI software supplied with this book includes a variety of data communications installation programs. All that is necessary is to select a network name during the network installation process. The designated communications program is then installed by the installation utility. A complete network installation procedure is provided in Chapter 8 of this book.

The Value-Added Network

EDI mail is exchanged by a variety of data communications means. Some companies host their own FTP sites, which permits trading partners to download purchase orders and functional acknowledgements and then upload invoices, catalogs, purchase order acknowledgements, functional acknowledgements, and a variety of other commercial documents. The move to Internet exchange is also maturing. Although growing rapidly, EDI document exchange by way of the Internet and FTP sites is still comparatively new. Today, the majority of transactions still occur over value-added networks (VANs). Following is a list of VANs that specialize in EDI. There are many more, especially VANs that concentrate on specific industries. For example, Pubnet is used by many publishing companies, book wholesalers, and book retailers.

Advanced Logic Resources, Inc.	Internet Commerce Corporation (ICC)
Advantis	KLEINSCHMIDT Inc.
Angle Incorporated	KTNET Korea Trade Network
ARI Network Services, Inc.	MCI
AT&T EasyLink Services	MPACT Immedia
Bell C\Global Solutions	Loren Data Corporation
Computer Network Corporation	POS-EDI (POSDATA Co, Ltd.)
Datamatix	Pubnet
ED-PLUS	Simplix
Electronic Data Transfer (EDT)	Singapore Network Services Pte Ltd.
GAP Information Corp.	Softshare
GE Information Services, Inc.	Sterling Commerce

GPAS, Inc.   TranSettlements

Harbinger Corporation   Vantree Systems

Charges

Paper-based business correspondence is exchanged using the services of the post office or a private courier. The sender pays postage based on the weight of the parcel. The service provided by a VAN is similar to an electronic post office. A VAN is a third-party organization that charges the sender a fee that is based on the number of characters (or kilobytes) sent. In addition to transaction costs, other fees are sometimes charged for connect time, monthly service fees, and taxes.

Electronic Mailboxes

The term network could be misleading. Network has nothing to do with either a local area network (LAN) or wide area network (WAN). In contrast, a VAN includes a network of private mailboxes that belong to subscribing trading partners. While a VAN may provide thousands of mailboxes to a variety of customers in different industries, you are only interested in your mailbox and those that belong to your trading partners.

Consider the following example. You want to obtain purchase orders from your trading partner and supply corresponding invoices in return. You and your trading partner each subscribe to private mailboxes hosted by the same VAN. Your computer is located in Houston and your trading partner's is located in Chicago. The VAN is located in Orlando. Your trading partner's computer sends the EDI purchase orders to the VAN. The transferred file's envelope includes the sender's mailbox address (like a return address label) and the recipient's (your) mailbox address.

When the VAN receives the EDI purchase order, the envelope is read to determine the document's destination. If the envelope has your address on it, it is placed in your electronic mailbox. Upon receipt of the EDI purchase order, the communications session between your trading partner's computer and the VAN's computer is concluded. Other trading partners may also send EDI purchase orders to you through the VAN. Therefore, several purchase orders along with other EDI documents may be stored in your mailbox, ready for you to pick up.

When convenient, you can launch a communications session between your computer and the VAN's to check your mailbox for possible EDI mail. Once logged on and verified, the VAN permits you to collect your EDI mail, which is downloaded to your computer ready for processing by your EDI system.

Checking for EDI Mail

Many VANs have Web sites that permit subscribers to check the status of their mailboxes before launching a communications session. However, it is not necessary to know if there is EDI mail in your electronic mailbox before checking. You can simply set up and launch communications sessions on an established schedule to *upload* (send) and *download* (receive) EDI mail. If no EDI mail is present in your mailbox, most EDI software packages will simply supply you with a "no mail" status.

Trading with Multiple Partners

A VAN permits you to exchange EDI mail with several trading partners at once. When you send EDI mail, the addresses contained in the header of the EDI mail are used by the VAN to sort and deliver the documents into the various destination mailboxes. This service eliminates the need for you to initiate separate communications sessions for each of your trading partners, and therefore greatly simplifies the process. Otherwise, you would have to prepare EDI mail for each trading partner and then launch separate communications sessions to exchange information with each of your trading partners.

VAN Interconnects

It is possible, even probable, for exchanging trading partners to use different VANs. When this happens, you may be required to subscribe to the services of two or more VANs. However, it is also likely, and certainly more economical, for different VANs to *interconnect* with each other. In other words, you can send your EDI mail to your VAN, who can deliver the EDI mail to an electronic mailbox that belongs to your partner's VAN. Once your VAN puts the EDI mail in the interconnecting VAN's mailbox, the destination VAN can retrieve, sort, and deliver the mail to addresses contained in the EDI mail headers. Interconnects between VANs is a common practice.

Communication Alternatives

In addition to using a VAN to exchange EDI mail, you can also exchange mail using the Internet or by communicating directly with your trading partner. These methods are discussed in the following paragraphs.

Internet FTP

The Internet has become a pervasive communications tool for all kinds of information exchanges. The Internet is a logical way to exchange EDI documents as long as the proper security and validation checks are in place. Several VANs are already using the Internet as a communications backbone, while others are working feverishly to develop Internet products. Internet Commerce Corporation (ICC) is one of the rapidly growing VANs that are making exclusive use of the benefits offered by Internet FTP. ICC is able to offer its service at the same reasonable rate 24 hours a day, seven days a week rather than charging prime time and nonprime time rates as many conventional VANs do. At this writing, QRS, which remarkets IBM's Advantis VAN, is developing an Internet FTP product that may be available by the time this book is distributed.

One of the advantages of Internet-based VANs is that they do not have to rely on a national or international network of dial-up telephone numbers. The expense of maintaining such a bank of telephone access numbers is high. Of course, this expense must be passed on in the form of fees and increased per kilobyte charges to their customers. Most if not all VAN customers, who may already have high-speed Internet connections, must rely on dial-up modems and comparatively slow asynchronous communications. By using their Internet connection, which they are already using for Web access and e-mail, the need for a dial-up connection is completely eliminated. Of course some small companies still use dial-up access to connect to the Internet. Nevertheless, they can upload and download EDI mail using their Internet service provider (ISP). Internet access permits companies to exchange EDI mail at DSL, ISDN, cable modem, T1, or, in the worst case, dial-up modem connection speeds.

An FTP site, where FTP stands for *File Transfer Protocol*, is nothing more than an Internet Protocol (IP) address on the Internet that can be accessed by an FTP client or modern Web browser. Every Windows 9x, NT, and 2000 operating system includes an FTP client utility. You can also log onto an FTP site from the MS DOS command line and upload and download files. Or, you can use a more elegant FTP client that features a graphical user interface with menus, dialog boxes, and a file explorer. Regardless of the client you use, the FTP site will have user name and password security. Once you enter the site, you can view, select, and download files. Similarly, you can select a target folder and upload (send) files. Using typical Internet connection speeds, this usually takes a matter of seconds.

When an FTP site is hosted by your VAN, the process of sorting and routing EDI mail to the addressee mailboxes works in the same way as it does for the traditional VAN configurations. If your trading partner uses a traditional VAN and you use an Internet VAN, an interconnect will occur as described previously. Therefore, the exchange works as before.

Point-to-Point

Point-to-point is best described as having your computer send EDI mail directly to your trading partner's computer without any intermediaries. In other words, a VAN is not involved in the exchange. Point-to-point can occur in many ways. Data can be exchanged using an electronic bulletin board system. This is typically done using asynchronous, dial-up data communications. The procuring trading partner can put EDI mail documents in secure folders within the bulletin board system that you can access with a user name and password. This is old technology and has all but disappeared with the advent of the Internet.

Some trading partners do enough business to warrant a direct communications link. This permits high-speed, reliable communications that can occur many times each day, if not continuously. Of course, this can be an expensive method and the transaction load must be large enough to justify the cost of a direct line.

Today, the most practical point-to-point data exchange method is Internet FTP. The consuming trading partner, such as a large distributor or retail chain, can host an Internet-based FTP server. Supplying trading partners access the site using common FTP client software. Just as with an Internet VAN, each supplier can provide a user name and password to gain access to a private section on the hard drive of the FTP server. Once access is established, the supplying partner can select and download purchase orders from an outbound folder. He can also select and upload invoices to an inbound folder. With the right equipment and software, this is a fast and reliable data communications method. Since large distributors and chains can fund substantial data processing resources, they are able to apply the same technologies that are used by Internet VANs. Therefore, the reliability factor is equally good. The data integrity checks, backup systems, and archives provided by most VANs can also be found in many company-hosted systems.

Some consuming trading partners tend to "invent" their own standards. When this happens, it is more difficult for supplying trading partners to automate the processing tasks associated with electronic business transactions. The EDI software, which is designed to comply with prevailing standards, cannot recognize the proprietary document format. Therefore, by definition, nonstandard, proprietary transaction sets are not EDI. For a trading partner to cope with this problem, custom software utilities must be written and installed. This can be expensive and time consuming and places an extra burden on those who are required to cooperate with the maverick trading partner. This situation takes a giant step backward into the early 1970s to a time when EDI standards were nonexistent.

Launching an Exchange

The supplying trading partner almost always initiates the communications link with the requisitioning trading partner. In fact, there is really no reason for a buying trading partner's computer to initiate a communications session with the selling partner's computer. The buying trading partner places their purchase order in the supplier's mailbox. That mailbox is either on the VAN's server, or on the supplier's server when point-to-point communication is used.

The supplying trading partner launches a communications session, uploading invoices and downloading purchase orders. Note that other EDI mail documents are also exchanged, such as functional acknowledgements, purchase order acknowledgements, product catalogs, and a host of other documents that serve the needs of the particular industry.

In summary, if you are a supplier, you will need communications software as well as EDI software to exchange EDI mail. If you have several trading partners that use different VANs, point-to-point, and Internet FTP, you will need several different communications packages. As long as your trading partners comply with the EDI standards, your EDI software should suffice. However, if one or more begin using nonstandard transaction sets, your work will be multiplied. Your IT staff will be required to write conversion utilities and modify control files to interface with your "maverick" trading partners.

Even if your trading partners fully comply with the standards and agree to use the same VAN (one that has been selected to serve your industry), your trading partners will probably use various transaction set versions. The author's company, which is on the supply side of the EDI exchange, presently uses four different transaction sets: 3010, 3020, 3060, and 4010. As more trading partners move to EDI, different sets are surely to be invoked. This is one reason for selecting Trading Partner Desktop from Mercator Software, Inc. More than 1,500 ANSI ASC X12 transaction set maps are available on a CD supplied by Mercator. This permits users to add and then map almost every available X12 transaction set in use today.

The product also comes with approximately 20 asynchronous communications packages that are compliant with numerous popular VANs. Finally, TPD also has an outstanding Map Editor feature so that users can select the segments and interior elements that are used by each of their trading partners. Within an hour or two, these powerful features can accommodate the requirements of virtually any trading partner. Of course, users must be familiar with the operation of the software, understand transaction set guidelines, and know which communications and processing tasks must be performed.

Security

Nothing is absolutely secure and probably never will be. If someone is intent on getting information and has the required resources to do so, they will. First, your data should be reasonably secure within the system of your VAN. Security is a hallmark of every good VAN. There's not a great deal that you can do about security once your data is in the hands of your trading partner. Of course, they have the same interest in security and data integrity that you do. And, you can always ask them to fill out a checklist or simply describe the security measures that they use. Therefore, your vulnerability exists in communications taps and unauthorized access to your in-house EDI systems.

Man Overboard!

Before discussing the plethora of available security measures, you can go overboard. Don't let what could be unwarranted paranoia plunge you into excessive investments in security systems. I believe that it was Henry Kissinger who said, "Paranoid people have enemies too." Who wants your data? What benefit can be gained from it? If you are a small supplier, your EDI data may just be a small piece of intelligence that is of no benefit to anyone. Why, then, would they want it? If you're a big distributor or retail chain with aggressive competitors, perhaps they can determine your strategic direction based on your buying trends. In this case, encryption might be called for. However, don't spend tens or hundreds of thousands of dollars building an impregnable fortress when disclosure is reasonably harmless. Having said all of this, you can and should implement a variety of precautions to attain a reasonable level of safety.

First, and perhaps foremost, your company must establish and enforce rigorous data backup and archiving policies. Be sure that your data is on redundant repository (tape or disk). If one system goes down, have your data stored on another system. If your building burns to the ground, have a copy of your data stored in another building. Redundancy is important, and it is not excessively expensive.

Security Issues

Several issues come to light when you ponder the security of both internal EDI systems and an EDI mail exchange. In addition to the disclosure of information to one or more unauthorized parties, there are many other factors to consider.

Validating the Sender When an EDI mail document is received, do you really know that it is from the organization that is identified as the sender? If not, the sender may repudiate the exchange and deny knowledge of the message and its content. Therefore, it is important to send a functional acknowledgement as soon as practical upon receipt of the EDI mail to notify the sending party that you are in receipt of their EDI mail.

Unauthorized Access/Disclosure You must also ensure that your EDI mail is received by the intended organization. Otherwise, a competitor could use EDI to obtain sensitive information. Although most often unlikely, it certainly is possible for an authentic message to be hijacked and critical data altered before it arrives at its destination. Also, messages may be duplicated either accidentally or intentionally. The duplicate message can appear genuine to the recipient, especially when it is a duplicate of the genuine EDI mail document.

Unauthorized Disclosure If a sensitive EDI mail document is sent, how can you ensure that the data is not disclosed during transit?

Delayed Messages Delays in EDI mail delivery could have significant adverse effects on your trades, including order cancellation.

Misrouted Messages Misrouted messages may never reach the intended recipient. Misrouting also increases the message's vulnerability to alternation.

EDI Service Loss Once your organization installs and begins trading using an EDI system, it may be extremely difficult to fall back on manual systems if you have a temporary EDI system failure or a communications outage. This is particularly true when the use of EDI has increased both your order processing and trading capacities over time. The task of manually entering orders can be overwhelming when it is compared with automated order processing that is provided by EDI.

In-House EDI System Security

The in-house systems used to transmit, store, and process messages are just as important to security as the transmission process itself. Some of these processes involve the:

- Secure creation of outbound messages
- Secure processing of incoming messages
- Secure retention of data

Secure Creation of Outbound Messages

Where manual input is used with an EDI system, there is a high potential for data entry errors caused by typographical errors. If automated input is used, the originating system may have a bug, which can also result in the generation of erroneous inputs to the EDI system. Internal bugs and even the incorrect implementation of EDI translation software can result in the transmission of messages that do not comply with the messaging standard in use (usually ANSI X12 or EDIFACT).

The sending organization is responsible for messages that are attributed to their origination. Therefore, they have a responsibility to prevent unauthorized messages from originating from their in-house EDI system. There is also a potential for a hacker to log into the company's computer systems in order to generate a seemingly authentic message. This underscores the obvious need to control the message creation process. This is achieved in several ways. First, the in-house system can be isolated from other systems that enable remote access. Development and maintenance of the system should also be applied with security in mind. The system must check to assure that all messages that should be sent are actually sent. In addition, very tight procedural controls should be established. This includes restricted access by employing EDI system log-on authentication. This typically requires user IDs and passwords.

Secure Processing of Incoming Messages

Once an EDI message reaches the recipient it is still only partially through its journey. The recipient must authenticate the sender's identity. In addition, the integrity of the message itself must be verified. Usually, the receipt of the message should be acknowledged. Returning a functional acknowledgement to the sender acknowledges receipt of the EDI mail. If the message is bogus, the trading partners can discuss the exchange and quickly resolve the situation before it becomes a problem.

Message Translation for Import/Export—EDI messages are usually translated (or converted) into formats that can be used by the recipients own order processing or inventory control systems. Each element within the received EDI mail flat file is extracted and rearranged into a format that the recipient's in-house order processing system can use. This is discussed in more detail in Part 2.

Rejected Messages—The in-house EDI system software should reject any EDI mail documents that it is unable to process. Rejected documents should be addressed quickly. In most cases, the sender will be asked to resend the document.

Error Detection and Correction—Many translation packages incorporate error detection and editing features that allow on-screen corrections. Often, this is as simple as opening the document in a text editor and making the changes that are required to produce a usable document. All changes and explanations for each should be recorded. Again, the sender should be contacted and a copy of the document sent to them so they can make corrections within their system.

Acting on Messages—It only takes a few seconds to check the integrity of an EDI document. Once checked, it is ready to process. Checks are usually automated, and happen so fast that the verification process is completely transparent to EDI system operators. The only time that an operator gets involved is when an error is detected.

Processing Messages—Incoming messages are typically processed using a combination of manual control and automation. For example, a group of EDI purchase orders from several different trading partners may be sorted to each trading partner's folder on the in-house system. The documents are then translated for use by the in-house EDI system. Next, it is common to reformat a purchase order document into a format that is compatible by the in-house order processing application. Once processed by that system, a corresponding invoice is returned to the EDI system. From there, it is processed and transmitted back to the originating trading partner.

Monitoring Controls—To make sure that the controls work, checks exist to ensure that no messages are lost between message receipt and the in-house destination application.

Secure Retention of Data

The primary purposes of data retention are to:

- Fulfill statutory and regulatory requirements
- Provide evidence of each transaction
- Provide records of business activity and for substantiating the organization's accounting records
- Provide information that can be used for planning and marketing

Every organization should assess its requirements for retaining data and develop a data-retention policy. This should be documented in the organization's operating procedures. Of course, it's possible to retain too much data. Where little data is produced, it may be easier to retain everything than to go through the process of identifying which records should be sorted and retained. The level of security over retained data depends upon the intended use. Finally, retained data should be protected against alteration, destruction, and unauthorized disclosure.

EDI Mail Security Mechanisms

There are a number of security mechanisms available today. Along with security, there are other authenticity techniques that are used to assure the validity and integrity of EDI mail documents. Here, security and related topics are examined.

Encryption

Encryption algorithms are used to scramble messages. When data is encrypted, it prevents it from being read by unauthorized persons. It can also prevent undetectable alterations to a message and check the identity of the originator. Most experts agree that encryption is the most effective protection against EDI document disclosure and tampering. Encryption may be used for:

- User authentication—Validate the identity of the sender.
- Message authentication—Verify that messages have not been lost or altered.
- Confidentiality—Prevent disclosure of the contents of the EDI mail document. Encrypted data cannot normally be understood by anyone other than the sender or the receiver.
- Error detection—Ensure that the content of the EDI mail document has not been accidentally modified.
- Proof of origin—Authenticate the identification of the sender of the EDI mail document.

There are many complex algorithms used for encryption. A simplified encryption example is briefly described and diagramed here.

In its original form, EDI mail is in easily read plaintext ASCII format. It can be opened and read with any simple text editor. An *encryption algorithm* and a corresponding variable, referred to as a *key*, are used to convert the document into unintelligible *cipher text* before it is sent over a public network. The recipient *decrypts* the cipher text to transform it back into plaintext using the encryption algorithm and key.

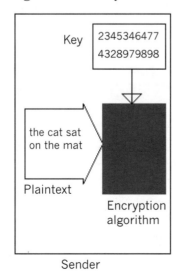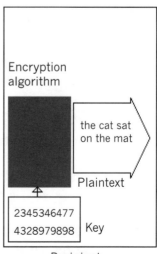

Encryption Example

Key Management

The procedures used to generate, store, exchange, archive, and delete keys are called *key management*. Key management is critical to the success of encryption. Requirements vary depending upon whether symmetric or asymmetric encryption is being used and whether the keys are key encrypting keys or data encrypting keys.

When a *symmetric* encryption system is used, it is vital for the trading partners who are exchanging enciphered data to maintain the secrecy of the keys. A symmetric system is shown in the preceding diagram. A symmetric system exists when compatible encryption utilities are used at each end of exchange.

In *asymmetric* encryption systems, encryption occurs in the interior of the exchange. A public key is used in asymmetric encryption. The decrypting party must ensure that the public key they receive is valid for the sending trading partner. If the wrong key is used, the recipient can mistakenly process EDI mail from a bogus sender.

Generation—Security measures are vital when a valid key is generated. It should never be possible for an unauthorized party to find out how a key is generated, because this can enable them to derive an identical key. Ideally, the initiation and controlling of the generation should be under dual control, i.e., no one person should be able to generate the keys.

Distribution—Security relies on how keys are distributed and whether the keys are public or private. Both manual and electronic distribution methods are used. Manually distributed keys should be split into two parts. Then each of the parts should be sent separately in secure envelopes. The envelopes used should be special, sealed envelopes that show if they have been opened. Regardless of whether a key is public or private, the recipient still has to be assured that it is genuine. This can be as simple as certifying an individual's written signature.

When a private key is distributed electronically, it is sent in encrypted format. Data encrypting keys are sent in cipher text that uses encrypting keys.

Certification

Third parties that are trusted by both senders and receivers, called certification authorities, are sometimes used to certify the authenticity of public keys. Another certification method is called *X.509 certification*. The X.509 is a part of the X.500 standard which sets out how directories are used to certify the public key of a sender. When the certifying message is received, the recipient requests the sender's public key. When requested, the certification authority sends the sender's public key to the recipient.

Archiving

Another step in the process is called *archiving*. When encryption is used for authentication, it is important to securely archive the involved keys for safe-keeping and later use in the event that a key is lost. Today, there are many kinds of media suitable for archiving important data. For example, CDs, WORM disks (write once, read many), or magnetic tape can be used to archive data. CDs and WORM disks are usually faster and more reliable than magnetic tape. The dramatic drop in the cost of hard drive storage devices is making them a popular choice for storage. They are fast, reliable, and can be "hot swapped" in many new computer systems.

Digital Signatures

Digital signatures use asymmetric encryption to authenticate the origin of a message. The digital signature can also authenticate the integrity of the contents of the message. The signature also prevents repudiation. The private key authenticates the signature of the sender and assures the recipient that the contents of the EDI mail have not been disclosed. Very briefly, a typical digital signature works like this:

- An algorithm, such as RSA, is used to generate a sender's signature. It can also be applied to some or all of the message contents.
- The recipient uses the sender's public key to decrypt and verify the signature of the sender.

Sealing

A message can also be *sealed* to show that the contents have not been changed, either accidentally or intentionally. Sealing is commonly achieved using a checksum value, which is either appended to the message or sent separately. A checksum value is calculated using data from the message. To check that the message has not been altered, the checksum is recalculated. If the data used in the calculation have been changed, then the result is different. This indicates that the seal has been broken. Most seals use encryption to increase the security of the checksum value.

Smart Cards

Smart cards are plastic cards that resemble credit cards. Rather than a magnetic strip, a smart card has an embedded microchip that contains a processor and memory. The smart card can check that a card reader is valid and perform the following processes:

- Identify and authenticate the EDI users
- Control the access to data and/or other available online resources

■ Conduct sealing and signing transactions

Biometrics

Biometric techniques take advantage of unique human attributes and provide a high level of authentication. The realm of biometrics includes, but is certainly not limited to, DNA, fingerprints, voice recognition patterns, the configuration of one's iris, and even the unique shape of an individual's hand. Although biometric systems are in place in extremely secure facilities, such as governmental agencies with extremely large budgets, most biometric applications for commercial use are meager. Many have only been pilot tested. However, as with most evolving technologies, it is only a matter of time before the costs associated with the installation of biometric security systems will reach a level that make them attractive to commercial users.

Concluding Thoughts about Security

If you are concerned about corporate espionage, "dirty tricks," or lost or corrupted EDI mail, then you should investigate the involved security issues and understand the risk. The first consideration is the security of the document itself—being sure that the integrity of the EDI mail is not violated. In today's world of hackers who gleefully produce virus programs that cost businesses billions in lost time, information, and software safeguards, there is always a fear that some unscrupulous individual might tamper with the content of exchanged EDI documents. Look at each of the issues above and measure the risk versus cost. It's easy to let paranoia elevate the costs, where there may be little risk and easy recovery. Many people have been warned about Internet credit card exchanges. However, their risk usually lies with their selection of a Web site that belongs to an unscrupulous owner, and not with the credit information itself. It's far riskier to engage in a paper transaction at the corner store or your teller machine than it is to perform an electronic transaction.

What's Next

Part 2 of this book walks you through the EDI software setup and exchange process. Even if you're completely new to EDI, if you read the descriptive information and then follow the step-by-step instructions, you will know a lot more about EDI than you do now. In fact, if you install and use TPD in your business, you will probably want to keep Part 2 of this book close by so you can use it as a handy reference. So, without further ado, let's get to the fun part—hands-on with your Windows PC.

Review Questions

1. Does an EDI system send and receive data? Explain your answer.

2. Describe some services offered by a value-added network.

3. What is a VAN interconnect?

4. List and describe two communications alternatives.

Part 2

Using EDI Software

(Trading Partner Desktop)

- Setting up Trading Partner Desktop
- Installing Trading Partner Desktop
- Configuring Communications and Adding a Trading Partner
- Configuring a Trading Partner and Adding Transaction Sets
- Mapping Transaction Sets
- EDI Files, Processing, and Exchanging Data with External Applications
- Exchanging and Examining EDI Mail
- Automating EDI Processing with Task Lists

Chapter 6

Setting Up Trading Partner Desktop

Introduction

The chapters in Part 2 guide you through the installation and use of Trading Partner Desktop (TPD), which is included on the CD at the back of this book. Note that the program on the CD is a 60-day evaluation version. It is full-featured and permits you to perform all operations required to install the software, set up trading partners and VANs, and even exchange EDI mail.

When the evaluation period ends, you can purchase the system from Mercator Software, Inc. They will supply you with a registration key. Once entered, you can resume your use of TPD.

What You Need

TPD is delivered on a program CD similar to the one supplied with this book. It is also available on floppy diskettes, but since all of today's Windows-based PCs are equipped with CD-ROM drives, this is probably not an issue. The CD supplied with this book includes the transaction sets used with the practice activities found in this book, so for now, at least, you won't need the ANSI Standard Set CD that is typically shipped with the TPD program. The ANSI Standard Set CD contains hundreds of standard transaction sets. This CD lets you add new transaction sets whenever needed to accommodate a trading partner's EDI requirements.

After TPD is installed by following the instructions in Chapter 7, you must perform the following steps.

- Add and configure a network mailbox. This lets you establish a communications link with your trading partner or with your trading partner's value-added network. The steps required to do this are described in Chapter 8.

- Add one or more trading partners to your system. You can obtain a *Trading Partner PC Kit* from Mercator Software, Inc. that provides preconfigured transaction sets and header information for a number of large companies. You can also configure your trading partners manually. To ensure that you know how to do this, a step-by-step configuration procedure is provided in Chapter 8.

- For each of your trading partners, you must also install and configure all transaction sets that are required. This includes Purchase Orders (850s), Invoices (810s), Purchase Order Acknowledgements (855s), Electronic Catalogs (832s), and any other transaction sets that may be needed. Note that when you use the *Trading Partner Desktop Kit*, the transaction sets are also included, which eliminates the need to manually install each transaction set. However, if your trading partner has not been "kitted," then you must rely on a manual installation. This process is described in Chapters 9 and 10.

- Once everything is properly set up, you can exchange EDI mail with a trading partner. Each step in the exchange process is described in Chapter 11.

- The task of interfacing TPD to an external order processing system varies with the particular order processing system being used. Chapter 11 also walks you through a general approach to exporting EDI purchase orders from TPD and importing invoices back into TPD from your order processing system.

- With an understanding of the steps involved in both ends of an EDI exchange (incoming and outgoing), you can automate your system using preconfigured task lists and the Scheduler. Chapter 12 shows you how to write transaction scripts.

Now proceed to Chapter 7 to install TPD on your computer.

Review Questions

1. Once you install Trading Partner Desktop, how long can you use it?

2. When the evaluation period ends, how is TPD reactivated?

3. What is required to add new transaction sets to the standard version of TPD?

4. What is the purpose of a network mailbox?

5. What is a benefit of a Trading Partner Desktop Kit?

6. What two items can be used to automate EDI system operations?

Chapter 7

Installing Trading Partner Desktop (TPD)

Introduction

This chapter steps you through the setup process. First, hardware and software requirements for TPD installation are described. Next, you perform the installation using the TPD setup program. Finally, it's time to take notes. Be sure to obtain the information required for EDI communications using the suggestions in the Thing to Do section of this chapter.

Hardware and Software Requirements

To set up TPD, you need a Pentium class PC. Almost any PC acquired within the past year should do, as they are typically equipped with a CD and hard disk drive, an SVGA display adapter and monitor, at least 32 MB of random access memory, a 28.8 to 56K modem, and a mouse. The basic program requires approximately 30 MB of hard disk space and 24 MB of memory, so almost any modern PC will suffice. However, when you begin adding trading partners, transaction set maps, and archives of EDI mail transactions, at least 40 MB of free disk space is advisable. The operating system must be Windows 95, 98, NT, or 2000. If you are using NT or 2000 server, you must be logged in with a user profile that has administrator privileges.

Installation

To install TPD, perform the following steps.

NOTE: If you wish to abort the installation, click Cancel. Then click Exit to stop the installation process.

Running Setup

1. Close all programs. If the Microsoft Office taskbar is displayed, close it.

2. Insert the Trading Partner Desktop CD in your CD drive. It should autorun. If it doesn't, click the Windows **Start** button, click **Run**, type **D:Setup.exe**, and press **Enter**. Note that D: is your CD-ROM drive designator; use the appropriate drive letter for your PC.

3. Click the icon to the left of Trading Partner in the Install | Update box.

4. Watch the progress bar as the InstallShield Wizard copies the setup files.

5. Read the Trading Partner Desktop End-User License Agreement (EULA) and click the **Yes** button to continue.

6. Enter the License Key in the space provided and click **Next**. This number can be found on the About the CD page at the back of the book.

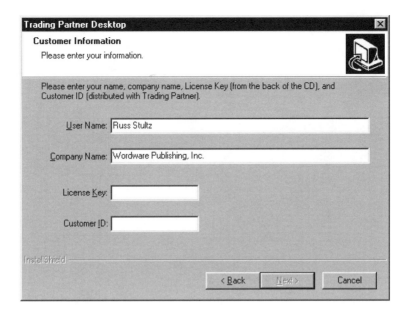

7. Respond to the Choose Destination dialog by clicking **Next** to accept the C:\Program Files\Trading Partner folder.

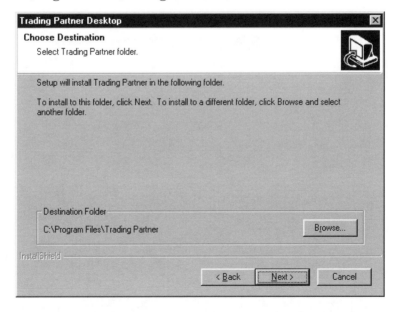

8. Respond to the second Choose Destination dialog by clicking **Next** to accept the C:\Program Files\Trading Partner\Edata folder.

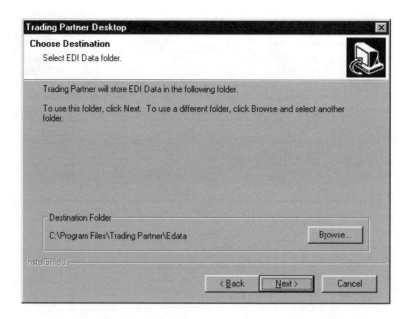

9. Respond to the third Choose Destination dialog by clicking Next to accept
    the C:\Program Files\Futrsoft\Dynacomm folder. Dynacomm is an asyn-
    chronous communications program.

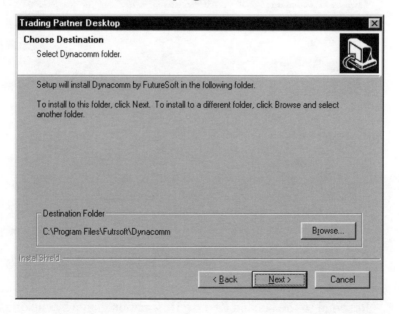

10. Check that the Typical option button is selected and click **Next** to accept
    the setup type.

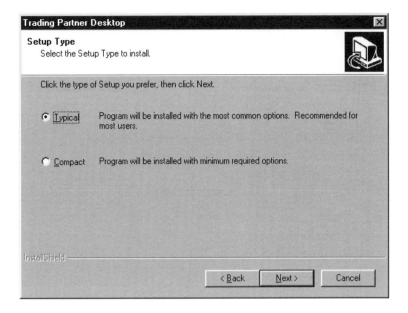

11. Watch the progress of the setup status by watching the following Setup Status dialog.

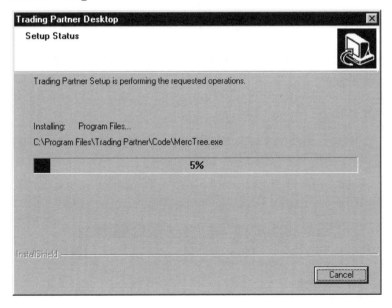

12. With the Yes I want to restart my computer now option button selected, click **Finish**.

Once your computer has restarted, continue on to the next installation procedure.

Installing Adobe Acrobat Reader

Adobe Acrobat Reader is used to read the online TPD help information, which is essentially an online instruction manual. You should find just about anything you need to know about TPD in the online help. Perform the following steps to install Adobe Acrobat Reader.

1. Put the Trading Partner Desktop CD in your CD-ROM drive. If the Setup screen is launched, click Exit.

2. Select **Run** from the Start menu. Click **Browse** and on your CD-ROM drive, select the D:\TP\Documentation\ar405eng.exe file.

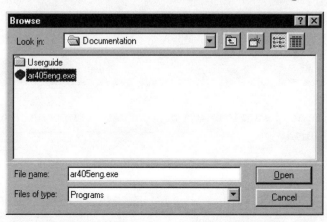

3. Click **Open**, then click **OK** to begin installing the Adobe Acrobat Reader.

4. Notice that the file is "unpacked." Then the first Setup dialog of the Adobe Acrobat Reader setup program is displayed. Click **Next**.

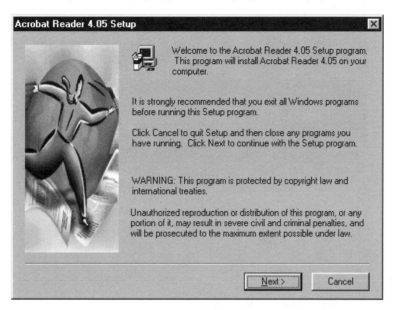

5. Click **Next** to accept the C:\Program Files\Adobe\Acrobat 4.0 folder.

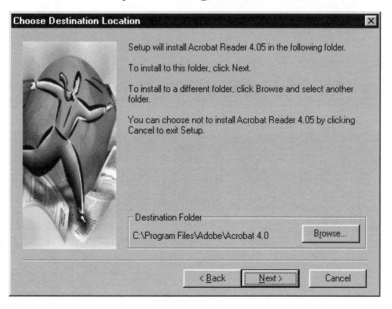

6. Notice that the file is installed. Click **OK** to finish the setup program.

Now you can read the online help information by clicking Help on the TPD main menu bar.

Some System Settings

In this section you start TPD and then make a few adjustments to the system settings. This includes checking the system's audit log, text editor, and archive settings.

1. Start TPD using the Windows **Start | Programs | Trading Partner** menu. Notice that the Desktop is displayed.

2. Click the **System Management** icon. Notice the System Management tasks.

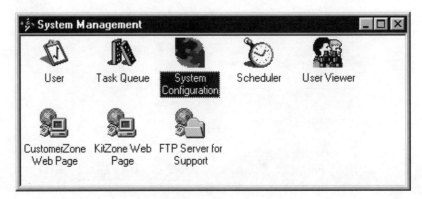

3. Click the **System Configuration** icon. This is where you enter the system's Audit Log Settings, Data File Settings, Registration Server, and system Preferences.

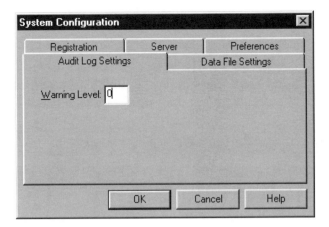

4. Type **1** in the Warning Level box of the Audit Log Settings tab. This "instructs" TPD to display a warning message for severe errors. A zero lets processes continue without displaying warnings. A 14 invokes warning messages for all errors. You can view a list of operations, warnings, and errors using the View | Audit Log selection on TPD's main menu bar.

5. Click **Data File Settings**. You can change the editor and archive level in this dialog. Type **Edit.com** as the Editor name and type **25** as the Archive Level. Leave TSIEdit.exe as the EDI Editor. This is my preferred editor for viewing EDI mail files because it shows row and column positions.

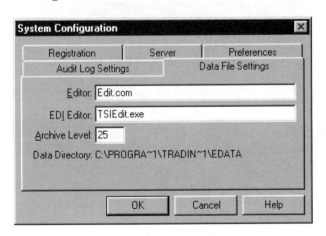

6. Click the **Preferences** tab to view the following dialog. Leave the first two check boxes checked. This permits single clicks and retains window sizes and arrangements each time you exit and restart TPD. Other entries are described in the following list:

   ■ **Hide Trading Partner Documents** Selecting this brings transaction set icons up one level in your trading partner window.

■ **Show Task List contents during install** This shows a list of tasks when you install new transaction sets. The default is to automatically install the most common tasks.

■ **Do not build Task Lists during install** This prevents TPD from building the default task list during a transaction set installation process.

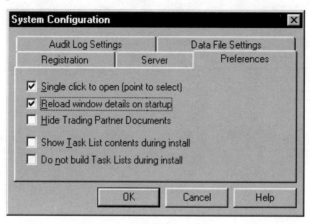

7. Click the **Registration** tab to view the next dialog. This is where you enter your License Key and Customer ID.

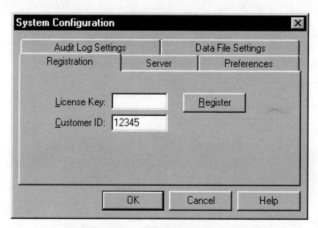

The customer ID is provided by Mercator Software, Inc. For now, you have a fully functional system that will operate for 60 days. When the time period expires, the program will stop working. Obtaining a user license and entering the supplied registration code restores operation.

8. Click **OK** to save the current settings and return to the Desktop.

You now have 60 days to use the program. If you decide to keep it, simply contact Mercator Software, Inc. to arrange for a permanent license and technical support. For now, use **File | Exit** to exit the program. Carefully review the following information in preparation for adding a communications link, trading partner, and transaction sets.

Things to Do

All of the information required to configure and use TPD is provided in the hands-on learning activities contained in the following chapters of this book. However, when you install the program in a production environment, you must obtain a number of values and IDs from your trading partners. Following is a checklist that will help you gather the required information.

1. Determine a method of communication that you can use to exchange EDI mail with your trading partner. Be sure that you are using a modem that is compatible with the agreed upon network. Once your modem is properly installed and tested, gather the following information about your network:

    ■ Type of communications you are using (asynchronous or bisynchronous—you should know this before installing a modem)

        ■ Data communications speed (e.g., 9,600 or 57,600 bps)

        ■ Network ID and password (or user ID and password)

        ■ Network phone number your modem will dial

        ■ If applicable, network specific interconnects (when the network you are using is connected to another network, it is commonly referred to as a "network interconnect")

2. In an EDI partnership, you should consult with your trading partner and:

    ■ Determine the EDI standard, such as ASC X12 or EDIFACT, and the transaction sets and versions (e.g., 850 Purchase Order and 810 Invoice version 003020) that are required to exchange EDI information. Note that the version you use usually corresponds to the industry that you serve. In this book, we use X12 asynchronous communications and version 003020 transaction sets.

    ■ Discuss electronic addresses, and mutually agree upon values for codes, qualifiers, and IDs to be used to identify you and your partner within the EDI data. The first two lines of an ASC X12 EDI mail document are called the ISA and the GS segments. These segments comprise the *header*, and identify the sender, receiver, and a number of other key parameters. For example, the header segments include the transaction set designator and version (e.g., 850 Purchase Order version 003020), a date and time stamp, a sequential number, and other information, such as:

■ Interchange ID Qualifier and Sender ID (ISA05 and ISA06) to identify the sender of the interchange.

■ Interchange ID Qualifier and Receiver ID (ISA07 and ISA08) to identify the receiver of the interchange.

■ Application Sender's/Receiver's Code (GS02 and GS03) to identify the sender and receiver of the group.

■ Optional Authorization Information Qualifier and ID (ISA01 and ISA02) to identify the sender of the interchange.

■ Optional Security Information Qualifier and ID (ISA03 and ISA04) to identify the sender and satisfy security requirements of the receiving trading partner.

TIP: One of the best ways to obtain the values you need in a transaction set, including both the header and interior elements, is to obtain an actual transaction set example from your trading partner. In addition to the examples, many large companies maintain a staff of experienced EDI professionals. Smaller companies use consultants. In either case, most trading partners can provide detailed guidelines for each of the transaction sets used. One of the goals of this book is to teach you how to interpret these guidelines so that you can map your trading partner's transaction sets to your system. As you move through the configuration process, you work with real transaction sets and learn their structures.

Following is an example of the first two segments of an ASC X12 EDI mail document—the ISA and GS segments. These two segments comprise the header of an ANSI ASC X12 transaction set. The asterisks are delimiters that are used to separate each of the elements within the ISA and GS segments. If you have experience with databases, you can think of each line as a record (called a segment in EDI circles) and each data element (called an element) as a field.

```
ISA*00*0000000000*00*0000000000*ZZ*MYADR12        *ZZ*ACME321
       *000922*0022*U*00302*000000104*0*P*>
GS*IN*MYADR12*ACME321*000922*0022*65*X*003040
```

In the preceding example notice that an asterisk (*) is used as a delimiter. *Delimiters* separate elements within each segment. Other characters are used as delimiters, but the asterisk is probably the most common. Note that some elements can be subdivided. By EDI definition, an *element* is the smallest possible entity within a transaction set. Segments are comprised of elements. However, even elements are sometimes subdivided. TPD calls them subelements, and a subelement delimiter, which could be a colon, greater than symbol (>), or other character, is used to separate one or more element subdivisions. However, if you're ever asked, "What is the smallest subdivision of a transaction set?" element is the technically correct answer. The term subelement is unique to TPD and only used to specify an element's subdividing delimiter, called a *component* by the ASC X12 specification. Components are rarely used in ASC X12 transaction sets. However, EDIFACT transaction sets make liberal use of components.

Each of the elements within the ISA and GS segments contain values that reveal information about the sender, receiver, transaction date and time, document identification (control number), and more. Following are descriptions of each of the elements of the ISA and GS segments.

ISA01—Authorization information qualifier; qualifies the value found in ISA02. The value is usually "00," meaning that no authorization information exists in the next element, i.e., element ISA02 is blank

ISA02—Authorization information; this is either blank or the sender's password

ISA03—Security information qualifier ("00" means that no security information exists in the next element, i.e., element ISA04 is blank)

ISA04—Security information (receiver's password)

ISA05—Interchange ID Qualifier; qualifies the next element. "ZZ" is used in the example

ISA06—Interchange sender's ID or EDI address

ISA07—Interchange ID Qualifier; qualifies the next element. "ZZ" is used in the example

ISA08—Interchange receiver's ID or EDI address

ISA09—Interchange date expressed in YYMMDD format

ISA10—Interchange time expressed in 24-hour format (HHMM).

ISA11—Interchange standard ID; "U" is the ANSI ASC X12 standard identifier code

ISA12—Interchange version ID; identifies the standard version/release for this interchange

ISA13—Interchange control number; this is a unique number used to track interchanges. This value is incremented by 1 for each subsequent interchange

ISA14—Functional acknowledgement request flag, where "0" signifies that the trading partner does not require an interchange acknowledgement

ISA15—Production or test indicator, where "P" signifies a production document and "T" signifies test

GS01—Functional identifier code, where IN=Invoice, PO=Purchase Order, FA=Functional Acknowledgement, etc.

GS02—Application sender's ID or EDI address (can differ from sender's interchange address found in ISA06)

GS03—Application receiver's ID or EDI address (can differ from receiver's interchange address found in ISA08)

GS04—Group date in YYMMDD format; this specifies when the document was sent

GS05—Group time in HHMM format

GS06—Group control number; a unique sequentially assigned number for each functional group

GS07—Responsible agency code; X signifies that the document is compliant with the ANSI ASC X12 standard

GS08—Version/release indicator; the 003040 transaction set version shown in the example

Chapter 9 examines these values again and steps you through an actual checklist. More information about the interior segments and elements found in an EDI transaction set and the purpose of each is presented in Chapter 10. In addition, actual examples of transaction set specifications are included in Appendix A.

3. Establish a communications link between you and your partner by adding and configuring a network mailbox. You may be required to establish a relationship with a VAN, which should supply dial-up numbers, a user name, and a user password.

4. Add one or more trading partners to your system. Although the procedures in this book walk you through a manual installation, you can obtain a TPD Kit for several large trading partners, which automates the process.

5. Install and configure all transaction sets you intend to trade with your partner. (Note: If you install a trading partner using a TPD Kit, you can skip this step, since your transaction sets are added when you install the kit.)

6. Familiarize yourself with the online help information. It provides a good overview of EDI in addition to walking you through the various components of TPD.

7. Familiarize yourself with the steps used to process inbound and outbound EDI documents. Also examine the directory structures and key filenames so that you know where files are kept and their purpose.

8. Learn how to automate your system using the preconfigured task lists and the scheduler.

9. Will you be importing or exporting EDI data from or to another application outside of TPD? If so, see Chapter 11 for complete details.

What's Next

Now that you've set up TPD and have reviewed the preceding checklist so that you know what information is required in a commercial environment, you are ready to proceed to the next phase. In the chapters that follow, you configure a communications link, add a trading partner, and then "map" some actual EDI transaction sets.

After you have configured the system for EDI exchanges, you must also consider how to exchange EDI files (purchase orders and invoices) between TPD and an external order processing system. This is discussed at length in Chapter 11. Additional chapters describe some of TPD's automation features that simplify many repetitive tasks that are performed during each EDI exchange.

Review Questions

1. How much disk space and memory should you have available before installing TPD?

2. How much disk space is advisable?

3. What should you do to any running programs before you install TPD?

4. Why do you need Adobe Acrobat Reader?

5. What happens when you put a value of 14 in the System Configuration Warning Level box?

6. What is the purpose of the first two check boxes of the System Configuration Preferences dialog?

7. Where are the ISA and GS segments found in a transaction set?

8. What is the purpose of the ISA and GS segments found in a transaction set?

Chapter 8

Configuring Communications and Adding a Trading Partner

Introduction

Now that TPD is set up, you are ready to begin configuring the system so you can exchange EDI mail with your trading partners. The first thing you must do is add a communications utility; then add the trading partners and their IDs, qualifiers, and delimiters. Finally, you must add the transaction set versions and identify the interior elements.

This chapter takes you through the steps required to configure communications and then add a trading partner. The next chapter walks you through the addition of two different transaction sets.

Configuring Communications

The communications program that you select is used to connect to your trading partner, usually through a value-added network (VAN), but there are some trading partners that support point-to-point EDI communications. Follow the steps in this hands-on activity to locate and set up a communications program.

1.   Start TPD. The Desktop should be displayed.

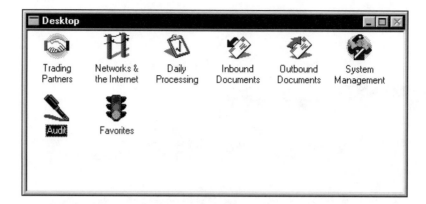

2. Double-click the **Networks & the Internet** icon.

3. Double-click the **Add New Network** icon. Notice the Network Wizard dialog.

4. With the Install pre-configured Network option button selected, click **Next**. Respond to the dialog that follows by inserting the companion CD into your CD-ROM drive.

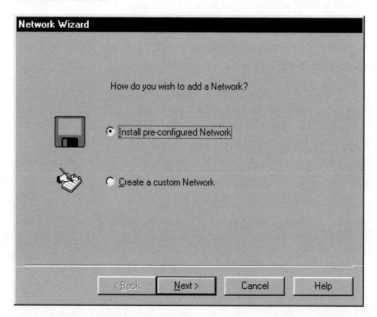

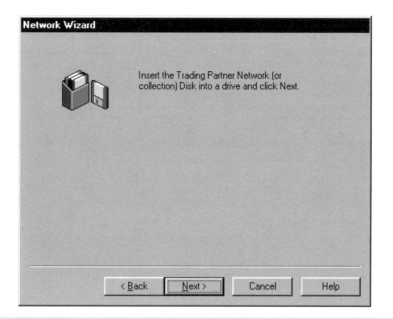

NOTE: If you choose to install a custom network, the Network Wizard is used to name and save it. Once saved, you can configure the communications parameters, name, password, modem, etc., using the Properties selection of the shortcut menu. The shortcut menu is displayed by right-clicking on the network name.

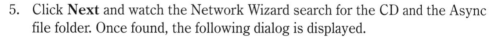

5. Click **Next** and watch the Network Wizard search for the CD and the Async file folder. Once found, the following dialog is displayed.

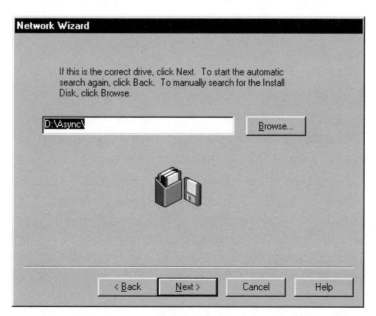

6. Click **Next** to view a list of supported networks. Although the companion CD only includes GEIS Async, the standard CD includes 22 popular value-added networks. These can be viewed in the list below the following illustration.

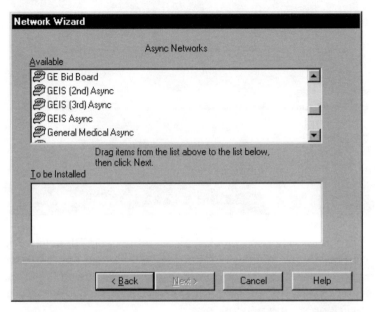

ACCESS Async	GEIS Async
Advantis	GEIS (2nd) Async
AirEx Async	GEIS (3rd) Async
Allegiance Async	General Medical Async
ATTPlus Async	GPCNet Async
Baxter Async	Kleinschmidt Async
BCSL Async	SCC Async
Beverage Data Network	Sprint Async
Commerce Network Async	TemplarC
EDINet Async	Transettlements Async
GE Bid Board	Wildcat BBS

7. Double-click **GEIS Async** and notice that GEIS Async moves to the To be Installed pane. If required, you can install multiple networks in support of multiple trading partners.

8. Click **Next**. Notice that the Network Wizard prompts you for a network name. This is used as a folder name. Keep the GEIS-A name.

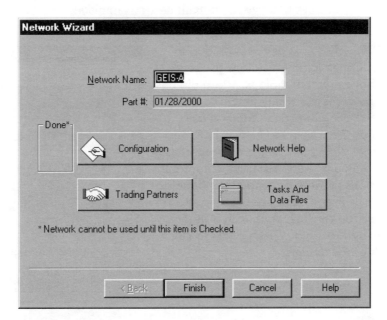

9. Click **Next**. Notice that the asynchronous communications files are copied to your hard drive. Next, you are presented with a Network Wizard dialog with four main buttons: Configuration, Trading Partners, Network Help, and Tasks And Data Files.

10. Click **Configuration** and examine the following dialog. Here, you can select those settings that are compatible with your computer and the network you are using. This includes such things as baud rate, data bits, stop bits, connection (or communications port), and other settings. The following dialog is specific to the Dynacomm asynchronous communications package. This dialog varies with the selected network. For example, the selections that you make will vary depending on the VAN.

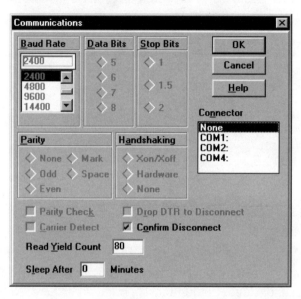

11. Click **Cancel** to leave the default settings in place.

NOTE: The next dialog is unique to GEIS. Other communications packages will have different dialogs. These dialogs can be accessed at any time by right-clicking the corresponding icon, such as GEIS-A, in the Networks & the Internet dialog and selecting Properties. This dialog is used to select the communications parameters, modem, phone number, user ID and password, and more. You can see what each button does by clicking it. Click Cancel to close each of the dialogs.

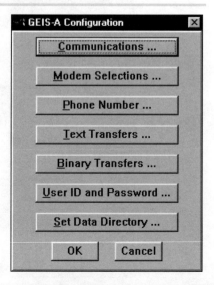

12. Click **OK**. Now click **Finish**. Notice that the GEIS-A icon is now in the Networks & the Internet dialog. Remember, you can right-click this icon and select Properties to change your asynchronous communications parameters at any time.

NOTE: You can uninstall a network, or other items for that matter, by selecting it and then using Edit | Uninstall on the TPD menu bar.

13. Close the Networks & the Internet dialog.

Now that one or more communications networks are installed, you can add one or more trading partners. Proceed to the next hands-on activity to learn how to add a trading partner to your system.

Adding a Trading Partner

You can add a trading partner in any of three ways:

- ■ Using a Mercator Software, Inc. Customized Kit
- ■ Manually
- ■ Using a customized kit over the mercator.com Web site. (This can only be done by licensed users. You cannot download a customization kit from Mercator's Web site without a user name and password. However, you can view a list of available customization kits.)

You can check with Mercator to determine if your trading partner has been kitted. If a kit exists for one of your trading partners, it will make the process much faster. In addition, valid transaction set maps will be installed for you when you install the kit.

In the following activity you add a new trading partner manually. This way, you will know how to set up virtually any trading partner. Be sure that you are at the TPD Desktop dialog.

1. Double-click the **Trading Partners** icon. Notice that an Add New Trading Partner icon is available.

2. Double-click the **Add New Trading Partner** icon; select the Create a custom Trading Partner option button on the first Trading Partner Wizard dialog.

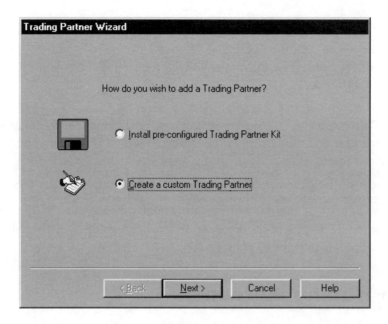

3. Click **Next** to display the next wizard dialog. Then select **GEIS-A**.

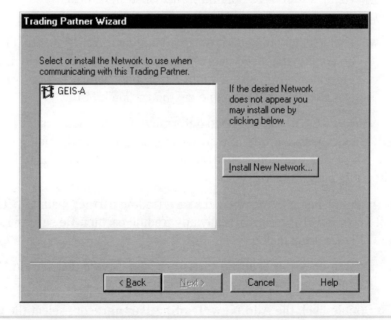

NOTE: Notice the Install New Network button. If you had not previously installed a network, you would be able to install it here.

4. Click **Next** to view the next dialog. Here, you enter a trading partner name and select the EDI standard to use with the trading partner. Type **Acme**. Notice that the name is mirrored in the Folder box. This is where all of Acme's files will be maintained. Then select **X12 ISA-IEA** as the EDI standard.

Trading Partner Wizard

Enter the name to Display for this Trading Partner

Name: Acme

Folder: Acme

X12 ISA-IEA
X12 BG-EG
X12 ICS-ICE
EDIFACT
TRADACOMS

Select the EDI Standard to use with this Trading Partner

< Back | Next > | Cancel | Help

TIP: Use a meaningful name. You may wish to keep it short, as any export and import programs that are written to interface TPD with an order processing system will likely have to include the folder name. Names like Acme, Kmart, Sams, Sears, and Target are ideal.

5. Click **Next** to display the next dialog of the Trading Partner Wizard. Here, you can begin configuring trading partner IDs, qualifiers, transaction sets, tasks, and data files.

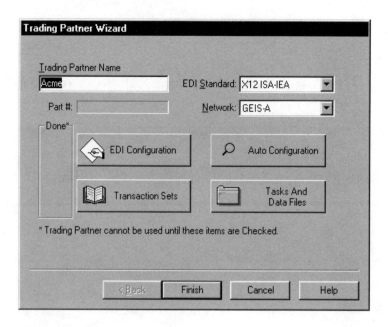

6. Click **EDI Configuration** to display the X12 ISA-IEA Envelope Configuration dialog. Here, you enter values that identify both you and your trading partner. The information is found in the elements of the first (ISA) and the last (IEA) segment of a transaction set. These two segments comprise the *envelope*. Therefore the values you type here go into the ISA segment described in the preceding chapter. The IEA segment is the last segment found in an ANSI ASC X12 standard transaction set. For every ISA segment, there is a matching IEA segment.

7. Type the following information in the indicated edit boxes:

    Your EDI Information:

    >   Qualifier: **ZZ** (This is used in the ISA05 or ISA07 elements.)

    >   Code: **1234567** (Type your EDI exchange ID found in ISA06 or ISA08.)

    Your Partner's EDI Information:

    >   Qualifier: **ZZ** (This is used in the ISA05 and ISA07 elements.)

    >   Code: **7654321** (Type your partner's EDI exchange ID found in ISA06 or ISA08.)

8. Notice the Standard ID "U" and the Standard Version "00302." These are found in the ISA11 and ISA12 elements. (See Chapter 7 for a list of the ISA and GS elements.)

9. Click **OK** to complete the envelope configuration. A checkmark is displayed next to the EDI Configuration button. This indicates that values have been entered. The absence of a checkmark indicates that the dialog is incomplete.

10. Notice the Auto Configuration button. If you have a valid transaction set in the network folder, you can click this button to automatically configure the transaction sets found in the transaction set file. If the GEIS-A network is used, the transaction set(s) would be in the file C:\Program Files\Trading Partner\Edata\Geis-a\Mail_in.new, where the file Mail_in.new is used for inbound transaction sets. The file Mail_out.new is used for outbound transaction sets. These filenames are used by TPD; the names are not part of any governing EDI standard. Chapter 11 describes TPD filename conventions.

11. Click **Finish** to complete the configuration. You will come back to this dialog to add transaction sets in the next chapter. Selecting a trading partner and then picking Properties in the shortcut menu accesses the configuration dialog.

12. Exit TPD. You are now ready to begin adding EDI transaction sets.

The Trading Partner Directory Structure

If you are reading this part of the book, you probably are an experienced Microsoft Windows user, and you probably use Windows Explorer on a regular basis. Here, you can examine TPD's directory structure in the following diagram. Note that some directories do not exist until you add trading partners and transaction sets.

```
C:\Program Files\Trading Partner\
    Code
    Documentation
    Edata
        <Network> (like Geis-a or Advantis)
            <Partner> (trading partner name)
                <Standard> (like Ansi)
                    <TransactionSet> (like 3040)
                        <Version> (like 810 and 850)
                            Archive (processed files archived
                                        here)
    Favorite
    Help (TPD help files)
    NetSetup (Workgroup Only) (networking security/permission files)
    Reports (reports)
    System (program files)
        Mask
        Template
        Maps
            Ansi (Ansi standard maps and transaction set control
                    files)
    Tasklists (script files that control repetitive tasks)
    User (user information and registration files)
```

What's Next

Now that you have configured a communications link and set up a trading partner, you can begin adding the transaction sets that are required by your trading partners. This is done in the next chapter. Although you are using a fictitious trading partner, the procedures are completely valid and can be used with valid partners. In particular, examining and setting up valid transaction sets and then studying the interior data elements will reveal a great deal about EDI documents and the systems that are used to process them.

Review Questions

1. What is the purpose of the communications package supplied with TPD?

2. How many popular value-added network communications programs are included with the standard TPD product?

3. What does the Networks & the Internet dialog's Properties button display?

4. How are networks and other items uninstalled from TPD?

5. List three ways to install a trading partner.

6. Where are the values used that you enter into the Envelope Configuration dialog?

Chapter 9

Configuring a Trading Partner and Adding Transaction Sets

Introduction

Now that you have a communications link and trading partner installed, you are ready to configure the trading partner and add the required EDI transaction sets. If you are a supplier, your trading partner should provide all necessary information relative to the communications link, transaction set version, and interior elements used. If you are the procuring trading partner, you must provide this information to your suppliers. In this book, assume that you are the supplying trading partner. You receive purchase orders (form 850s) from your trading partners and send functional acknowledgements (form 997s) and invoices (form 810s) to them.

Although you assume the role of a supplying trading partner in this book, remember that TPD can easily handle outbound purchase orders and inbound invoices just as easily. In fact, TPD lets you assume the roles of both a supplying and acquiring trading partner, as is often the case of manufacturing companies that work with both suppliers and distributors.

Using Your Checklist

Before you can configure a trading partner, it is necessary to collect the information found in the checklist described in Chapter 7. You may also have to establish a relationship with the value-added network. Your trading partner can usually supply contact information. The VANs customer support organization will provide one or more access (dial-up) numbers, a user name and password, and a rate schedule.

TIP: Note that VANs typically bill a flat monthly fee, connection fees, and charge for each kilobyte exchanged. Some VANs discount exchanges made at off-hour times (nights and weekends). Most established VANs have Web sites that let you look at your inbox for pending EDI mail before you connect. You can also browse your outbox to verify that your EDI mail was successfully received by the VAN. Inbox and outbox archives are also maintained so you can check EDI mail documents that were sent in the past 30 to 60 days.

Following is a checklist that is designed to help you collect the values needed for the first two segments of a transaction set, i.e., the ISA and GS header segments. Provisions are also made for communications values needed to link to your VAN. If you enter the field of EDI, feel free to use the checklist for gathering your own information.

Many of the values in the checklist have been filled in and should be used when configuring your trading partner in the activities that follow. Also notice that many values are automatically entered by TPD; these values are derived from the system date and time and the type of transaction set being processed.

Element	Description	Value
ISA01	Authorization information qualifier	00
ISA02	Authorization information	blank (or null)
ISA03	Security information qualifier	00
ISA04	Security information (receiver's password)	blank (or null)
ISA05	Interchange identification qualifier	ZZ
ISA06	Interchange sender's (trading partner's) identification	ACME321
ISA07	Interchange identification qualifier	ZZ
ISA08	Interchange receiver's (your) identification (or address)	MYADR12
ISA09	Interchange date (entered at processing time)	Entered by TPD
ISA10	Interchange time (entered at processing time)	Entered by TPD
ISA11	Interchange standard ID	U
ISA12	Interchange version ID	00200
ISA13	Interchange control number (entered at processing time)	Entered by TPD
ISA14	Functional acknowledgement request flag	0
ISA15	Production or test indicator (entered at processing time)	P or T
GS01	Functional identifier code (PO, IN, FA, etc.)	Entered by TPD

Element	Description	Value
GS02	Application sender's ID (trading partner's) (may differ from ISA06)	ACME321
GS03	Application receiver's (your) ID (may differ from ISA06)	MYADR12
GS04	Group date (YYMMDD) (entered at processing time)	Entered by TPD
GS05	Group time (HHMM) (entered at processing time)	Entered by TPD
GS06	Group control number	Entered by TPD
GS07	Responsible agency code; X=ANSI ASC X12 standard	Entered by TPD
GS08	Version/release indicator; 003040 version	Entered by TPD
VAN-1	General Electric Information Systems	GEIS-A
VAN-2	Telephone number (voice)	888-555-5555
VAN-3	Telephone number (fax)	972-555-1234
VAN-4	Web site address	www.geis.com
VAN-5	Dial-up number (57.6 kflex)	214-555-5432
VAN-6	User name	MYADR12
VAN-7	User password	MYADR999

In addition to the information found in the checklist, you must also obtain detailed transaction set specifications. Your trading partner should provide you with a detailed layout of each required transaction set. The partner can usually send you layout specifications by e-mail or you can download the specifications from your trading partner's Web site. These layouts will be similar to the ones shown in Appendix A. However, they may not be as complete.

In the examples used in this and following chapters, you use the 003040 version 850 (PO) and 810 (invoice). The 850 and 810 are among the most common transaction sets in use today. There are a large number of different transaction set types including electronic catalogs (SC832), purchase order acknowledgements (PR855), and many others.

Version 003040 is one of hundreds of possible formats. In fact, the publisher of this book uses versions 003010, 003020, and 003040 in order to trade with major book retailers and distributors. Each industry has one or more versions that fit their unique requirements. In addition to these, you will also send and receive functional acknowledgements (FA997s), which acknowledge the receipt of an EDI document. TPD automatically prepares and sends a 997 for each inbound document received. The program also receives and saves inbound 997s that are sent by trading partners.

Configuring a Trading Partner and Adding Transaction Sets

Now that you've gathered the information found in the checklist, you're ready to enter configuration information for Acme. Begin by starting TPD. Once at the Desktop, proceed as follows.

1. Click the **Trading Partners** icon. Then select **Acme**, right-click, and click **Properties**. (Note that you can also select a trading partner and press **Alt+Enter** to view the Trading Partner Wizard dialog.)

2. Click the **EDI Configuration** button. Enter the information shown in the following dialog and click **OK**.

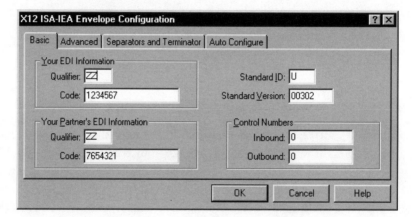

3. Add the 003040 850 and 003040 810 transaction sets as follows:

NOTE: Mercator Software, Inc. supplies an ASC X12 Standards Collection CD when you purchase TPD. This CD contains more than 1,500 different transaction sets. The CD used in this book contains the 003040 version with the 850, 810, and 997 transaction sets. These are the only ones that are required for the activities in this book.

Click the **Transaction Sets** button on the Trading Partner Wizard dialog and look at the following dialog.

Click **Install**. The following dialog is displayed.

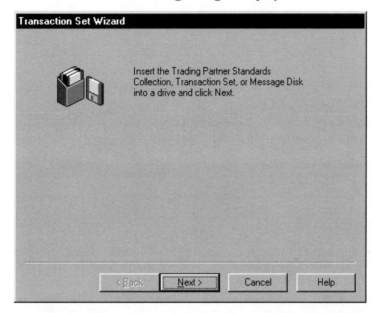

Insert the companion CD in your CD-ROM drive.

Click **Next**. Wait for the Transaction Set Wizard to find the D:\X12 directory.

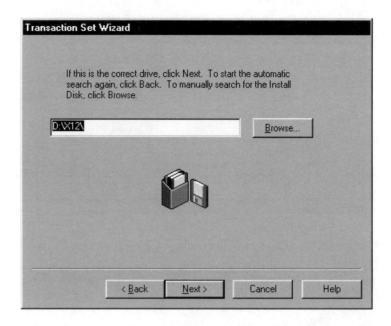

Click **Next.** Then double-click (or drag) the 810 3040, 850 3040, and 997 lines from the Available to the To be Installed pane. This dialog typically contains a list of transaction sets beginning with 100 4010 Insurance Plan Desc. and ending with 999 ALL UCS Functional Acknowledgement.)

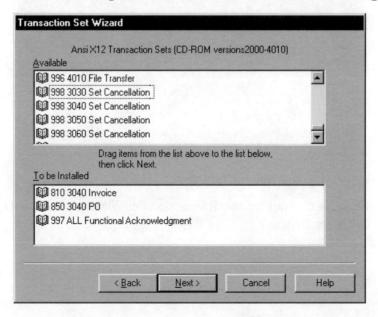

Click **Next.** Using the following dialog, install the 810Ver3040 transaction set.

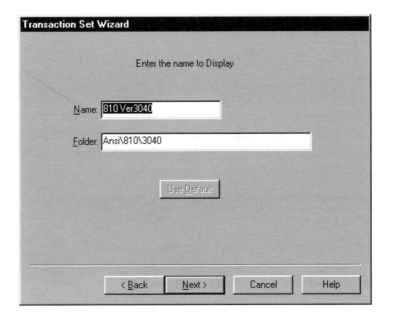

Click **Next**. Notice the dialog that follows and the progress bar. When finished, the Task List Direction dialog is displayed. This dialog lets you
differentiate between inbound and outbound documents. Click **Outbound**
(sent to Trading Partner) since this is an invoice (810).

Click **Next** to view the 850 Ver3040 dialog. Click **Next** and make it an
Inbound transaction set. Then install the 997VerALL transaction set and
click **Finish** to complete the job.

4. Compare your dialog with the following illustration.

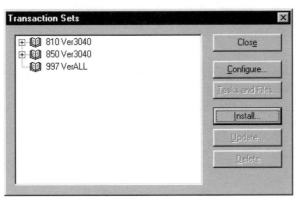

5. Click **Close** to finish the job. Notice that the Transaction Set button still
doesn't have a checkmark by it, which indicates that the transaction set has
not yet been configured. This is done in the next chapter. For now click
Finish and then exit TPD.

Automatic Configuration

TPD includes a feature called *automatic configuration*. To use this feature you must have a valid transaction set from your trading partner. This file must be named Mail_in.new and be located in the folder \Program Files\Trading Partner\Edata*vanname*, where *vanname* is the name of your value-added network provider, such as Geis or Advantis. When the Mail_in.new file is available, you can open the Trading Partners dialog, right-click the trading partner's icon, and then select Properties from the shortcut menu.

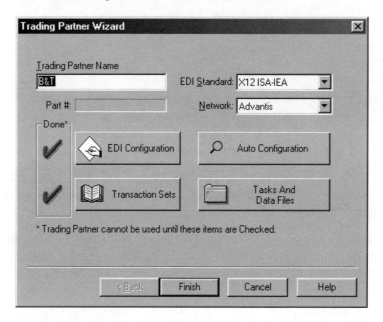

Notice the Auto Configuration button. When you click this button, TPD displays an additional dialog where you can add the header segments and elements, i.e., ISA and GS, of the selected transaction set. The configuration data is based on what exists in the header segments of the transaction set contained in the Mail_in.new file. This is the easy way to configure your trading partner, and only takes a few seconds from start to finish. Of course you must have valid transaction sets in the Mail_in.new file.

Looking Back

In the preceding activity you configured a trading partner and added three version 003040 transaction sets, i.e., an 850 (purchase order), 810 (invoice), and 997 (functional acknowledgement). The transaction sets reside in the Program Files\Trading Partner\System\Maps\Ansi folder.

Two files now exist for each transaction set. These are:

8103040.tm (translator map)
8103040.dbm (database map)
8503040.tm
8503040.dbm
997all.tm
997all.dbm

Neither the dbm nor the tm files have been configured yet. This is done in the next chapter. The dbm file contains all possible segments and elements found in the ANSI ASC X12 standard. When you map these transaction sets in the next chapter, the dbm files are used as a source. The final mapped dbm file is found in a unique trading partner folder. When mapped, it will only contain those elements required by the trading partner. The mapping process omits unused elements. In the case of Acme, you would find the resulting mapped file in the Program Files\Trading Partner\Edata\Geis-a\Acme\Ansi\810\3040 folder. The tm files are control files that are used to validate values found in the interior elements of a transaction set. Although most trading partners use standard code values, if your trading partner chooses to use a nonstandard value, you can add it to the corresponding segment line in the tm file. You are alerted to non-standard codes by an error message that includes the line number within the transaction set where the error occurred. Next, you must determine the element number such as PO105. Then look at the corresponding translator map file and locate the offending segment and element. Finally, you can open the translator map file and find the element code line. The element number is located at the end of the line. Add the required code as necessary. This is described in more detail in the discussion about tm files in Chapter 10.

What's Next

In the next chapter you map the 850 transaction set using the transaction set guidelines included in Appendix A. This is where the "rubber meets the road," as you will quickly see how a transaction set is organized, mapped, and used to exchange commercial information. In addition to the mapping activity, Chapter 10 also guides you through the creation of a cross reference file using the Fieldlst.exe utility that is provided with TPD. The cross reference file is an essential reference when writing export and import utilities that permit TPD to exchange information with external applications.

Review Questions

1. What items are typically considered as a basis for the charges billed by a VAN?

2. What is the purpose of the checklist found near the beginning of this chapter?

3. How do you use TPD to access a trading partner's EDI configuration properties?

4. What is contained on the ASC X12 Standards Collection CD that is distributed by Mercator Software?

5. What are dbm and tm files?

Chapter 10

Mapping Transaction Sets

Introduction

This chapter shows you how to use the information contained in the 8503040 and 8103040 transaction set guidelines found in Appendix A. Once you have this information in hand, using TPD's convenient DB Map Editor makes mapping easy. Begin by looking at the transaction set guidelines found in the appendix. Then follow the hands-on activity, which guides you through the transaction set mapping process.

The transaction set guideline examples in the appendix are thorough and extremely informative. Unfortunately, most guidelines are not always as complete. Therefore, to see every possible segment and element available in a transaction set, you can create and view a *cross reference file* (extension .xrf). An 8503040 cross reference file is created near the end of this chapter in preparation for the activities in Chapter 11.

After you add the 8503040 transaction set and create the cross reference file, an understanding of the contents of an xrf file is necessary. In addition to showing you every possible segment and element within a transaction set, it is an essential reference for those who want to know more about export and import files—the subject of Chapter 11.

Examining the Specifications

Appendix A contains two transaction set guidelines, or specifications, prepared by a trading partner. Use these guidelines to determine which segments and elements your trading partner requires. You can quickly see that only a small portion of the available segments and elements are used. Frequently a trading partner's guideline only includes those segments and elements that are required; those segments and elements that are not used are omitted.

Following is an excerpt from the 8503040 guidelines. Notice that there is a Heading, Detail, and Summary table. This is followed by a detailed description of each segment within the transaction set.

Heading:	Pos. No.	Seg. ID	Name	Req. Des.	Max. Use	Loop Repeat	Notes and Comments
Must Use	010	ST	Transaction Set Header	M	1		
Must Use	020	BIG	Beginning Segment for Invoice	M	1		
Not Used	030	NTE	Note/Special Instruction	F	100		
	040	CUR	Currency	O	1		
Not Used	050	REF	Reference Numbers	O	12		
Not Used	060	PER	Administrative Communications Contact	O	3		
			LOOP ID - N1			200	
	070	N1	Name	O	1		
	080	N2	Additional Name Information	O	2		
	090	N3	Address Information	O	2		
	100	N4	Geographic Location	O	1		

Detail:	Pos. No.	Set. ID	Name	Req. Des.	Max. Use	Loop Repeat	Notes and Comments
			LOOP ID - IT1			200000	
	010	IT1	Baseline Item Data (Invoice)	O	1		
Not Used	012	CRC	Conditions Indicator	O	1		
Not Used	015	QTY	Quantity	O	5		n2
Not Used	020	CUR	Currency	O	1		
Not Used	030	IT3	Additional Item Data	O	5		
	040	TXI	Tax Information	O	10		
Not Used	050	CTP	Pricing Information	O	25		
Not Used	059	MEA	Measurements	O	40		
			LOOP ID – PID			1000	
	060	PID	Product/Item Description	O	1		

Summary:	Pos. No.	Set. ID	Name	Req. Des.	Max. Use	Loop Repeat	Notes and Comments
Must Use	010	TDS	Total Monetary Value Summary	M	1		
	020	TXI	Tax Information	O	10		
	030	CAD	Carrier Detail	O	1		
			LOOP ID – SAC			25	
	040	SAC	Service, Promotion, Allowance, or Charge Information	O	1		
	050	TXI	Tax Information	O	10		
Not Used	060	ISS	Invoice Shipment Summary	O	5		
Must Use	070	CTT	Transaction Totals	M	1		n3
Must Use	080	SE	Transaction Set Trailer	M	1		

Heading and Summary

The segments that reside in the header and summary sections of a transaction set encase the segments that are used in the detail section. There may be thousands of header-summary pairs within an EDI document. Within each of these, thousands of detail entries can exist. Note that the ST and SE segments come in pairs. The header and summary section will always have a common control number. This makes it easy to locate the beginning and ending of each transaction set.

Detail

The segments within the detail section include descriptive elements for each of a *line item*'s SKU (stock-keeping unit) or part number, quantity, unit of measure, price, weight, etc.

Notice the Must Use and Not Used entries in the first column. This tells you which segments within the transaction set are required or not used. Those that are not annotated are available for use as needed. However, in many instances these elements are optional, depending on the type of product, the countries in which the trading partners reside, and similar factors. For example, if both trading partners are in the same country, the CUR (currency) entry may be unnecessary. However, if they are in different countries, currency may be important.

Following are descriptions of what each column includes:

Pos. No.—Position number is for reference only. It indicates the order of the segments within the transaction set's header, detail, or summary sections.

Seg. ID—Segment identification is used to identify each segment. ST is the transaction set header, BIG is the beginning segment for an invoice, and so on. Note that for every ST there must be a corresponding SE segment. In the ST-SE pair, each component contains an identical transaction set control number. The next ST-SE pair will contain the next transaction set control number, i.e., the value will be incremented by one.

Name—This is either the name or a text description of each segment.

Req. Des.—Data Segment Requirement Designation uses a number of syntactical requirement codes to specify the use of a data element.

M=mandatory; you must use this segment/element.

O=optional; the segment/element can be used or omitted.

Part 2

F=floating; the segment can be placed anywhere within the detail section of the transaction set, unlike other segments that must be placed in a particular position within the set, i.e., N2 must follow N1, etc.

P=paired; to be used, the element must always be paired with one or more other elements.

C=conditional; if one particular element exists, all other elements must also exist.

R=required; this element exists if at least one other specified element exists.

L=list condition; if the first element exists, then at least one more element should also exist.

E=exclusion; only one of the defined data elements can be present (rarely used).

X=special; the X usually means that you should read the supporting notes for this element to determine the syntactical requirements. The X is not part of the ANSI ASC X12 standard.

Max. Use—Maximum use specifies how many times the corresponding segment can be used within the detail set.

Loop Repeat—Looping is used when several descriptive codes are needed to describe an item. For example, an element may have codes for size, weight, color, and more. The same element may repeat (loop) many times to provide all necessary information about an item. Loops are a familiar concept to programmers who use loops to perform multiple events. A counter or an event is used to control the duration of a loop.

Looking More Closely

Now let's drill down a little deeper into the transaction set. Following is an excerpt from the transaction set specifications shown in Appendix A.

Segment:	**ST Transaction Set Header**
Position:	010
Loop:	
Level:	Heading
Usage:	Mandatory
Max Use:	1
Purpose:	To indicate the start of a transaction set and to assign a control number
Syntax Notes:	
Semantic Notes:	1 The transaction set identifier (ST01) used by the translation routines of the interchange partners to select the appropriate transaction set definition (e.g., 810 selects the Invoice Transaction Set).
Comments:	

Data Element Summary

	Ref. Des.	Data Element	Name		Attributes	
Must Use	ST01	143	Transaction Set Identifier Code		M	ID 3/3

Code uniquely identifying a Transaction Set

    810   X12.2 Invoice

	Ref. Des.	Data Element	Name		Attributes	
Must Use	ST02	329	Transaction Set Control Number		M	AN 4/9

Identifying control number that must be unique within the transaction set functional group assigned by the originator for a transaction set

Use to transmit a unique number assigned by the originator of the transaction set. This number may be system generated.

Segment:	**BIG** Beginning Segment for Invoice
Position:	020
Loop:	
Level:	Heading
Usage:	Mandatory
Max Use:	1
Purpose:	To indicate the beginning of an invoice transaction set and transmit identifying numbers and dates
Syntax Notes:	
Semantic Notes:	1 BIG10 indicates the consolidated invoice number. When BIG07 contains code CI, BIG10 is not used.
Comments:	1 BIG07 is used only to further define the type of invoice when needed.

Data Element Summary

	Ref. Des.	Data Element	Name		Attributes	
Must Use	BIG01	245	Invoice Date		M	DT 6/6

Invoice Issue Date.

Use to identify the date the transaction set was created. In the context of a commercial invoice, this date will represent the date of the invoice.

	Ref. Des.	Data Element	Name		Attributes	
Must Use	BIG02	76	Invoice Number		M	AN 1/22

Identifying number assigned by issuer

Use to uniquely identify the invoice transaction to an issuer. The invoice number may not be duplicated by an issuer in an original transaction (BIG08, code 00) within a 12-month period. Same number can be used if issuing an amended invoice (BIG08 is code 02, 03, or 04).

	Ref. Des.	Data Element	Name		Attributes	
	BIG03	323	Purchase Order Date		O	DT 6/6

Date assigned by the purchaser to Purchase Order

When BIG05 is used, cite the date of the delivery order, call or release. When BIG05 is not used, cite the date of the procurement instrument in BIG04.

	Ref. Des.	Data Element	Name		Attributes	
Must Use	BIG04	324	Purchase Order Number		O	AN 1/22

Identifying number for Purchase Order assigned by the orderer/purchaser

Use to identify the procurement instrument identification number (PIIN) other than an order against a basic procurement instrument, e.g., delivery order, release, or call. For purchase orders, cite the order number. For delivery, cite the basic procurement instrument identification number (e.g., the contract, grant, cooperative agreement, etc., number) and cite the delivery order or call number in BIG05.

	Ref. Des.	Data Element	Name		Attributes	
	BIG05	328	Release Number		O	AN 1/30

Number identifying a release against a Purchase Order previously placed by the parties involved in the transaction

Use to identify a delivery or task order, call or release number, (e.g., the Supplemental PIIN) against the basic procurement instrument cited in BIG04.

	BIG06	327	Change Order Sequence Number		O	AN 1/8

Number assigned by the orderer identifying a specific change or revision to a previously transmitted transaction set

Use, as applicable, to identify a modification number to the instrument in BIG05. If BIG05 is blank, use the PIIN in BIG04.

	BIG07	640	Transaction Type Code		O	ID 2/2
Must Use						

Code specifying the type of transaction

	CI	Consolidated Invoice
	CN	Credit Invoice
	CR	Credit Memo
	DI	Debit Invoice
	DR	Debit Memo

	BIG08	353	Transaction Set Purpose Code		O	ID 2/2
Must Use						

Code identifying purpose of transaction set

00 Original

Use to indicate the initial submission of an original invoice.

01 Cancellation

Use to indicate the cancellation of a previously submitted invoice.

02 Add

Use to indicate an amended invoice that contains only additions to a previously transmitted invoice.

03 Delete

Use to indicate an amended invoice that contains only deletions from a previously transmitted invoice.

04 Change

Use to indicate an amended invoice that contains a combination of additions and deletions to a previously transmitted invoice. This code is also used to indicate data in a previously transmitted invoice has changed, e.g., the quantity invoiced and the total invoiced amount. In effect, the old quantity and invoiced amount are deleted and the new quantity and invoiced amount are added.

05 Replace

07 Duplicate

Use to indicate a duplicate submission. Use only when informed that the original invoice was not received.

	BIG09	306	Action Code		O	ID 1/2

Code indicating type of action

F Final

Use to indicate the final invoice. Leave blank for partial invoices.

	BIG10	76	Invoice Number		O	AN 1/22
Not Used						

Identifying number assigned by issuer

First, notice the ST segment and the ST01 and the ST02 elements. The ST01 element contains the transaction set identifier code. This is a three-digit value such as 810, 832, 850, 997, etc., which identifies the type of transaction set being sent. The ST02 element contains the transaction set control number. As described above, this is a unique sequential number that identifies the current transaction set. The companion SE02 also includes this control number. The SE01 element (see one of the SE elements in Appendix A) contains a count of the total number of segments included in the transaction set. This count includes the ST and SE segments too.

All segments and elements are described in the table. To better understand what some of the information within the table means, some descriptions of the less obvious table headings and interior data follow.

Ref. Des.—The reference designator is an identifier that is assigned to each element within a segment by the ANSI X12 standard. BIG01, N102, and CTT02 are examples of reference designators.

Data Element—The ANSI X12 standard assigns a unique number to each data element within a transaction set.

Attributes—The attributes M, O, F, P, C, R, L, and E are mandatory, optional, floating, paired, conditional, required, list condition, and exclusion as described in the preceding Req. Des. entry description. X is sometimes used to indicate either "not used" or to designate that a syntactical relationship exists between two or more elements. The relationship should be described in supporting notes. Each of these data segment requirement designations are discussed above. The next code can be any of the following:

N=Number (an integer)

R=Real number (a decimal value)

DT=Date value

TM=Time value

ID=Code value (Code values are found in the ANSI X12 standard.)

C, Z, or X=Conditional value, usually used in pairings; if one value exists, one or more companion values must also exist. An example would be if N101 is BT (for bill to), a bill-to address must also be included.

1/22—This is a fractional value that specifies the minimum and maximum number of characters that can reside within an element. The value 1/22 means that a value containing anywhere from 1 to 22 characters or digits is permitted within the element. The value 6/6 means that the value must be six characters long. Note that a minus sign is not counted as a placeholder. Therefore, –24.95 is only five characters long and would fit within an element having an R 1/5 attribute.

Having the preceding definitions and a trading partner's transaction set table like the ones found in Appendix A make it fairly easy to map a transaction set. This is especially true when you have a mapping tool like the one provided with TPD. The transaction set map shows you every segment and element required. You may also want to examine the xrf files created at the end of this chapter.

Manual Mapping

You now have some background in how transaction sets are described. You are also familiar with much of the terminology that is used for mapping. With this background in place, you can begin mapping the 850 transaction set added in Chapter 9. You use the 8503040 table in Appendix A as a guide. Just work your way through the steps contained in the following hands-on mapping activity.

NOTE: In most cases some optional segments are used. However, for the purpose of experiencing the manual mapping process, you only add the Must Use segments and elements in the hands-on activity.

Hands-On Mapping Activity

In Chapter 9, you added two transaction sets. In this activity you start TPD and manually map the 8503040 transaction set.

1. Start TPD. If the Trading Partners dialog is not displayed, just click the **Trading Partners** icon to open it.

2. Double-click **Acme** to display the following dialog.

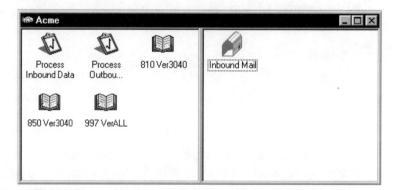

Notice that the 850 Ver3040 and the 810 Ver3040 transaction sets that you added in Chapter 9 are displayed.

3. Right-click on the **850 Ver3040** icon to display the shortcut menu. Then click **Properties**. Notice the following Transaction Set Wizard dialog. This is where you can create and edit database maps.

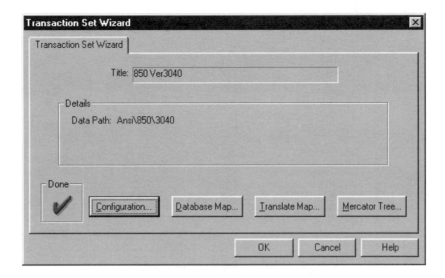

4. Click the **Database Map** button to launch the Database Map dialog.

5. Click **Create** to create a blank 850 Ver3040 map. Then click **Edit** to launch the DB Map Editor. Examine this dialog carefully.

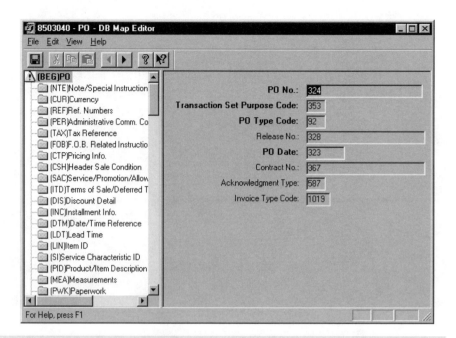

TIP: The pane on the left displays a list of ANSI ASC X12 segment reference designators. These correspond to the Ref. Des. column of the guidelines (the table in Appendix A). The right pane shows each of the elements that belong to the selected (highlighted) segment. In the illustration, the BEG segment is selected. Notice which elements are boldfaced and the number value that resides in each of the element fields. The boldface elements are selected for use; they correspond to "Must Use." The number is a value that corresponds to the ASC X12 standard. The guidelines in Appendix A include these values in the Data Element column.

The DB Map Editor can also be used to hide those elements and/or segments that you do not use. This is done by right-clicking on the element or segment and selecting Hidden. This removes unused segments and elements from the screen facilitating easy data entry.

At this point you can follow the Heading, Detail, and Summary tables at the top of the 850 guidelines to identify the required (Must Use) segments. Right-click on the optional segments to display the shortcut menu. This menu is illustrated in step 9 of this activity. Click Required to display the optional segment in boldface. Boldface entities are included in your transaction set map. Conversely, you can uncheck optional segments in the same way to exclude them from the map. You can also work your way down the segment pane one segment at a time. As you encounter each segment, you can edit each of the corresponding elements in accordance with the transaction set guidelines. Just check or uncheck the Required line in the shortcut menu.

6. After all required segments are properly identified in the left pane, go back to the top of the segment list and select the **(BEG)PO** line.

7. Compare the right pane to the BEG information found in the corresponding 8503040 Data Element Summary section of the guidelines table. An excerpt from the 8503040 table is shown here for your convenience.

	Ref. Des.	Data Element	Name		Attributes
Must Use	BEG01	353	**Transaction Set Purpose Code**		M ID 2/2
			Code identifying purpose of transaction set		
			00	Original	
				Use to indicate an original procurement instrument. This code is used only after the contractor has agreed to all terms and conditions to be contained in the procurement instrument transmitted.	
			07	Duplicate	
				Use to indicate the re-transmission of a previously transmitted procurement instrument.	
			22	Information Copy	
				Use to indicate that this is an informational copy of an original procurement instrument. This informational copy is sent to addresses other than the selling party, e.g., the Contract Administration Office.	
Must Use	BEG02	92	**Purchase Order Type Code**		M ID 2/2
			Code specifying the type of Purchase Order		
			Use to identify the type of procurement instrument represented by this transaction set.		
			LS	Lease	
			NE	New Order	
				Use to indicate a Purchase Order. A request has been submitted to ASC X12 to add a code for Purchase Order. We expect this code will be available for use in ASC X12 Version/Release 3050. In the meantime, use this code.	
			RL	Release or Delivery Order	
				An order for goods and services placed against a pre-existing contract or blanket order	
				Use to indicate releases, calls, or delivery orders against existing indefinite procurement instruments.	
			RT	Rental	
			ZZ	Mutually Defined	
				Use to indicate that a type of procurement instrument other than a lease, purchase order or delivery order is being issued. When used, use the following NTE segment to explain the type of procurement instrument being issued. A request has been submitted to ASC X12 to add codes for Agreement, Blanket Purchase Agreement, Contract, Basic Agreement, Basic Ordering Agreement, Grant, Indefinite Delivery Indefinite Quantity (IDIQ), Indefinite Delivery Definite Quantity (IDDQ), Requirements, Task Order, and Letter Contract. We expect these codes will be available for use in ASC X12 Version/Release 3050. Do not use for releases or delivery orders. When applicable, use code RL.	
Must Use	BEG03	324	**Purchase Order Number**		M AN 1/22
			Identifying number for Purchase Order assigned by the orderer/purchaser		

Use to identify the procurement instrument identification number (PIIN) not the order against a basic procurement instrument, e.g., delivery order, release, or call. For purchase orders, cite the order number. For delivery orders, cite the basic procurement instrument identification number (e.g., the contract or schedule number) and cite the delivery order or call number in BEG04. Federal numbers will not exceed 15 characters in length in order to comply with Federal Procurement Data System requirements.

	BEG04	328	**Release Number**	O	AN 1/30

Number identifying a release against a Purchase Order previously placed by the parties involved in the transaction

Use to identify the delivery order, call or release number, (e.g., the Supplemental PIIN) against the basic procurement instrument cited in BEG03.

Must Use	BEG05	323	**Purchase Order Date**	M	DT 6/6

Date assigned by the purchaser to Purchase Order

When BEG04 is used, cite the date of the delivery order, call, or release. When BEG04 is not used, cite the date of the procurement instrument in BEG03.

Not Used	BEG06	367	**Contract Number**	O	AN 1/30

Contract number

	BEG07	587	**Acknowledgment Type**	O	ID 2/2

Code specifying the type of acknowledgment

		AC	Acknowledge - With Detail and Change

Use to indicate acknowledgment of this 850 is required using the available segments in the 855 and retransmitting the same data in the corresponding segments in the 850. Changes are permitted.

		AD	Acknowledge - With Detail, No Change

Use to indicate acknowledgment of this 850 is required using the available segments in the 855 and retransmitting the same data in the corresponding segments in the 850 without change.

		AK	Acknowledge - No Detail or Change

Use to indicate acknowledgment by acceptance or rejection of this 850 is required.

Not Used	BEG08	1019	**Invoice Type Code**	O	ID 3/3

Code defining the method by which invoices are to be processed

Refer to 003040 Data Element Dictionary for acceptable code values.

TIPS: Notice that the Must Use elements are already selected. This often occurs. However, you should carefully compare the guidelines and the boldfaced elements to ensure that they track each other. There will almost always be segments and elements that you must edit.

Also, compare the data element numbers. These must match the element numbers found in the guideline. Some transaction sets include two or more reference designators with the same name. However, the element numbers will differ. You can verify that you are mapping the right entity by ensuring that the data element numbers match.

Finally, the element sequences may not match. For example, the DB Map Editor lists the first three BEG elements in BEG03, BEG01, and BEG02 order. Therefore, check the data element numbers to make sure that you map the correct entities. The top to bottom sequence takes care of itself when TPD processes the transaction set. In the case of the BEG03 element, it is a "key field" which is used for sorting. Hence, TPD lists it first.

Now examine each of the BEG elements as they are listed in the guidelines.

Required	Ref. Des.	Element #	Name	Attributes	(Use/Type/Length)	
Must Use	BEG01	353	Trans. Set Purpose Code	Mandatory	ID	2/2
Must Use	BEG02	92	PO Type Code	Mandatory	ID	2/2
Must Use	BEG03	324	PO No.	Mandatory	AN	1/22
	BEG04	328	Release No.	Optional	AN	1/30
Must Use	BEG05	323	Purchase Order Date	Optional	DT	6/6
Not Used	BEG06	367	Contract Number	Optional	AN	1/30
	BEG07	587	Acknowledgement Type	Optional	ID	2/2
Not Used	BEG08	1019	Invoice Type Code	Optional	ID	3/3

TIPS: Notice that a series of acceptable ID codes are listed below the ID-type segments. These codes are used by your trading partner and should comply with the ASC X12 standard. TPD can process any standard code. However, if your trading partner chooses to use a nonstandard ID code (and some do), you must use an ASCII text editor to add that code to the line in the corresponding 8503040.tm file. Following is an example of this line in the 8503040.tm file for BEG07, element number 587.

`587,AC|AD|AE|AH|AK|AP|AT|NA|RD|RF|RJ|RO|ZZ`

Look at the transaction set guideline and check the required codes. The guideline instructs you to use the standard codes AC, AD, and NA. These are acceptable standard codes because they are included in the 587 line in the 8503040.tm file.

If a nonstandard code is required by your trading partner, open the 8503040.tm file, locate the element line, and type the required code. Be sure to separate it from adjacent codes using the vertical bar symbol.

8. Mandatory elements are boldface, and cannot be removed. You can view their properties by right-clicking and then clicking on **Properties**.

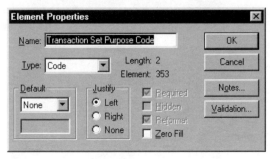

9. To add or remove an optional element from the map, right-click to display the shortcut menu.

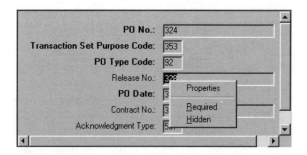

Then click on **Required** to display a checkmark. The required element is now displayed in boldface. To remove an element, right-click again and then click on **Required** to remove the checkmark. (You can also use the Required line on the Edit menu as well.)

Recall from above that optional segments are added and removed from the transaction using the shortcut menu's Required line. If you advance to each of the segments and their elements one at a time, you can designate all required entities as you work your way from top to bottom.

10. Examine the guidelines to see which segments are used. This is a simple transaction set that includes the BEG, PO1, and CTT segments. These are displayed in boldface in the left pane.

11. Now click **(BEG)PO** and ensure that the required elements are mapped (boldface).

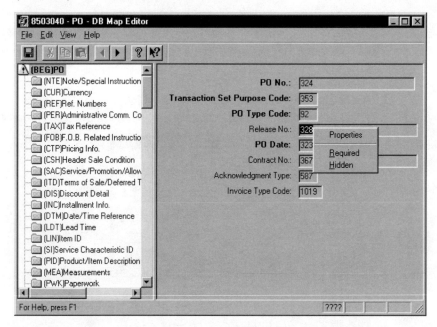

12. Scroll down to the (PO1)Baseline Item Data segment in the left pane and click on it to select it.

13. Read the Purpose and Syntax Notes. These tell you which elements are used in this segment. It also explains how element pairs are used.

Segment:	**PO1** Baseline Item Data
Position:	010
Loop:	PO1
Level:	Detail
Usage:	Mandatory
Max Use:	1
Purpose:	To specify basic and most frequently used line item data
Syntax Notes:	1 If PO103 is present, then PO102 is required.
	2 If PO105 is present, then PO104 is required.
	3 If PO106 is present, then PO107 is required.
	4 If PO108 is present, then PO109 is required.
	5 If PO110 is present, then PO111 is required.
	6 If PO112 is present, then PO113 is required.
	7 If PO114 is present, then PO115 is required.
	8 If PO116 is present, then PO117 is required.
	9 If PO118 is present, then PO119 is required.
	10 If PO120 is present, then PO121 is required.
	11 If PO122 is present, then PO123 is required.
	12 If PO124 is present, then PO125 is required.
Semantic Notes:	
Comments:	1 See the Data Dictionary for a complete list of ID's.
	2 PO101 is the line item identification.
	3 PO106 through PO125 provide for ten (10) different product/service ID's per each item
	For example: Case, Color, Drawing No., UPC No., ISBN No., Model No., SKU.

14. The 24 elements that correspond to those shown in the Syntax Notes section of the guideline should be set as Required. Use the following list of element numbers to set the corresponding element fields to Required.

PO102	330	Quantity Ordered
PO103	355	Unit or Basis for Measurement Code
PO104	212	Unit Price
PO105	639	Basis of Unit Price Code
PO106	235	Product/Service ID Qualifier
PO107	234	Product/Service ID
PO108	235	Product/Service ID Qualifier
PO109	234	Product/Service ID
PO110	235	Product/Service ID Qualifier
PO111	234	Product/Service ID
PO112	235	Product/Service ID Qualifier
PO113	234	Product/Service ID
PO114	235	Product/Service ID Qualifier

PO115	234	Product/Service ID
PO116	235	Product/Service ID Qualifier
PO117	234	Product/Service ID
PO118	235	Product/Service ID Qualifier
PO119	234	Product/Service ID
PO120	235	Product/Service ID Qualifier
PO121	234	Product/Service ID
PO122	235	Product/Service ID Qualifier
PO123	234	Product/Service ID
PO124	235	Product/Service ID Qualifier
PO125	234	Product/Service ID

The Comments section describes the use of these elements. Notice that up to ten different product/service IDs for each line item may exist.

15. Look at the right pane in the following dialog illustration. The elements that correspond to PO102 through PO109 have been mapped as required.

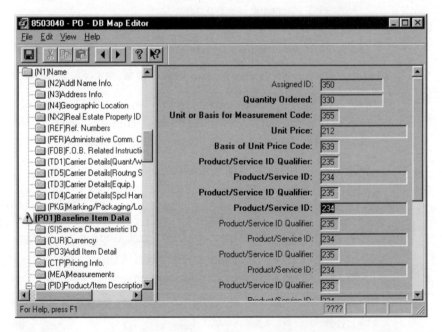

When you are finished, all remaining 234 and 235 elements should be boldfaced.

16. Scroll down and select the **(CTT)Transaction Totals** segment in the left pane.

17. Set the following elements as Required.

CTT01   354   Number of Line Items

CTT02   347   Hash Total (sum of the values in all PO102 elements)

The other CTT elements are not used. However, when they are, be sure to read the notes to determine if they contain necessary information.

18. Compare your screen to the following illustration. If elements 354 and 347 are boldfaced, you are finished.

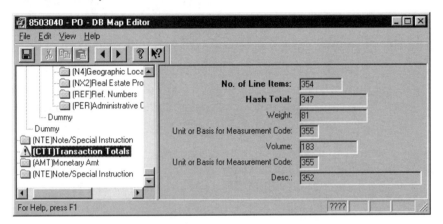

19. Click the **Save** button (the diskette icon) to save your map.

20. Click **File | Exit** to close the DB Map Editor. Click **Close** and then click **OK** in the Transaction Set Wizard dialog.

21. Close the Acme and Trading Partners dialogs. Then exit the TPD program by clicking **File | Exit**.

Concluding Comments about Mapping

This completes the hands-on mapping activity. Before exiting the TPD program, you could have also mapped the 8103040 transaction set by right-clicking the 810 Ver3040 icon in the Acme trading partner dialog. For additional mapping practice, you may wish to do this. Also remember that most transaction set guidelines call for a number of optional segments. The guidelines will almost always tell you which ones are recommended for use, which takes the guesswork out of your mapping task.

Creating a Cross Reference (XRF) File

Now that you've mapped the 8503040 transaction set, you can create a *cross reference file* (extension .xrf) for the transaction set. This file lists all segments and elements in a selected transaction set.

The cross reference file is derived from the dbm file using a program called Fieldlst.exe. Cross reference files are used as a transaction set reference and provide complete layout information by showing all segments and elements. Once created and saved you can use the printed layouts and your trading partner's transaction set guidelines to help you develop export/import utilities that exchange EDI information with external programs.

To use the Fieldlst.exe utility supplied with TPD with the 8503040.dbm (map file), proceed as follows:

1. Open Windows Explorer (or go to the MS-DOS prompt if you prefer).

2. Change directory to the "C:\Program Files\Trading Partner\System\Maps\Ansi folder or type **CD "\Program Files\Trading Partner\System\Maps\Ansi** and press **Enter** from the DOS prompt. (Note that the quotation mark is required to type filenames greater than eight characters.)

3. Copy the Fieldlst.exe program from the Code directory. Use **COPY "\Program Files\Trading Partner\Code\Fieldlst.exe** and press **Enter** from the DOS prompt.

4. Exit Windows Explorer. Type **CD "\Program Files\Trading Partner\System\Maps\Ansi** and press **Enter.**

5. Type **FIELDLST 8503040** and press **Enter.** The 8503040.dbm (database map) file is used to produce an 8503040.xrf (cross reference) file.

6. Type **FIELDLST 8103040** and press **Enter.** The 8103040.dbm file is used to produce an 8103040.xrf file.

You can now display and print the xrf files using an ASCII editor such as Edit.com. Just type EDIT 8503040.xrf and press Enter to open the 8503040 file in the DOS Edit program. The files can also be inserted into a Microsoft Word document so that they can be arranged into a two-column, landscape format before they are printed. This reduces their size. You can also use the View | Headers and Footers feature to add page numbers to the footer and a title to the header. It is advisable to begin collecting your specifications and xrf printouts in a three-ring binder. The interpreted maps are required references for Chapter 11, where export/import utilities are described.

You can also create the 810 3040 database map (dbm) file by performing steps 1 through 5 of the Hands-On Manual Mapping activity. Just right-click on the 810 Ver3040 icon, click the Database Map button, and then click Create. You do not have to edit and save this file to create it. Once created, you can use the Fieldlst.exe utility to create a cross reference file for this transaction set.

Print each of the xrf files and bind them with a staple. Note that the cross reference files already exist on the companion CD in both xrf and doc format. Look for the 8103040 and 8503040 files with file extensions xrf and doc.

Examining the XRF Files

An 8503040.xrf file was created in the above Creating a Cross Reference (XRF) File section. Recall that the xrf files can be viewed and printed with nearly any text editor including Windows Notepad, Windows WordPad, and Edit.com. For your convenience, these files were created as Microsoft Word document files, organized, and then saved on the companion disk with the names 8103040.doc and 8503040.doc. You may open and print these documents and use them in the activities found in Chapter 11. If you don't have Word, you can open and print the 8103040.xrf and 8503040.xrf files, also on the companion CD, using a common ASCII text editor.

The xrf file shows the entire transaction set including element offsets and lengths. An element's *offset* equals the offset value plus 1, which specifies where the first column (or character) of the element begins. For example, an offset of 32 and a length of 8 means that an element should begin on column 33 and occupy the next 8 characters. Hence, the next element would start at column 41 (33+8=41). Now look at the following 8103040.doc (or xrf) file excerpt.

```
----- BIG  Seg # 0001  Level 0 --------
----- (BIG)Invoice --

    Name Type    Seg  Off Len    Description
    ==== ====    ===  === ===    ===========
     SEQ S       0001  4  6       Seq. No.
   BIG01 D       0001 10  6       Invoice Date
   BIG02 A       0001 16 22       Invoice No.
   BIG03 D       0001 38  6       PO Date
   BIG04 A       0001 44 22       PO No.
```

The BIG segment is the first one found in the transaction set map. Notice that each element, i.e., BIG01, BIG02, etc., is shown. This is the way TPD parses and interprets a transaction set for processing. The cross reference does not include the envelope or group headers and trailers (ISA, GS, ST, SE, etc.). Now look at the entries found in the cross reference file.

Name	BIG01, BIG02, etc.	This is the element name as defined in the ANSI ASC X12 standard.
Type	S, D, A, C, etc.	Data type, where S=sequence number, D=date, A=ASCII value, T=time, C=code.

Segment	Segment number	TPD assigns segment number 0001 to this line. This is an internal value that is used by TPD; it is not part of the ANSI X12 standard. Following segment numbers in the cross reference file are 0002, 0003, etc.
Offset	4, 10, 16, etc.	The offset is the column number in which each element begins. A value of 16 specifies that the element begins in column 16.
Length	6, 6, 22, etc.	A value of 6 specifies that the length of an element is 6 characters.
Description		A descriptive name for each element. Note that each element has a sequence number that occupies the first 10 characters (or columns) of the segment (line).

The cross reference is used extensively in the next chapter. There, you see how it serves as an essential reference for programmers who are responsible for writing import and export utilities that tie an external order processing program to TPD.

What's Next

Now that you've installed transaction sets and mapped them, you can exchange EDI mail with your trading partner. Of course, to send a transaction set, you must create it. And when you receive transaction sets from your trading partner, you must process them. The next chapter delves into these processes. In particular, it steps you through receiving, processing, and sending EDI mail. It also describes file structures and provides guidelines for importing and exporting data between TPD and external programs.

Review Questions

1. How can you see all segments and elements within a transaction set?
2. What do the segments within the detail section of a transaction set typically contain?
3. Describe the purpose of the ST-SE segments.
4. What is a transaction set control number?
5. Describe three of the Data Segment Requirement Designations.
6. Why is looping used?

7. What is a reference designator within an EDI transaction set?

8. When manually mapping a transaction set, describe how you select and deselect segments and elements within the transaction set.

9. What does the Auto Configuration button do and what must be present for it to function properly?

10. What are types, segments, offsets, and lengths as used in a cross reference (xrf) file?

Chapter 11

EDI Files, Processing, and Exchanging Data with External Applications (Export and Import Utilities)

Introduction

This chapter introduces you to the files that are processed by TPD. It describes their locations, structures, and how they are exchanged with external applications, such as an in-house order processing or inventory control system.

Once you can successfully exchange EDI information with a trading partner, you are well on your way to deriving the benefits afforded by EDI. However, having a valid transaction set in a folder on your computer is only the first step in a multiple-step process. You must still be able to use the information within the transaction sets. This usually means parsing the data into useful formats, where *parsing* means to extract and rearrange data in a usable format. TPD provides translation utilities so that the raw EDI mail files can be read in plaintext format. In addition, TPD prepares ASCII export files and can read and import properly formatted ASCII source files. Often, export file format can be used by an in-house order processing or invoicing system. This chapter describes the steps in the process, file formats, and how you can export and import information between TPD and an external application.

Processing Tasks and Files

Before delving into the export and import processes themselves, it is important to understand the steps in receiving, processing, and sending EDI transaction sets. It is also necessary to understand what the files that are being processed look like.

File Processing Overview

Following is an explanation of the files and processes conducted by TPD. Included are the names of each file and task that is performed.

Inbound EDI Mail

To obtain your EDI mail files, perform the following steps.

1. From the TPD Desktop, open the Networks & the Internet dialog and then click the communications folder you wish to use, such as Geis or Advantis. An Advantis dialog is shown in the following illustration. Notice that the status flags are up. This tells you that both incoming and outgoing mail is ready to be processed.

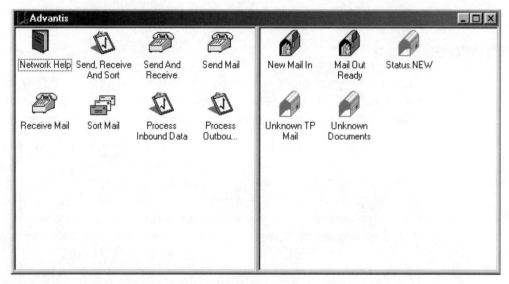

2. With the network folder open, check the New Mail In and Mail Out Ready status flags. At this point, the status flags should be down.

3. Click the **Receive Mail** icon to log onto the installed network. This checks your EDI mailbox (on the network) for inbound mail.

4. If inbound mail exists, it is automatically downloaded to the New Mail In box and the status flag pops up to show you that new mail has been received.

TIP: The new EDI mail file is named Mail_in.new. This file contains all inbound transaction sets. The file can contain several different transaction sets from two or more trading partners. You can find this file in the network folder; the complete folder and file name is:

C:\Program Files\Trading Partner\Edata\Geis\Mail_in.new.

You can click the New Mail In box to display the file in the system editor (Notepad, WordPad, Edit.com, etc.). Do not make any changes to the information (in other words, quit without saving).

NOTE: When mail is sorted in the next step, TPD extracts each trading partner's portion of the EDI mail file and places it in the trading partner's inbound folder. TPD knows where to put each portion of incoming mail based on the trading partner's identification code, which is found in the ISA header segment. Once the mail is in the trading partner's inbound dialog, you can see it by checking the status of the Sorted Mail flag. The presence of mail is indicated by a raised red flag.

5. Click **Sort Mail** to distribute the inbound mail to the different trading partner folders on your computer. For example, 850 3040 transaction sets received from Acme are sorted to the folder C:\Program Files\Trading Partner\Edata\Geis\Acme\Ansi\850\3040. The filename of the sorted transaction set will be MAIL_IN.srt. When successfully sorted, the Mail_in.new file is also automatically archived to the Geis\Archive folder. The first file is named IN_01.new. Following files are incremented to IN_02.new, IN_03.new, and so on up to a maximum value that corresponds to the established archive level value.

TIP: The total number of archive files maintained depends on how many you wish to keep for future review and/or reuse. You can set the archive level (the number of files you wish to retain) in the System Management | System Configuration dialog. Reuse occurs when a trading partner requests that you resend a particular transaction set or if you need to reprocess or review a specific transaction set for any reason.

Inbound EDI mail files received from other trading partners that have been added to TPD are put in their respective folders. For example, an 850 3010 transaction set from the Ingram company would be sorted to the folder:

C:\Program Files\Trading Partner\Edata\Geis\Ingram\Ansi\850\3010.

An example of a sorted file is shown in the File Examples section found later in this chapter.

6. After you've sorted the mail, close the Networks & the Internet dialog and return to the TPD Desktop. Then open the Trading Partners dialog. Click the desired trading partner icon, then **850 Ver3020**, 3040, or whichever version that trading partner uses. In the example, a 850 Ver3020 is shown. Finally, Click **850 Ver3020 Inbound**. Notice that the trading partner's Sorted Mail status flag is up.

7. Now that you've sorted the mail, you're ready to *interpret* it. This essentially converts the mail into a format that can be processed by TPD. Click **Interpret Sorted Mail**. The Sorted Mail status flag drops and the Translated Mail status flag pops up to show that the file has been interpreted (or translated).

8. The sorted mail file is automatically archived. At this point you can run a Raw Data Report to display the translated transaction set information in the Notepad editor. Once displayed, you can use File | Print if you want to print the information.

9. Close the Notepad editor. Return to the trading partner's 850 dialog.

10. Click **Put Translated to Export File** to create an export file. The translated file is automatically archived. The export file, which is given the filename Mail_in.rfm (where rfm stands for reformatted), is located in the trading partner's ...\850\3020 folder.

This completes the inbound processing tasks. In summary, here's what you did.

■ **Receive Mail** (Network dialog)

- **Sort Mail** (Network dialog)
- **Interpret Sorted Mail** (Trading Partner's 850 Inbound dialog)
- Optionally run **Raw Data Report** (Trading Partner's 850 Inbound dialog)
- **Put Translated to Export File** (Trading Partner's 850 Inbound dialog)

The export file is now ready to be processed by an external utility. A description of how the export file can be parsed and reformatted is provided later in this chapter. For now, continue reading how to process outbound EDI mail transaction sets.

Outbound EDI Mail

Outbound files that are imported from an external application are typically placed in the Imported File mailbox. For the Imported File mailbox status flag to pop up, the file must be in the trading partner's …810\3040 folder with the name Mail_out.rfm. Recall that rfm means reformatted. Once a valid reformatted import file exists, you can process it as follows:

1. Click the trading partner's icon to open the trading partner's transaction set dialog.

2. Click the **810 Ver***nnnn* icon, where *nnnn* is the ASC X12 version number being used, such as 3010, 3020, 3040, etc. (We'll use 3020 for sake of illustration.) Now click the 810 Ver3020 Outbound icon to open the processing dialog shown below.

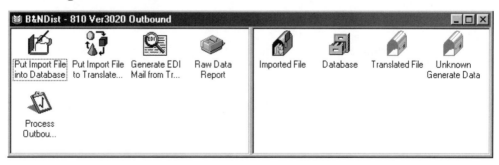

3. Click **Put Import File to Translated File**. The Translated File status flag pops up and the Imported File status flag drops. The translated file takes on the filename MAIL_OUT.trn. The import file is automatically archived as OUT_01.rfm.

4. Click **Generate EDI Mail from Translated** to put the mail in the network dialog's Mail Out Ready box. The translated file is used to produce an ASC X12 transaction set with all proper header, trailer, and detail segments and elements. The transaction set is combined with other transaction sets, if

any, in a Mail_out.new file located in the network folder (the same place that the original Mail_in.new file was produced). The translated file is put in the archive folder.

5. Close the trading partner's transaction set dialog and open the network dialog. Check to ensure that the Mail Out Ready status flag is up to verify that your outbound mail is ready to send. You can click the Mail Out Ready mailbox to examine the file contents in the system editor.

WARNING: Do not change the contents of the file unless you know exactly what you're doing. During processing, TPD conducts a variety of checks to ensure that all required segments and elements exist, are organized properly, and are assigned valid control numbers.

6. Click **Send Mail** to connect to your installed network. When sent, the mail is put in the network's outbox ready to be picked up by your trading partners. The Mail_out.new file is automatically archived as OUT_01.new, where the 01 depends on the number of files in your archive.

This completes the outbound processing tasks. In summary, here's what you did.

- **Put Import File to Translated** (Trading Partner's 810 Outbound dialog)
- **Generate EDI Mail from Translated** (Trading Partner's 810 Outbound dialog)
- **Send Mail** (Network dialog)

This whirlwind tour of the processing tasks and the files that we used, created, and archived is essentially all that is required when each of your trading partners have been properly added and their transaction sets accurately mapped. TPD checks and rechecks the information to ensure that all segments and elements are in the proper sequence and comply with the ASC X12 ANSI standard. In the next chapter, you are shown how these tasks can be scripted to achieve a degree of automation.

The entire export and import process was omitted, as this part of the process is a bit more involved. That's why an entire section is dedicated to the process later in this chapter.

File Examples

The files that are processed and archived are shown in the following list along with their locations. Then a few transaction set examples serve as a basis to a better understanding of the file formats discussed in this chapter. Therefore, some examples of raw EDI transaction files, a sorted file, a translated file, and an export and import file are described. Following is a list of TPD transaction set filenames and definitions.

Filename	Description
Mail_in.new	Received EDI mail file
In_01.new, in_02. New, etc.	Archived Mmail_in.new files
Mail_in.srt	Sorted Mail_in.new file
In_01.srt, in_02.srt, etc.	Archived Mail_in.srt files
Mail_in.trn	Translated Mail_in.srt file
In_01.trn, in_02.trn, etc.	Archived Mail_in.trn files
Mail_in.rfm	Export file
In_01.rfm, in02.rfm, etc.	Archived Mail_in.rfm files
Mail_out.rfm	Import file
Out_01.rfm, out_02.rfm, etc.	Archived Mail_out.rfm files
Mail_out.trn	Translated Mail_out.rfm file
Out_01.trn, out_02.trn, etc.	Archived Mail_out.trn files
Mail_out.new	Mail out ready file
Out_01.new, out_02.new, etc.	Archived Mail_out.new Files

Other Files

You can use the Windows Explorer's Tools | Find | Files or Folders feature to locate these files within the C:\Program Files\Trading Partner folders.

8503020.dbm, 8103040.dbm, etc.—These are examples of a database map file. It is created and saved when you add a transaction set. The raw database map resides in the ...System\Maps\Ansi folder. The modified version of this file, which is created and saved using the Database Map section of TPD's Transaction Set Wizard, is saved in the trading partner's version folder, i.e., ...850\3020.

8503020.tm, 8103040.tm, etc.—These are transaction set control files. It is created in concert with the dbm control file. This file is used in conjunction with the dbm file to validate the EDI files, including such things as valid ASC X12 ID codes. These files are found in the ...System\Maps\Ansi folder.

8503020.xrf, 8103040.xrf, etc.—These are the cross reference files created with the Fieldlst.exe utility. They are also found in the ...System\Maps\Ansi folder.

Status.new—This file records and displays a list of communications events achieved in the last transaction session. If a problem exists, you must sometimes correct it and then delete this file before retrying a communications session.

Unmapin.rpt—This is a report file that is created when you view and/or print a Raw Data Report. It is found in the trading partner's version folder, i.e., ...850\3020.

Mail_out.edt, Mail_in.edt—These are edited transaction set files. They are located in the trading partner's version folders, i.e., ...810\3020 or ...850\3020.

Mail_in.new File Example

First, look at the following example of a Mail_in.new file. It contains FA997s (functional acknowledgements) and PO850s (purchase orders) that were received from two different trading partners. (The trading partner's ID codes in the ISA and GS segments have been changed to protect the innocent.)

```
ISA*00*          *00*          *ZZ*1234567     *ZZ*7654321
*990922*1051*U*00300*000000567*0*P*>
GS*FA*1234567*7654321*990922*1051*285*X*003020
ST*997*000000285
AK1*IN*1144
AK9*E*660*660*660
SE*4*000000285
GE*1*285
IEA*1*000000567
ISA*00*          *00*          *ZZ*1234567     *ZZ*7654321
*990922*1052*U*00300*000000568*0*P*>
GS*FA*1234567*7654321*990922*1052*286*X*003020
ST*997*000000286
AK1*IN*1144
AK9*E*660*660*660
SE*4*000000286
GE*1*286
IEA*1*000000568
ISA*00*          *00*          *ZZ*2468024     *ZZ*7654321
*990922*2027*U*00300*000000086*0*P*>
GS*PO*2468024*7654321*990922*2027*82*X*003040BISAC
ST*850*000000085
BEG*00*NE*00260412**990922**AE
CSH*0
DTM*001*000322***20
N1*ST**15*1919191
N1*BT**15*9292929
PO1*1*8*UN*29.95*SR*IB*155622592X
CTP*****DIS*.45
PO1*2*1*UN*12.95*SR*IB*1556222580
```

```
CTP*****DIS*.45
PO1*3*1*UN*15.95*SR*IB*1556221339
CTP*****DIS*.45
PO1*4*1*UN*12.95*SR*IB*1556221754
CTP*****DIS*.45
CTT*4*11
SE*16*000000085
GE*1*82
IEA*1*000000086
```

Examining the Mail_in.new File

It's not difficult to interpret these files if you have a roadmap. The transaction set guidelines and the cross reference file both serve as excellent navigation tools when trying to determine what's contained within an EDI transaction set file.

The Mail_in.new file contains three transaction sets: two functional acknowledgments (FA997s) and one purchase order (PO850). Each of the transaction sets begin with ISA and GS header segments and end with GE and IEA trailer segments. Notice that the ISA and IEA segments include a matching control number. In the case of the first transaction set, which is an FA997, the control number is 567. Although not part of the transaction set, underlines are included to help you separate the three transaction sets within the Mail_in.new file.

Next, check the interior segments. A set header and trailer (ST and SE) also have matching control numbers. When multiple transaction sets exist from the same trading partner, the control numbers are automatically incremented by one as each new transaction set is added. To help you find them in the example, the ST-SE pairs are italicized. The detail segments within each ST-SE set contain the detail descriptive information for the items being ordered.

In a PO850 transaction set, N1 lists the ship-to and bill-to information. This is typically an official *store address number* (SAN). Each PO1 segment includes quantity ordered, unit of measure (UN), a price qualifier code (SR=suggested retail), a price (15.95, etc.), a part number qualifier code (IB=ISBN), and a part number (155622....). The CTP segment includes a discount qualifier (DIS) and a discount value (.4). The CTT segment includes the total number of line items ordered and a *hash total*, which is the total number of units counted in the group. Now see if you can look at the raw Mail_in.new file example to see how it's organized.

Finally, notice the asterisk (*) delimiters that are used to separate each of the elements. When two or more asterisks are strung together, it indicates that interior elements are not used. Therefore, the line CTP*****DIS*.4 has five blank elements, i.e., CTP01 through CTP05. CTP06 and CTP07 include the code DIS and the value .4.

Mail_out.new File Example

Now look at an example of a Mail_out.new file. It contains an FA997 and an IN810 (invoice).

```
ISA*00*          *00*          *ZZ*7654321        *ZZ*2468024
*990930*0847*U*00300*000000023*0*P*>
GS*IN*7654321*2468024*990930*0847*23*X*003040
ST*810*000230001
BIG*990930*99091465**00245658
N1*ST**15*9090909
IT1**56*UN*7.63**IB*1556223196
IT3***AS
CTP**SLP*16.95***DIS*.45
TDS*42714**42714
CTT*1*56
SE*9*000230001
ST*810*000230002
BIG*990930*99091466**00255074
N1*ST**15*1919191
IT1**1*UN*7.63**IB*1556223773
IT3***AS
CTP**SLP*16.95***DIS*.45
IT1**45*UN*7.63**IB*1556223773
IT3***AS
CTP**SLP*16.95***DIS*.45
TDS*35087**35087
CTT*2*46
SE*12*000230002
GE*2*23
IEA*1*000000023
```

Examining the Mail_out.new File

Unlike the Mail_in.new EDI mail file, only one transaction set is included in the file. However, it does contain multiple groups—one for each invoice. It also includes the necessary header and trailer segments for the transaction set along with individual set header and trailer segments (ST-SE). Envelope, group, and set control numbers are automatically assigned by TPD. These numbers are maintained in each trading partner's properties dialogs, and can be updated as necessary.

Sorted Mail File (Mail_in.srt) Example

```
;Sorted
;
;ENVELOPE MAIL Receipt Tag=
;Network=Advantis
;TP=Acmeinc(,,2468024,7654321)
;Env Control=000000083,990920,2026
;Env Tag1=
;Env Tag2=
;
;Grp Tag1=
;Grp Tag2=
GS*PO*2468024*7654321*990920*2026*81*X*003040BISAC
ST*850*000000084
BEG*00*NE*00258404**990920**AE
CSH*0
DTM*001*000320***20
N1*ST**15*1919191
N1*BT**15*2468024
PO1*1*48*UN*12.95*SR*IB*1556223986
CTP*****DIS*.45
PO1*2*19*UN*15.95*SR*IB*1556226489
CTP*****DIS*.45
PO1*3*36*UN*24.95*SR*IB*1556225970
CTP*****DIS*.45
PO1*4*19*UN*34.95*SR*IB*1556225954
CTP*****DIS*.45
PO1*5*14*UN*39.95*SR*IB*1556225458
CTP*****DIS*.45
PO1*6*56*UN*16.95*SR*IB*1556223196
CTP*****DIS*.45
PO1*7*64*UN*18.95*SR*IB*1556225695
CTP*****DIS*.45
PO1*8*40*UN*18.95*SR*IB*1556225377
CTP*****DIS*.45
CTT*8*296
SE*24*000000084
```

Examining the Sorted Mail File

When you sort a trading partner's inbound EDI mail, it is extracted from the Mail_in.new file and placed in the folder that corresponds to the trading partner's transaction set. The preceding file is a purchase order (PO850) and resembles the Mail_in.new file in structure. Notice that the header begins with ;Sorted and several lines that identify the network, trading partner information, a control number, and a date and time stamp. This information is used by TPD to link the file to the trading partner's configuration information.

Also notice that when the EDI mail is sorted, the envelope header and trailer segments (ISA, GE, IEA) are removed. The GS segment is retained. However, the set headers and trailers (ST and SE segments) and the interior detail segments still exist. The ST and SE control numbers also remain intact, as this information is used by TPD. Finally, notice that as in the raw Mail_in.new and Mail_out.new transaction sets, delimiters (*) are used to separate the elements within each segment. In the translated file that follows, you'll see that these delimiters disappear.

Translated Mail File (Mail_out.trn) Example

```
;Interpreted
;
;ENVELOPE MAIL Receipt Tag=990922,2133
;Network=Advantis
;TP=Ingram(,,INGX   INGXABC,WP01   WP01A)
;Env Control=000000007,990923,1615
;Env Tag1=
;Env Tag2=
;
;START SET 810 VERSION=003010 GROUP=IN
;Module=(1616161,WP01A)
;Set Control=000000007
;Grp Control=1,990923,1615
;Grp Tag1=
;Grp Tag2=
;
000100000199092399091356                     DZ26568R
0006000001BT                                 151697978
0006000002VN                                 152914786
0020000001      2           EA22.48            IB155622558X
0024000001   SLP49.95                      DIS.55
0020000002     10           EA15.73            IB1556225954
0024000001   SLP34.95                      DIS.55
005100000120223               20223
00570000012      12
;END SET 810 VERSION=003010 GROUP=IN
;Module=(1616161,WP01A)
;Set Control=000000007
;Grp Control=1,990923,1615
;Grp Tag1=
;Grp Tag2=
;
```

```
;START SET 810 VERSION=003010 GROUP=IN
;Module=(1616161,WPO1A)
;Set Control=000000007
;Grp Control=1,990923,1615
;Grp Tag1=
;Grp Tag2=
;
000100000199092399091357                        EZ265F3R
0006000001BT                                     151697978
0006000002VN                                     152914786
0020000001        1          EA7.18               IB1556224486
0024000001   SLP15.95                            DIS.55
0020000002        1          EA7.18               IB1556224559
0024000001   SLP15.95                            DIS.55
0020000003        1          EA14.83              IB1556225822
0024000001   SLP32.95                            DIS.55
00510000012918                       2918
00570000013        3
;END SET 810 VERSION=003010 GROUP=IN
;Module=(1616161,WPO1A)
;Set Control=000000007
;Grp Control=1,990923,1615
;Grp Tag1=
;Grp Tag2=
;
```

Examining the Translated Mail File

This file begins with ;Interpreted, which tells TPD that the file has been translated and is ready for use. Once translated, you can produce a raw data report,
display the information in a database mask, or put it in a reformatted export file.
The ST and SE set header and trailer are replaced with ;START SET and ;END
SET segments. It also replaces the segment identification (N1, PO1, CTP, etc.)
with 4-digit numbers such as 0001, 0006, 0020, and 0024. That is followed by a
6-digit value such as 000001, 000002, 000003, etc. This is where the cross reference files (extension .xrf) become invaluable. Each segment in the cross
reference file lists the segment name and the corresponding 4-digit reference
number. The offset and length values also tell you where to find each element
and the type of information contained in the element. You can check the column
counter of your editor (such as Edit.com) to determine the position and length
of each element.

Export File (Mail_in.rfm) Example

```
;Reformatted
;
```

```
;ENVELOPE MAIL Receipt Tag=,
;Network=Advantis
;TP=Acmeinc(,,2468024,7654321)
;Env Control=000000086,990922,2027
;Env Tag1=
;Env Tag2=
;
;START SET 850 VERSION=003040BISAC GROUP=PO
;Module=(2468024,7654321)
;Set Control=000000085
;Grp Control=82,990922,2027
;Grp Tag1=
;Grp Tag2=
;Accept+
000100000100NE00260412                              990922        AE
00100000010
0014000001001000322        20
0029000001ST                            151923552
0029000002BT                            151925334
00410000011        8        UN29.95        SRIB155622592X
0044000001                        DIS.4
00410000022        1        UN12.95        SRIB1556222580
0044000001                        DIS.4
00410000033        1        UN15.95        SRIB1556221339
0044000001                        DIS.4
00410000044        1        UN12.95        SRIB1556221754
0044000001                        DIS.4
00910000014        11
;END SET 850 VERSION=003040BISAC GROUP=PO
;Module=(2468024,7654321)
;Set Control=000000085
;Grp Control=82,990922,2027
;Grp Tag1=
;Grp Tag2=
;
```

Examining the Export File

The reformatted export file is identical to the translated file except for the first line. The expression ;Reformatted replaces the expression ;Interpreted. The status flag of the Export File mailbox pops up when a Mail_in.rfm file exists in the trading partner's inbound transaction set folder, such as …\850\3040. The presence of a Mail_out.rfm file in the outbound transaction set dialog (…\810\3020) pops up the Import File status flag.

Exporting to and Importing from an External Application

Following is a list of the steps that must be performed in the export/import process.

Exporting:

1. Put Translated to Export File (creates Mail_in.rfm in trading partner's inbound transaction set folder).

2. Copy Mail_in.rfm file to working folder where a data extraction (parsing) utility can excerpt data.

3. Find all required data and convert it into a format that can be used by the external program.

4. Read the converted data into the external program and process the information.

Importing:

1. Produce a file that includes all necessary segments and elements.

2. Extract the segments and elements and combine them with the required headers and trailers into a valid Mail_out.rfm file.

3. Copy or move the Mail_out.rfm file to the trading partner's outbound transaction set folder, i.e., …\810\3020.

4. Put Import File to Translated File.

Once the import file has been translated, you can generate EDI mail and send it to the trading partner. If you have additional import files ready to process, you can process each by performing steps 1 through 8 in the Inbound EDI Mail section. As you generate EDI mail for each trading partner, it is appended to the Mail_out.new file. If you use a single network for all trading partners, then you can send all EDI mail at once. However, if you use two or more networks, then you will have to send your EDI mail on each of the installed networks that have pending outbound transaction sets.

Part 2

Taking a Closer Look

The Mail_in.rfm file is an ASCII text file that can be opened and read by any text editor. It can also be opened by a program and the information within it extracted and arranged in a format that can be used by an external program. Several Mail_in.rfm files can exist at the same time for different trading partners. As mentioned above, the files are found in the trading partner's inbound transaction set folder (such as …\850\3020\Mail_in.rfm). You can process each file one at a time, returning a Mail_out.rfm file for each, which must be placed in the trading partner's outbound transaction set folder, i.e., …\810\3020.

Each Mail_in.rfm file contains a number of envelope and group control lines that begin with semicolons. There are also START SET and END SET control segments that correspond to the ST and SE header and trailer segments. Other control lines include trading partner ID numbers, the network name, and date and time stamps. The interior segments, which are all numbered, correspond to each of the required segments found in the detail section of the transaction set. The numbers are listed in the cross reference file so you can quickly look up each segment's reference designation (BEG01, N101, PO101, CTT01, etc.). The numbers are arranged sequentially in the cross reference file, making it easy to find corresponding segments.

The elements within each segment are arranged so that their positions correspond to the offset and length values found in the cross reference file. For example, you can find the contents of the BEG02 element by simply looking at the offset and length values listed for BEG01 in the cross reference file. Note that segment and sequence numbers occupy the first ten columns of each segment line. Therefore the first element of each segment, such as BEG01, N101, CTT01, etc., starts at column 11 (an offset value of 10) in the reformatted file.

Knowing the segment identification numbers and the exact positions, or offset values, of each element makes programming a conversion utility reasonably straightforward. Programmers can write utilities to parse the information from the reformatted file and rearrange the information into a file format that can be fed to an order processing or reporting system. Once the information (quantities, part numbers, etc.) is converted, then you can begin processing the transaction in the same way that you would if you received the information by other means. The advantage, of course, is that the information has not been entered using error-prone manual means. Therefore, if the conversion utility has been tested for accuracy, the resulting information will be an accurate reproduction of your trading partner's transaction set.

Parsing the Reformatted File

As indicated in the previous paragraph, being able to extract, or *parse*, the information within the reformatted data file is a fairly rudimentary process. First, the information is arranged in a reliable and predictable sequence. The cross reference file includes segment names and numbers and the column location and length of each interior element. With a sample file and a printout of the cross reference file as a guide, almost any programmer can locate and extract information such as purchase order dates, purchase order numbers, ship-to and bill-to addresses, quantities, and part numbers. Common search routines and substring functions are used to find and copy values. When multiple line items are included within a transaction set, looping routines can be written to extract all information.

Once all necessary information is extracted and reformatted so that an external program can use it, another utility must be developed. This one must present the reformatted information to the external program so that the data can be processed to produce an invoice and packing slip.

Producing the Import File

Once the external order processing program processes the data, an invoice must be produced. It can be a paper invoice, an electronic invoice, or both. When working with TPD, it is necessary to produce an electronic invoice in a valid Mail_out.rfm format. The Mail_out.rfm file must include all required segments and elements. Segments must be in the correct sequence and include the reference and sequence numbers found in the cross reference file. In the example below, notice that two 0006 segments exist. The first occurrence has sequence 000001 (positions 5 through 10), while the second has sequence 000002. Repeating (or looped) segments must be labeled with incremental sequence numbers.

Interior elements must comply with the offset and length guidelines found in the corresponding cross reference file. All control lines, including the set header/trailer lines, must be inserted in the correct locations within the file. The following example of a small Mail_out.rfm file shows the necessary control lines and one set of interior detail (lines 0001 through 0057).

```
;Reformatted
;
;ENVELOPE MAIL Receipt Tag=000412,2055
;Network=Advantis
;TP=Bigmart(,,7654321,5525525)
;Env Control=000000085,000416,1419
;Env Tag1=
;Env Tag1=
;
;START SET 810 VERSION=003020 GROUP=IN
;Module=(7654321,5525525)
;Set Control=000000085
;Grp Control=1,000416,1419
;Grp Tag1=
;Grp Tag1=
;
0001000001000416000040195                    CZ1035DR
0006000001BT                                  552552500
```

```
0006000002VN                                      333222111
0020000001        10        EA22.48               IB155622639X
0024000001  SLP49.95                              DIS.55
005100000122478                      22478
00570000011       10
;END SET 810 VERSION=003010 GROUP=IN
;Module=(7654321,5525525)
;Set Control=000000085
;Grp Control=1,000416,1419
;Grp Tag1=
;Grp Tag1=
;
```

Finally, the file must be copied or moved to the corresponding trading partner's inbound transaction set folder (…810\3020), which pops up the Import File status flag. When the status flag is up, and the file is properly crafted, TPD can process it successfully.

Program Complexity

As one who has written interface programs between TPD and a company's internal order processing system, I can assure you that the basic program is not very complex. However, as more trading partners and transaction sets are added, the complexity increases. You must write internal routines that examine and extract a different set of information for each trading partner's transaction set. Although each routine is similar, the data locations and values differ for each new transaction set. Even when the transaction sets are the same version, different trading partners use different segments, elements, and internal values such as ID codes. This requires that you identify the trading partner to the program and then develop routines for each of the different transaction set permutations.

Branching statements (typically IF and CASE) are used to select different sections of program code for each trading partner. Different header and trailer segments must also be prepared for each trading partner. These can be hard coded inside the program, placed in an external table, or a combination of both used. The main header and trailer segments include network name, transaction set number, version number, and group type. The trading partner name, sender and receiver identification numbers, and date and time stamps are also included.

So as not to get carried away with more programming details than necessary, the subject of export/import utilities must end. However, if you are a programmer or if you plan to collaborate with one, the file structures, cross reference files, and a knowledge of your external order processing program plus some of the suggestions found above should get you started. Obviously, you can use any legitimate programming language. This can include Visual Basic, C, C++, C#, Object Pascal (Delphi), Access, SQL, dBASE, Paradox, or even QBasic.

What's Next

Now that you have an understanding of the processes involved in exchanging and processing EDI mail, including export and import routines, you should be able to run the TPD system processes. You also know what has to be done to get files ready to exchange between external programs. When you're ready to write an export/import program yourself or collaborate with a programmer who can write the program, the preceding descriptions and file examples should give you a starting place.

In the next chapter you are returned to the tasks involved in processing EDI mail. There, you see how these can be scripted. Scripting eliminates the need to perform each task in the process one step at a time. Instead, you can perform a series of tasks with a single initiating click.

Review Questions

1. What does parsing mean?
2. What kind of files can TPD exchange with external applications?
3. What is contained in the Mail_in.new file and where is it located?
4. What happens when you click the Sort Mail icon?
5. What does the Archive Level setting control and how is it used?
6. What is meant by a raised mailbox flag?
7. List the three steps performed within TPD to process a Mail_out.rfm (import) file.
8. What must be written to exchange files between TPD and an external application?

Chapter 12

Automating EDI Processing with Task Lists

Introduction

You can process your EDI documents manually by clicking each of the task icons in the network and trading partner inbound and outbound dialogs. This includes such tasks as receiving mail, sorting it, translating it, and converting the translated mail to an export file. When an import file has been prepared, you can put the import file to a translated file, generate EDI mail, and finally send the mail to a network. These steps require that you execute each task one at a time.

There is a better way—using task lists, which are easily created scripts that identify each task to be performed. Of course, before you can automate one or more tasks, you must know which tasks are required and the sequence in which they must occur. This is presented in the Processing Tasks and Files section of Chapter 11.

Task Lists and the Scheduler

The task lists and the Scheduler are both available to automate TPD processes. The task lists feature is used to create and save one or more list of tasks in the required order. The Scheduler is used to launch one or more desired task lists at a predetermined time. Therefore, the Scheduler lets you perform EDI trans-actions unattended. Both the task lists and the Scheduler are described in the balance of this chapter.

Task Lists Overview

TPD permits you to build a series of individual tasks within a single list using the Tasklist Editor. A task is either a system-defined program, such as Sort Mail or Interpret Sorted Mail, or an external Windows or DOS program or a DOS batch file. Adding an external program is described in the Launching External Programs section of this chapter. When you first install a communications network, trading partner, or transaction set, individual tasks are automatically created for you. When you collect them within a task list, they run from top to bottom in the order encountered in the list, unless a fatal data error occurs in the case of a missing or corrupted EDI file. For example, if the first task is Receive Mail and none is found in the mailbox, an error will occur, causing the program to exit the task list. Any tasks that remain in the list are ignored.

You should avoid creating large task lists that are intended to do everything in a single pass. Instead, create and save small task lists for each trading partner and then call them from your network task lists. This simplifies the process, makes it easier to maintain each task list, and is more reliable. If one trading partner has no mail, then the next trading partner's task list can be called, and so on until all tasks have been run. In contrast, if you put all network and trading partner tasks in a single list, the entire process will be aborted when a "no file" error occurs.

Blank task lists are created automatically when you install TPD. You only need to edit the existing task lists to control their behavior. You can also create and save your own task lists, and use them to call external programs and batch files. Each network, trading partner, and transaction set dialog contains Process Inbound Data or Process Outbound Data icons. When a task list has been created and saved, you can select and open the Process Inbound Data or Process Outbound Data icon to see a list of tasks to be performed.

Using the Tasklist Editor

You can use the Tasklist Editor to create or modify any task list. This includes adding new entries, changing the order of the listed entries, and deleting entries from the task list. Perform the following steps.

1. Click the **Daily Processing** icon to open the Daily Processing window.

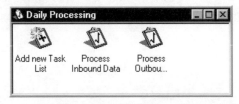

2. Click **Add new Task List** to launch the Tasklist Editor.

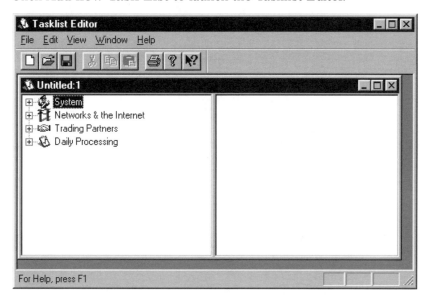

3. Click on the plus sign [+] button on the Trading Partners line and then expand the Tasklist Editor until you view Acme's 850 Ver3040 Inbound task list.

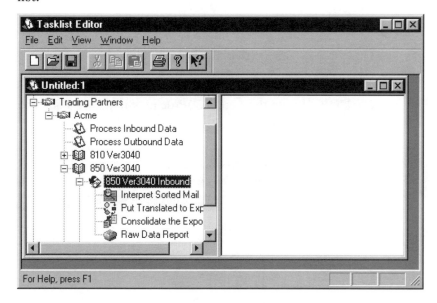

4. Arrange the tasks as shown in the following illustration by selecting and dragging **Interpret Sorted Mail** and **Put Translated to Export File** to the right pane.

Part 2

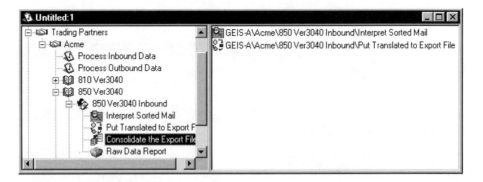

5. Click **File | Save**, select the **Acme 850 Ver3040 Inbound** line in the Position pane, and then type **Acme850Proc** as the filename. This saves the task list in the Acme 850Ver 3040 Inbound window.

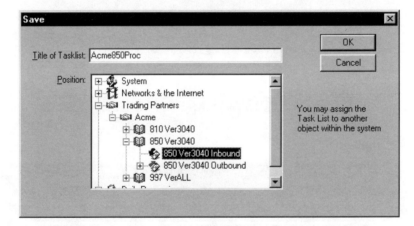

6. Click **OK** to save the Acme850Proc task list. Now click **File | Exit** to close the Tasklist Editor.

NOTE: Now that the Acme850Proc task list is available, you can call it by name in other task lists. Opening the Acme's 850 Ver3040 Inbound list does this. An icon is also added to the window for this task list.

In the hands-on activity you created and saved a task list in the trading partner's 850 Ver3040 Inbound dialog. Now you can create and save task lists for system-wide or network tasks and call the Acme850Proc task list from the other lists. This gives you a hierarchical structure, keeping each task list brief and succinct.

Launching External Programs

As mentioned earlier, you can create and add external program calls to a task list. This is done by creating and saving a valid command line and giving it a descriptive name when it is saved. The name, just like other saved tasks, shows up as a valid task that can be inserted in one of your task lists. The command line can be a call to a DOS batch file or an external Windows or DOS program. Perform the following steps to familiarize yourself with this process.

1. Click the **Acme** icon in the Trading Partners window and work your way down to Acme's 850 Ver3040 Inbound window.

2. Click **File | New** and notice that the Task Wizard is displayed.

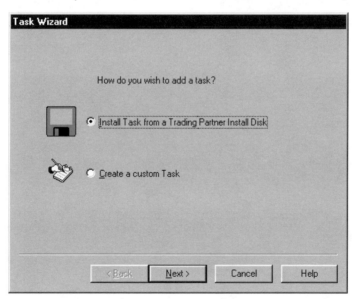

3. Click **Create a custom Task** and then click **Next**.

4. Click **User Tracked Task** and type **Proc850** as the Task Name.

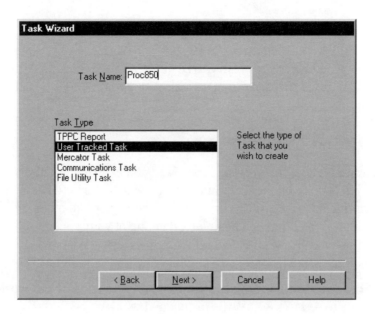

5. Click **Next.** Then type **C:\Proc850.bat** as the command line.

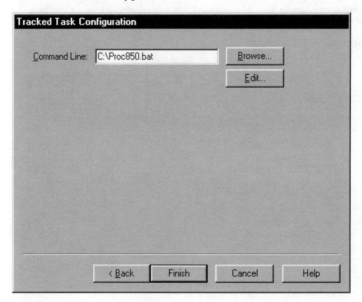

6. Click **Finish** to save the task. Return to the 850 Ver3040 Inbound dialog and notice that the task has been added.

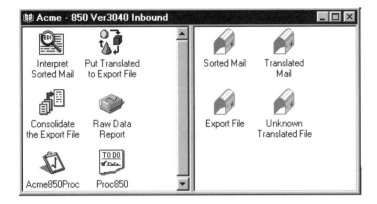

7. Then close the windows and return to the TPD Desktop.

The internal and external tasks are now available for use and can be placed in any task list. You can delete a task by selecting it and then using Edit | Uninstall to remove it.

The Scheduler

As mentioned earlier you can use TPD's Scheduler to run task lists at predetermined times. This essentially achieves unattended operation using the system clock and one or more task lists that you have created and saved. Following is a brief hands-on activity that describes the use of the Scheduler. However, before you can run the Scheduler, you must obtain a list of the task list names that you want to use and determine the schedule time that you want to use.

1. Click **System Management** to display the following dialog.

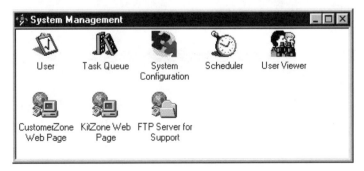

2. Click the **Scheduler** icon to display the Scheduler window.

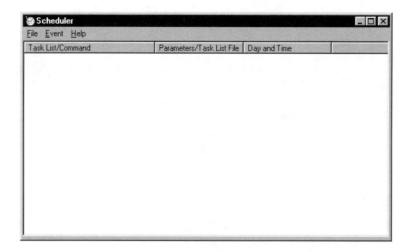

3. Click **Event | Add** (or press **Shift+Ins**) to display the Schedule Event dialog.

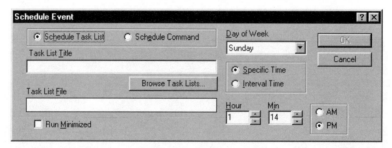

4. At this point you can schedule either a task list or a command, depending on the active option button. The Browse Task Lists button displays a list of available task lists. Selecting the Schedule Command option button changes the dialog.

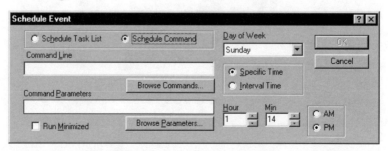

5. Read the following dialog descriptions:
   a. Browse Commands—Helps you find an executable file.

b.   Browse Parameters—Helps you find and schedule a parameter file
that is used by the file located in the Command Line.

c.   Run Minimized—Normally, task lists are displayed on the screen as
they execute. When minimized, the task list is not displayed during
execution.

6. Click the **Schedule Task List** option button. Then click **Browse Task
Lists** and select the **GEIS-A – Send, Receive And Sort** task. Click **OK**.
Then select **Sunday at 1:00 PM** and click **OK** to save the schedule.

7. Press **Shift+Ins** again to redisplay the Schedule Event dialog. Again, click
Browse, and select the **850 Ver3040 Inbound – Acme850Proc** task.
Click **OK**, set the schedule for **Sunday at 1:25 PM**, and click **OK** again.

8. Compare your Scheduler dialog to the following illustration.

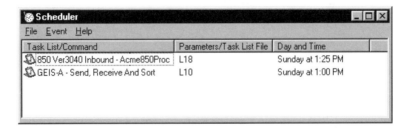

9. To avoid executing these tasks, remove both lines from the Scheduler by
right-clicking on each line and clicking **Delete**.

10. Click **File | Exit** and then click **No** in response to the Save changes
prompt.

11. Exit TPD, as this completes your tour of task lists and the Scheduler.

What's Next

As you can see, TPD has a broad repertoire of tools to help you perform EDI
exchanges. The task lists and Scheduler features make processing EDI mail
even easier. By now, you should have realized that EDI is not a complex technology. It is straightforward and uses standards that most people can read and
understand with a little background information.

At this point in the book the benefits of EDI should be quite obvious. The benefits of EDI are enhanced with a full-featured system like TPD. The next chapter
provides some conclusions and food for thought.

Review Questions

1. What is the purpose of a task list?

2. How is the Scheduler used?

3. When a task list is running, what happens if a fatal error occurs?

4. Explain why it is best to have several small task lists rather than one large one.

5. When a task list is created and saved, what shows up in the trading partner's Inbound processing window?

6. Explain how an external program can be controlled from a task list.

7. What can you use to automatically download EDI mail late at night or on weekends when long-distance rates are at their lowest point?

Chapter 13

What's Next

Introduction

If you completed the material in the preceding twelve chapters, you should have a fairly good grasp of EDI and many of the features provided by the Trading Partner Desktop EDI software. Although you may not be an "expert" yet, you're certainly conversant in what EDI does, its benefits, how it works, and what a full-featured EDI software program should do. The goal of this book is to familiarize you with both EDI and the central features associated with a full-featured EDI software system. The online help provided with TPD provides much more detailed information about the software and covers product features that were not addressed in detail in the basics provided in this book.

Moving Ahead

At this point you should appreciate the fact that installing, upgrading, or simply maintaining an EDI system is not a trivial task. If you work for a large enterprise, the complexities increase because of the number of transactions that must be handled each day. In addition, you may find yourself using dozens of different transaction set versions, adding them, modifying them, and even customizing them at the whim of important trading partners. Fortunately, TPD provides all the configuration tools that you need to make these kinds of adjustments.

Some large enterprises employ a staff of EDI professionals. Smaller organizations may use a data processing professional on a part-time basis. Very small enterprises often use consultants. It doesn't take a math genius to calculate the most economical approach. Regardless of which approach you find yourself or your enterprise taking, you should now know what to expect from EDI. If you worked your way through the hands-on activities contained in Part 2, you should know what you can expect from a good EDI software program.

Some questions to ask yourself when you are considering a system include:

- Does your system handle both ASC X12 and EDIFACT transaction sets?
- Can you add and/or reconfigure trading partners?
- Can you add and/or reconfigure communications networks?
- Can you add and/or reconfigure transaction sets?
- Can you map the transaction sets yourself?
- Can you automatically configure your maps to comply with a variety of transaction set configurations?
- Can you automate common tasks using task lists or scripts?
- Can you schedule tasks to be run unattended so they can take advantage of lower night and weekend telephone and processing rates?
- Can you export and import information between your EDI program and external applications?
- Does your EDI software program supplier offer both dial-up and online technical support?
- Are you dependent on an outside service for any of these tasks?

With TPD, you know that you can provide a positive answer to these questions. You should also know that Mercator Software Inc., the publisher of Trading Partner Desktop, also sells EDI software for PC networks as well as larger systems. Mercator Software, Inc. also sells a Commerce Chain Transformation Solution called *Mercator*. This powerful solution can make it easier to transform information through your commerce chain. You can obtain more information about these products from Mercator Software Inc. by logging onto their Web site at www.mercator.com.

Review Questions

1. Where can you find more detailed information about TPD?
2. Name three ways that companies, large and small, typically staff their EDI technical support needs.
3. Where can you find more information about Mercator Software's EDI products?

Part 3

Appendixes

- Transaction Set Guidelines
- Glossary of EDI Terms

Transaction Set Guidelines

This appendix contains a few examples of transaction set guidelines used by the U.S. government. The guidelines included in this appendix are specifically for the 003040 810 Invoice and the 003040 850 Purchase Order transaction sets. These and other 003040 transaction set guidelines can be viewed at:

http://snad.ncsl.nist.gov/dartg/edi/3040-ic.html

Other transaction set specifications that can be viewed on and/or downloaded from this site include:

- 820 Payment Order/Remittance Advice
- 824 Application Advice
- 836 Contract Award
- 840 Request for Quotation
- 843 Response to Request for Quotation
- 852 Product Activity Data
- 855 Purchase Order Acknowledgement
- 864 Text Message
- 997 Functional Acknowledgement

810 Invoice

Functional Group ID=IN

Introduction

This Draft Standard for Trial Use contains the format and establishes the data contents of the Invoice Transaction Set (810) for use within the context of an Electronic Data Interchange (EDI) environment. The transaction set can be used to provide for customary and established business and industry practice relative to the billing for goods and services provided.

Notes

1. Use this transaction set to transmit commercial invoices to a Federal Government activity responsible for initiating the payment.

2. Use a single occurrence of this transaction to invoice or provide adjustments for one or more deliveries or service performances, provided to the Federal Government on one or more shipments.

3. Use to transmit commercial invoice data only from one invoice preparing party to one invoice receiving party.

4. Use to send a replacement invoice when a previously submitted invoice is incorrect. When used, cite code 05 in BIG08.

Heading:	Pos. No.	Seg. ID	Name	Req. Des.	Max. Use	Loop Repeat	Notes and Comments
Must Use	010	ST	Transaction Set Header	M	1		
Must Use	020	BIG	Beginning Segment for Invoice	M	1		
Not Used	030	NTE	Note/Special Instruction	F	100		
	040	CUR	Currency	O	1		
Not Used	050	REF	Reference Numbers	O	12		
Not Used	060	PER	Administrative Communications Contact	O	3		
			LOOP ID - N1			200	
	070	N1	Name	O	1		
	080	N2	Additional Name Information	O	2		
	090	N3	Address Information	O	2		
	100	N4	Geographic Location	O	1		
	110	REF	Reference Numbers	O	12		
	120	PER	Administrative Communications Contact	O	3		
	130	ITD	Terms of Sale/Deferred Terms of Sale	O	5		
	140	DTM	Date/Time Reference	O	10		
	150	FOB	F.O.B. Related Instructions	O	1		
Not Used	160	PID	Product/Item Description	O	200		
Not Used	170	MEA	Measurements	O	40		
Not Used	180	PWK	Paperwork	O	25		
Not Used	190	PKG	Marking, Packaging, Loading	O	25		
Not Used	200	L7	Tariff Reference	O	1		
	210	AT	Financial Accounting	O	3		

Not Used	212	BAL	Balance Detail	O	2		n1	
			LOOP ID - LM			10		
Not Used	220	LM	Code Source Information	O	1			
Not Used	230	LQ	Industry Code	M	100			
			LOOP ID - N9			1		
Not Used	240	N9	Reference Number	O	1			
Not Used	250	MSG	Message Text	M	10			

Detail:	Pos. No.	Seg. ID	Name	Req. Des.	Max. Use	Loop Repeat	Notes and Comments
			LOOP ID - IT1			200000	
	010	IT1	Baseline Item Data (Invoice)	O	1		
Not Used	012	CRC	Conditions Indicator	O	1		
Not Used	015	QTY	Quantity	O	5		n2
Not Used	020	CUR	Currency	O	1		
Not Used	030	IT3	Additional Item Data	O	5		
	040	TXI	Tax Information	O	10		
Not Used	050	CTP	Pricing Information	O	25		
Not Used	059	MEA	Measurements	O	40		
			LOOP ID – PID			1000	
	060	PID	Product/Item Description	O	1		
Not Used	070	MEA	Measurements	O	10		
Not Used	080	PWK	Paperwork	O	25		
Not Used	090	PKG	Marking, Packaging, Loading	O	25		
Not Used	100	PO4	Item Physical Details	O	1		
	110	ITD	Terms of Sale/Deferred Terms of Sale	O	2		
	120	REF	Reference Numbers	O	>1		
Not Used	130	PER	Administrative Communications Contact	O	5		
Not Used	140	SDQ	Destination Quantity	O	500		
	150	DTM	Date/Time Reference	O	10		
	160	CAD	Carrier Detail	O	>1		
Not Used	170	L7	Tariff Reference	O	>1		
Not Used	175	SR	Advertising Schedule Requested	O	1		
			LOOP ID – SAC			25	
	180	SAC	Service, Promotion, Allowance, or Charge Information	O	1		
	190	TXI	Tax Information	O	10		
			LOOP ID – SLN			1000	
Not Used	200	SLN	Subline Item Detail	O	1		
Not Used	210	REF	Reference Numbers	O	>1		
Not Used	220	PID	Product/Item Description	O	1000		
Not Used	230	SAC	Service, Promotion, Allowance, or Charge Information	O	25		
Not Used	235	TC2	Commodity	O	2		
			LOOP ID - N1			200	

Part 3

	240	N1	Name	O	1	
	250	N2	Additional Name Information	O	2	
	260	N3	Address Information	O	2	
	270	N4	Geographic Location	O	1	
Not Used	280	REF	Reference Numbers	O	12	
Not Used	290	PER	Administrative Communications Contact	O	3	
			LOOP ID – LM			10
Not Used	300	LM	Code Source Information	O	1	
Not Used	310	LQ	Industry Code	M	100	

Summary:	Pos. No.	Seg. ID	Name	Req. Des.	Max. Use	Loop Repeat	Notes and Comments
Must Use	010	TDS	Total Monetary Value Summary	M	1		
	020	TXI	Tax Information	O	10		
	030	CAD	Carrier Detail	O	1		
			LOOP ID – SAC			25	
	040	SAC	Service, Promotion, Allowance, or Charge Information	O	1		
	050	TXI	Tax Information	O	10		
Not Used	060	ISS	Invoice Shipment Summary	O	5		
Must Use	070	CTT	Transaction Totals	M	1		n3
Must Use	080	SE	Transaction Set Trailer	M	1		

Transaction Set Notes

1. The BAL segment is to be used only if the code in BIG07 indicates that the transaction is a "Monthly Adjustment" or "Special Handling Adjustment" invoice.

2. The QTY segment is used to specify a quantity of units which are expected as payments, e.g., trade-ins or returns.

3. Number of line items (CTT01) is the accumulation of the number of IT1 segments. If used, hash total (CTT02) is the sum of the value of quantities invoiced (IT102) for each IT1 segment.

Segment:	**ST** **Transaction Set Header**
Position:	010
Loop:	
Level:	Heading
Usage:	Mandatory
Max Use:	1
Purpose:	To indicate the start of a transaction set and to assign a control number
Syntax Notes:	
Semantic Notes:	1 The transaction set identifier (ST01) used by the translation routines of the interchange partners to select the appropriate transaction set definition (e.g., 810 selects the Invoice Transaction Set).
Comments:	

Data Element Summary

	Ref. Des.	Data Element	Name	Attributes	
Must Use	ST01	143	**Transaction Set Identifier Code**	M	ID 3/3

Code uniquely identifying a Transaction Set

      810   X12.2 Invoice

	Ref. Des.	Data Element	Name	Attributes	
Must Use	ST02	329	**Transaction Set Control Number**	M	AN 4/9

Identifying control number that must be unique within the transaction set functional group assigned by the originator for a transaction set

Use to transmit a unique number assigned by the originator of the transaction set. This number may be system generated.

Segment:	**BIG** Beginning Segment for Invoice
Position:	020
Loop:	
Level:	Heading
Usage:	Mandatory
Max Use:	1
Purpose:	To indicate the beginning of an invoice transaction set and transmit identifying numbers and dates
Syntax Notes:	
Semantic Notes:	1 BIG10 indicates the consolidated invoice number. When BIG07 contains code CI, BIG10 is not used.
Comments:	1 BIG07 is used only to further define the type of invoice when needed.

Data Element Summary

	Ref. Des.	Data Element	Name	Attributes	
Must Use	BIG01	245	**Invoice Date**	M	DT 6/6

Invoice Issue Date.

Use to identify the date the transaction set was created. In the context of a commercial invoice, this date will represent the date of the invoice.

	Ref. Des.	Data Element	Name	Attributes	
Must Use	BIG02	76	**Invoice Number**	M	AN 1/22

Identifying number assigned by issuer

Use to uniquely identify the invoice transaction to an issuer. The invoice number may not be duplicated by an issuer in an original transaction (BIG08, code 00) within a 12-month period. Same number can be used if issuing an amended invoice (BIG08 is code 02, 03, or 04).

	Ref. Des.	Data Element	Name	Attributes	
	BIG03	323	**Purchase Order Date**	O	DT 6/6

Date assigned by the purchaser to Purchase Order

When BIG05 is used, cite the date of the delivery order, call, or release. When BIG05 is not used, cite the date of the procurement instrument in BIG04.

	Ref. Des.	Data Element	Name	Attributes	
Must Use	BIG04	324	**Purchase Order Number**	O	AN 1/22

Identifying number for Purchase Order assigned by the orderer/purchaser

Use to identify the procurement instrument identification number (PIIN) other than an order against a basic procurement instrument, e.g., delivery order, release, or call. For purchase orders, cite the order number. For delivery, cite the basic procurement instrument identification number (e.g., the contract, grant, cooperative agreement, etc., number) and cite the delivery order or call number in BIG05.

	Ref. Des.	Data Element	Name	Attributes	
	BIG05	328	**Release Number**	O	AN 1/30

Number identifying a release against a Purchase Order previously placed by the parties involved in the transaction

Use to identify a delivery or task order, call or release number, (e.g., the Supplemental PIIN) against the basic procurement instrument cited in BIG04.

	Ref. Des.	Data Element	Name	Attributes	
	BIG06	327	**Change Order Sequence Number**	O	AN 1/8

Part 3

Number assigned by the orderer identifying a specific change or revision to a previously transmitted transaction set

Use, as applicable, to identify a modification number to the instrument in BIG05. If BIG05 is blank, use the PIIN in BIG04.

Must Use	BIG07	640	**Transaction Type Code**		O	ID 2/2

Code specifying the type of transaction

CI	Consolidated Invoice	
CN	Credit Invoice	
CR	Credit Memo	
DI	Debit Invoice	
DR	Debit Memo	

Must Use	BIG08	353	**Transaction Set Purpose Code**		O	ID 2/2

Code identifying purpose of transaction set

00   Original

Use to indicate the initial submission of an original invoice.

01   Cancellation

Use to indicate the cancellation of a previously submitted invoice.

02   Add

Use to indicate an amended invoice that contains only additions to a previously transmitted invoice.

03   Delete

Use to indicate an amended invoice that contains only deletions from a previously transmitted invoice.

04   Change

Use to indicate an amended invoice that contains a combination of additions and deletions to a previously transmitted invoice. This code is also used to indicate data in a previously transmitted invoice has changed, e.g., the quantity invoiced and the total invoiced amount. In effect the old quantity and invoiced amount are deleted and the new quantity and invoiced amount are added.

05   Replace

07   Duplicate

Use to indicate a duplicate submission. Use only when informed that the original invoice was not received.

	BIG09	306	**Action Code**		O	ID 1/2

Code indicating type of action

F   Final

Use to indicate the final invoice. Leave blank for partial invoices.

Not Used	BIG10	76	**Invoice Number**		O	AN 1/22

Identifying number assigned by issuer

Segment:	**CUR** Currency
Position:	040
Loop:	
Level:	Heading
Usage:	Optional
Max Use:	1
Purpose:	To specify the currency (dollars, pounds, francs, etc.) used in a transaction
Syntax Notes:	1 If CUR08 is present, then CUR07 is required.
	2 If CUR09 is present, then CUR07 is required.
	3 If CUR11 is present, then CUR10 is required.
	4 If CUR12 is present, then CUR10 is required.

	5	If CUR14 is present, then CUR13 is required.
	6	If CUR15 is present, then CUR13 is required.
	7	If CUR17 is present, then CUR16 is required.
	8	If CUR18 is present, then CUR16 is required.
	9	If CUR20 is present, then CUR19 is required.
	10	If CUR21 is present, then CUR19 is required.

Semantic Notes:

Comments: 1   See Figures Appendix for examples detailing the use of the CUR segment.

Notes: *Use this 1/CUR/040 segment to identify the currency in which payment will be made if in other than U.S. dollars.*

Data Element Summary

	Ref. Des.	Data Element	Name		Attributes	
Must Use	**CUR01**	**98**	**Entity Identifier Code**		**M**	**ID 2/2**
			Code identifying an organizational entity, a physical location, or an individual			
			BY	Buying Party (Purchaser)		
				Use to indicate that the purchasing office (e.g., in the contract or order), authorized payment in the currency cited in CUR02.		
			PR	Payer		
				Use to indicate that the paying office authorized payment in the currency cited in CUR02.		
Must Use	**CUR02**	**100**	**Currency Code**		**M**	**ID 3/3**
			Code (Standard ISO) for country in whose currency the charges are specified			
			Use the appropriate code to specify the currency that will be used to make payment.			
Not Used	**CUR03**	**280**	**Exchange Rate**		**O**	**R 4/6**
			Value to be used as a multiplier conversion factor to convert monetary value from one currency to another			
Not Used	**CUR04**	**98**	**Entity Identifier Code**		**O**	**ID 2/2**
			Code identifying an organizational entity, a physical location, or an individual			
Not Used	**CUR05**	**100**	**Currency Code**		**O**	**ID 3/3**
			Code (Standard ISO) for country in whose currency the charges are specified			
Not Used	**CUR06**	**669**	**Currency Market/Exchange Code**		**O**	**ID 3/3**
			Code identifying the market upon which the currency exchange rate is based			
Not Used	**CUR07**	**374**	**Date/Time Qualifier**		**X**	**ID 3/3**
			Code specifying type of date or time, or both date and time			
Not Used	**CUR08**	**373**	**Date**		**O**	**DT 6/6**
			Date (YYMMDD)			
Not Used	**CUR09**	**337**	**Time**		**O**	**TM 4/8**
			Time expressed in 24-hour clock time as follows: HHMM, or HHMMSS, or HHMMSSD, or HHMMSSDD, where H = hours (00-23), M = minutes (00-59), S = integer seconds (00-59) and DD = decimal seconds; decimal seconds are expressed as follows: D = tenths (0-9) and DD = hundredths (00-99)			
Not Used	**CUR10**	**374**	**Date/Time Qualifier**		**X**	**ID 3/3**
			Code specifying type of date or time, or both date and time			
Not Used	**CUR11**	**373**	**Date**		**O**	**DT 6/6**
			Date (YYMMDD)			
Not Used	**CUR12**	**337**	**Time**		**O**	**TM 4/8**
			Time expressed in 24-hour clock time as follows: HHMM, or HHMMSS, or HHMMSSD, or HHMMSSDD, where H = hours (00-23), M = minutes (00-59), S = integer seconds (00-59) and DD = decimal seconds; decimal seconds are expressed as follows: D = tenths (0-9) and DD = hundredths (00-99)			

Part 3

Not Used	CUR13	374	Date/Time Qualifier	X	ID 3/3

Code specifying type of date or time, or both date and time

Not Used	CUR14	373	Date	O	DT 6/6

Date (YYMMDD)

Not Used	CUR15	337	Time	O	TM 4/8

Time expressed in 24-hour clock time as follows: HHMM, or HHMMSS, or HHMMSSD, or HHMMSSDD, where H = hours (00-23), M = minutes (00-59), S = integer seconds (00-59) and DD = decimal seconds; decimal seconds are expressed as follows: D = tenths (0-9) and DD = hundredths (00-99)

Not Used	CUR16	374	Date/Time Qualifier	X	ID 3/3

Code specifying type of date or time, or both date and time

Not Used	CUR17	373	Date	O	DT 6/6

Date (YYMMDD)

Not Used	CUR18	337	Time	O	TM 4/8

Time expressed in 24-hour clock time as follows: HHMM, or HHMMSS, or HHMMSSD, or HHMMSSDD, where H = hours (00-23), M = minutes (00-59), S = integer seconds (00-59) and DD = decimal seconds; decimal seconds are expressed as follows: D = tenths (0-9) and DD = hundredths (00-99)

Not Used	CUR19	374	Date/Time Qualifier	X	ID 3/3

Code specifying type of date or time, or both date and time

Not Used	CUR20	373	Date	O	DT 6/6

Date (YYMMDD)

Not Used	CUR21	337	Time	O	TM 4/8

Time expressed in 24-hour clock time as follows: HHMM, or HHMMSS, or HHMMSSD, or HHMMSSDD, where H = hours (00-23), M = minutes (00-59), S = integer seconds (00-59) and DD = decimal seconds; decimal seconds are expressed as follows: D = tenths (0-9) and DD = hundredths (00-99)

Segment:	**N1** Name
Position:	070
Loop:	N1 Optional
Level:	Heading
Usage:	Optional
Max Use:	1
Purpose:	To identify a party by type of organization, name, and code
Syntax Notes:	1 At least one of N102 or N103 is required.
	2 If either N103 or N104 is present, then the other is required.
Semantic Notes:	
Comments:	1 This segment, used alone, provides the most efficient method of providing organizational identification. To obtain this efficiency the "ID Code" (N104) must provide a key to the table maintained by the transaction processing party.
	2 N105 and N106 further define the type of entity in N101.
Notes:	*1. Whenever possible, address information should be transmitted using code values contained in a combination of the N101 and N103/4 data elements. Use N102 and N2-N4 segments only when it is necessary to transmit the full address. For example, if a vendor can be identified by a DUNs number, it is not necessary to transmit the vendor's full address since the relationship between the DUNs number and the vendor's address can be established by accessing a data base in which the information is stored, having been put there at the time the vendor electronically registered as a federal government trading partner.*
	2. At least two iterations of this 1/N1/070 loop are required using codes PE and PO.
	3. Use to identify a ship-to-addressee when the invoice contains multiple line items and the address is applicable to all line items. Use the 2/N1/240 loop when the invoice or the ship-to address varies among the line items.
	4. Use the 1/N1/070 loop to identify organizations or people that apply to all of the line items, or are not applicable at the line item level. When the addresses vary by line item, use the 2/N1/240 loop.

Data Element Summary

	Ref. Des.	Data Element	Name	Attributes	
Must Use	N101	98	**Entity Identifier Code**	M	ID 2/2

Code identifying an organizational entity, a physical location, or an individual

	MQ	Metering Location
		Use to indicate the location of the meter applicable to the invoice.
	PE	Payee
		Use to indicate the party submitting the invoice.
	PO	Party to Receive Invoice for Goods or Services
		Use to indicate where the invoice should be mailed.
	RI	Remit To
		Use to indicate a specific remit-to address when multiple remit-to addresses were provided as a part of the trading partner registration process. Do not use when only a single remit-to address was provided as a part of the registration process.
	ST	Ship To
		Use to indicate the ship-to address when the invoice contains multiple line items and the address is the same for all. When the invoice varies by line item, use the 2/N1/240 loop.
	SV	Service Performance Site
		When services are contracted for, this describes the organization for whom or location address at which those services will be performed
		Use to indicate a location where a service, (e.g., data entry) was performed.

	Ref. Des.	Data Element	Name	Attributes	
	N102	93	**Name**	X	AN 1/35

Free-form name

Use only when N101 is either code ST or code SV to provide a text name. Do not use when the ship-to address can be identified by a code in N103/04.

	Ref. Des.	Data Element	Name	Attributes	
Must Use	N103	66	**Identification Code Qualifier**	X	ID 1/2

Code designating the system/method of code structure used for Identification Code (67)

	1	D-U-N-S Number, Dun & Bradstreet
		Use in all transmissions to identify the DUNS number of the invoicing party and Federal Facility.
	10	Department of Defense Activity Address Code (DODAAC)
		Use to indicate either a Department of Defense Activity Address Code or a Civilian Agency Activity Address Code.
	33	Commercial and Government Entity (CAGE)
		Use to indicate vendors with CAGE codes.
	A2	Military Assistance Program Address Code (MAPAC)
		Contained in the Military Assistance Program Address Directory (MAPAD); represents the location of an entity
		Use to indicate a MAPAC address.
	FA	Facility Identification
		Use to indicate a vendor facility that cannot be identified by either a CAGE code or a DUNs number.

	Ref. Des.	Data Element	Name	Attributes	
Must Use	N104	67	**Identification Code**	X	AN 2/17

Code identifying a party or other code

	Ref. Des.	Data Element	Name	Attributes	
Not Used	N105	706	**Entity Relationship Code**	O	ID 2/2

Code describing entity relationship

	Ref. Des.	Data Element	Name	Attributes	
Not Used	N106	98	**Entity Identifier Code**	O	ID 2/2

Code identifying an organizational entity, a physical location, or an individual

Segment:	**N2** Additional Name Information
Position:	080
Loop:	N1 Optional
Level:	Heading
Usage:	Optional
Max Use:	2
Purpose:	To specify additional names or those longer than 35 characters in length
Syntax Notes:	
Semantic Notes:	
Comments:	
Notes:	*1. This segment is not necessary when the cited party can be identified by a code value in N101/03/04.*
	2. Use, as needed, only when N101 is code ST or SV and that party cannot be identified by coded means.

Data Element Summary

	Ref. Des.	Data Element	Name		Attributes	
Must Use	N201	93	**Name**		M	AN 1/35
			Free-form name			
	N202	93	**Name**		O	AN 1/35
			Free-form name			

Use only when N101 is either code ST or code SV to provide a text name. Do not use when the ship-to address can be identified by a code in N103/04

Segment:	**N3** Address Information
Position:	090
Loop:	N1 Optional
Level:	Heading
Usage:	Optional
Max Use:	2
Purpose:	To specify the location of the named party
Syntax Notes:	
Semantic Notes:	
Comments:	
Notes:	*1. This segment is not necessary when the cited party can be identified by a code value in N101/03/04.*
	2. Use, as needed, only when N101 is code ST or SV and that party cannot be identified by coded means.

Data Element Summary

	Ref. Des.	Data Element	Name		Attributes	
Must Use	N301	166	**Address Information**		M	AN 1/35
			Address information			
	N302	166	**Address Information**		O	AN 1/35
			Address information			

Segment:	**N4** Geographic Location
Position:	100
Loop:	N1 Optional
Level:	Heading
Usage:	Optional
Max Use:	1
Purpose:	To specify the geographic place of the named party
Syntax Notes:	1 If N406 is present, then N405 is required.

Semantic Notes:

Comments: 1 A combination of either N401 through N404, or N405 and N406 may be adequate to specify a location.

2 N402 is required only if city name (N401) is in the USA or Canada.

Notes: *1. This segment is not necessary when the cited party can be identified by a code value in N101/03/04.*

2. Use, as needed, only when N101 is code ST or SV and that party cannot be identified by coded means.

3. When identifying a APO/FPO, N401 carries the APO/FPO city name and N403 carries the ZIP code of the city.

Data Element Summary

	Ref. Des.	Data Element	Name		Attributes	
	N401	19	**City Name**		O	AN 2/30
			Free-form text for city name			
	N402	156	**State or Province Code**		O	ID 2/2
			Code (Standard State/Province) as defined by appropriate government agency			
	N403	116	**Postal Code**		O	ID 3/9
			Code defining international postal zone code excluding punctuation and blanks (zip code for United States)			
	N404	26	**Country Code**		O	ID 2/3
			Code identifying the country			
			A conversion table may be required to convert agency codes to ASC X12 codes.			
Not Used	N405	309	**Location Qualifier**		X	ID 1/2
			Code identifying type of location			
Not Used	N406	310	**Location Identifier**		O	AN 1/30
			Code which identifies a specific location			

Segment:	**REF** Reference Numbers
Position:	110
Loop:	N1 Optional
Level:	Heading
Usage:	Optional
Max Use:	12
Purpose:	To specify identifying numbers.
Syntax Notes:	1 At least one of REF02 or REF03 is required.
Semantic Notes:	
Comments:	
Notes:	*This 1/REF/110 segment can be used to identify numbers that apply to either the cited party or all of the line items. When the reference number does not apply to a cited party, or varies by line item, use the 2/REF/120 segment.*

Data Element Summary

	Ref. Des.	Data Element	Name		Attributes	
Must Use	REF01	128	**Reference Number Qualifier**		M	ID 2/2
			Code qualifying the Reference Number.			
			1. Use, as applicable, to identify the shipment number, replacement shipment number and final shipment indicator.			
			2. Use, as applicable, to identify reference numbers such as the shipment number, customer reference number, etc., applicable to the cited party.			
		45	Old Account Number			
			Identifies accounts being changed			
			Use only when applicable, and only when agreed to by the trading partners.			

46	Old Meter Number	
	Identifies meters being removed	
	Use only as applicable, and only when agreed to by the trading partners.	
55	Sequence Number	
	Use to indicate the suffix letter associated with a replacement shipment (i.e., when transmitting the letter A to indicate the first replacement shipment). (Applicable to DoD invoice only.)	
AA	Accounts Receivable Statement Number	
BL	Government Bill of Lading	
CR	Customer Reference Number	
	Use to indicate a customer's internal reference number.	
FS	Final Sequence Number	
	Use to indicate the suffix letter associated with a final shipment number (i.e., when transmitting the letter Z to indicate a final shipment). (Applicable to DoD invoice only.)	
MG	Meter Number	
OI	Original Invoice Number	
PQ	Payee Identification	
RB	Rate code number	
SE	Serial Number	
SI	Shipper's Identifying Number for Shipment (SID)	
	A unique number (to the shipper) assigned by the shipper to identify the shipment	
	Use to identify the shipment number.	

Must Use	REF02	127	**Reference Number**	X	AN 1/30

Reference number or identification number as defined for a particular Transaction Set, or as specified by the Reference Number Qualifier.

Not Used	REF03	352	**Description**	X	AN 1/80

A free-form description to clarify the related data elements and their content

Segment:	**PER** Administrative Communications Contact
Position:	120
Loop:	N1 Optional
Level:	Heading
Usage:	Optional
Max Use:	3
Purpose:	To identify a person or office to whom administrative communications should be directed
Syntax Notes:	1 If either PER03 or PER04 is present, then the other is required.
	2 If either PER05 or PER06 is present, then the other is required.
Semantic Notes:	
Comments:	

Data Element Summary

	Ref. Des.	Data Element	Name	Attributes	
Must Use	PER01	366	**Contact Function Code**	M	ID 2/2

Code identifying the major duty or responsibility of the person or group named

AF	Authorized Financial Contact
	Use to indicate the communication number to be contacted with questions arising from the submission of this invoice. Use only when the contact differs from one provided as a part of the registration process.

Not Used	PER02	93	**Name**	O	AN 1/35

Free-form name

PER03	365	**Communication Number Qualifier**		X	ID 2/2
		Code identifying the type of communication number			
		EM	Electronic Mail		
		EX	Telephone Extension		
		FX	Facsimile		
		IT	International Telephone		
		TE	Telephone		
PER04	364	**Communication Number**		X	AN 1/80
		Complete communications number including country or area code when applicable			
PER05	365	**Communication Number Qualifier**		X	ID 2/2
		Code identifying the type of communication number			
		EM	Electronic Mail		
		EX	Telephone Extension		
		FX	Facsimile		
		IT	International Telephone		
		TE	Telephone		
PER06	364	**Communication Number**		X	AN 1/80
		Complete communications number including country or area code when applicable			

Segment:	**ITD** Terms of Sale/Deferred Terms of Sale
Position:	130
Loop:	
Level:	Heading
Usage:	Optional
Max Use:	5
Purpose:	To specify terms of sale
Syntax Notes:	1 If ITD03 is present, then at least one of ITD04 ITD05 or ITD13 is required.
	2 If ITD08 is present, then at least one of ITD04 ITD05 or ITD13 is required.
	3 If ITD09 is present, then at least one of ITD10 or ITD11 is required.
Semantic Notes:	1 ITD15 is the percentage applied to a base amount used to determine a late payment charge.
Comments:	1 If the code in ITD01 is "04", then ITD07 or ITD09 is required and either ITD10 or ITD11 is required; if the code in ITD01 is "05", then ITD06 or ITD07 is required.
Notes:	*1. Use this 1/ITD/130 segment when the discount terms apply to all of the line items. If the discount terms vary by line item, use the 2/ITD/110 segment.*
	2. Payment method was provided at time of registration. Changes to that data must be made by submitting a registration data change using the 838 transaction set.
	3. Use only when a discount is applicable. Do not transmit this segment when a discount is not applicable.

Data Element Summary

Ref. Des.	Data Element	Name		Attributes	
ITD01	336	**Terms Type Code**		O	ID 2/2
		Code identifying type of payment terms			
		21	Fast Pay		
			Code indicating that an invoice is subject to accelerated payment		
			Use to indicate FAST PAY procedures are applicable only when that procedure has been authorized in the contract or order for which this invoice is being submitted.		
ITD02	333	**Terms Basis Date Code**		O	ID 1/2

Code identifying the beginning of the terms period

Use the same code as the one indicated in ITD02 of the Contract Solicitation Response (843 transaction set). Use of this segment shall not override the terms and conditions of the contract, order, or Prompt Payment Act.

Refer to 003040 Data Element Dictionary for acceptable code values.

	ITD03	338	**Terms Discount Percent**	O	R 1/6

Terms discount percentage, expressed as a percent, available to the purchaser if an invoice is paid on or before the Terms Discount Due Date

The amount shown is in percent, e.g., two and a half percent should be shown as 2.5 (two point five). Do not write the percent as .025.

Not Used	ITD04	370	**Terms Discount Due Date**	X	DT 6/6

Date payment is due if discount is to be earned

	ITD05	351	**Terms Discount Days Due**	X	N0 1/3

Number of days in the terms discount period by which payment is due if terms discount is earned

Not Used	ITD06	446	**Terms Net Due Date**	O	DT 6/6

Date when total invoice amount becomes due

	ITD07	386	**Terms Net Days**	O	N0 1/3

Number of days until total invoice amount is due (discount not applicable)

	ITD08	362	**Terms Discount Amount**	O	N2 1/10

Total amount of terms discount

Use, if needed, to prevent differences that can result from rounding off methods.

Not Used	ITD09	388	**Terms Deferred Due Date**	O	DT 6/6

Date deferred payment or percent of invoice payable is due

Not Used	ITD10	389	**Deferred Amount Due**	X	N2 1/10

Deferred amount due for payment

Not Used	ITD11	342	**Percent of Invoice Payable**	X	R 1/5

Amount of invoice payable expressed in percent

Not Used	ITD12	352	**Description**	O	AN 1/80

A free-form description to clarify the related data elements and their content

Not Used	ITD13	765	**Day of Month**	X	N0 1/2

The numeric value of the day of the month between 1 and the maximum day of the month being referenced

Not Used	ITD14	107	**Payment Method Code**	O	ID 1/1

Code identifying type of payment procedures

Not Used	ITD15	954	**Percent**	O	R 1/10

Percentage expressed as a decimal

Segment:	**DTM** Date/Time Reference
Position:	140
Loop:	
Level:	Heading
Usage:	Optional
Max Use:	10
Purpose:	To specify pertinent dates and times
Syntax Notes:	1 At least one of DTM02 DTM03 or DTM06 is required.
	2 If either DTM06 or DTM07 is present, then the other is required.
Semantic Notes:	
Comments:	

Notes: *1. Use this 1/DTM/140 segment to specify dates if they apply to all of the line items in the invoice. When the dates vary by line item, use the 2/DTM/150 segment.*
2. Use two iterations of the segment when a range of dates (expressed as period start - period end, is required).

Data Element Summary

	Ref. Des.	Data Element	Name		Attributes	
Must Use	DTM01	374	Date/Time Qualifier		M	ID 3/3

Code specifying type of date or time, or both date and time

011	Shipped	
035	Delivered	
135	Booking	

Use to indicate a billing revenue period. When used, cited the last day of the period.

150	Service Period Start	

Use to indicate the performance commencement date for a line item that is ordering a service.

151	Service Period End	

Use to indicate the performance completion date for a line item that is ordering a service.

186	Invoice Period Start	

When the billing period covered by an invoice begins

187	Invoice Period End	

When the billing period covered by an invoice ends

266	Base	

The start of base date for a calendar reference - all dates fall after it

Use to indicate a billing demand month. When used, cite the last day of the applicable month.

	Ref. Des.	Data Element	Name		Attributes	
	DTM02	373	Date		X	DT 6/6

Date (YYMMDD)

	DTM03	337	Time		X	TM 4/8
Not Used						

Time expressed in 24-hour clock time as follows: HHMM, or HHMMSS, or HHMMSSD, or HHMMSSDD, where H = hours (00-23), M = minutes (00-59), S = integer seconds (00-59) and DD = decimal seconds; decimal seconds are expressed as follows: D = tenths (0-9) and DD = hundredths (00-99)

Not Used	DTM04	623	Time Code		O	ID 2/2

Code identifying the time. In accordance with International Standards Organization standard 8601, time can be specified by a + or - and an indication in hours in relation to Universal Time Coordinate (UTC) time; since + is a restricted character, + and - are substituted by P and M in the codes that follow

Not Used	DTM05	624	Century		O	N0 2/2

The first two characters in the designation of the year (CCYY)

Not Used	DTM06	1250	Date Time Period Format Qualifier		X	ID 2/3

Code indicating the date format, time format, or date and time format

Not Used	DTM07	1251	Date Time Period		X	AN 1/35

Expression of a date, a time, or range of dates, times or dates and times

Part 3

Segment:	**FOB** F.O.B. Related Instructions		
Position:	150		
Loop:			
Level:	Heading		
Usage:	Optional		
Max Use:	1		
Purpose:	To specify transportation instructions relating to shipment		
Syntax Notes:	1	If FOB03 is present, then FOB02 is required.	
	2	If FOB04 is present, then FOB05 is required.	
	3	If FOB07 is present, then FOB06 is required.	
	4	If FOB08 is present, then FOB09 is required.	
Semantic Notes:	1	FOB01 indicates which party will pay the carrier.	
	2	FOB02 is the code specifying transportation responsibility location.	
	3	FOB06 is the code specifying the title passage location.	
	4	FOB08 is the code specifying the point at which the risk of loss transfers. This may be different than the location specified in FOB02/FOB03 and FOB06/FOB07.	
Comments:			
Notes:	*This segment is not necessary when the order is for service.*		

Data Element Summary

	Ref. Des.	Data Element	Name	Attributes
Must Use	FOB01	146	**Shipment Method of Payment**	M ID 2/2
			Code identifying payment terms for transportation charges	
			BP Paid by Buyer	
			The buyer agrees to the transportation payment term requiring the buyer to pay transportation charges to a specified location (origin or destination location)	
			Use to indicate that the FOB point is origin.	
			PE Prepaid and Summary Bill	
			Use to indicate that the contract or order authorizes the selling party to prepay and add transportation charges to the invoice.	
			PS Paid by Seller	
			The seller agrees to the transportation payment term requiring the seller to pay transportation charges to a specified location (origin or destination location)	
			Use to indicate that the FOB point is destination.	
Not Used	FOB02	309	**Location Qualifier**	X ID 1/2
			Code identifying type of location	
Not Used	FOB03	352	**Description**	O AN 1/80
			A free-form description to clarify the related data elements and their content	
Not Used	FOB04	334	**Transportation Terms Qualifier Code**	O ID 2/2
			Code identifying the source of the transportation terms	
Not Used	FOB05	335	**Transportation Terms Code**	X ID 3/3
			Code identifying the trade terms which apply to the shipment transportation responsibility	
Not Used	FOB06	309	**Location Qualifier**	X ID 1/2
			Code identifying type of location	
Not Used	FOB07	352	**Description**	O AN 1/80
			A free-form description to clarify the related data elements and their content	
Not Used	FOB08	54	**Risk of Loss Qualifier**	O ID 2/2
			Code specifying where responsibility for risk of loss passes	
Not Used	FOB09	352	**Description**	X AN 1/80
			A free-form description to clarify the related data elements and their content	

			Segment:	**AT** Financial Accounting

	Segment:	**AT** Financial Accounting
	Position:	210
	Loop:	
	Level:	Heading
	Usage:	Optional
	Max Use:	3
	Purpose:	To transmit financial accounting data
	Syntax Notes:	
	Semantic Notes:	
	Comments:	1 AT09 identifies unique local activity financial accounting information.
	Notes:	*1. Use this 1/AT/210 segment to identify the appropriation reimbursed and disbursed when the cited appropriation data applies to all line items. When the appropriation data varies by line item use the 2/REF/120 segment.*
		2. Only use when the purchase order has appropriation data in the 1/REF/050 segment, code AT.

Data Element Summary

	Ref. Des.	Data Element	Name		Attributes	
Not Used	AT01	1281	**Fund Code**		O	ID 2/2
			Code identifying a specific appropriation or fund account to be charged or credited			
Not Used	AT02	1282	**Treasury Symbol Number**		O	AN 7/21
			Number identifying a department, fiscal year, and appropriation limit for a standard accounting classification coding structure			
Not Used	AT03	1283	**Budget Activity Number**		O	AN 1/16
			Number identifying an administrative subdivision of funds against which a transaction is to be charged for a standard accounting classification coding structure			
Not Used	AT04	1284	**Object Class Number**		O	AN 3/12
			Number identifying the nature of the goods or services acquired and a specific office or organization using resources for a standard accounting classification coding structure			
Not Used	AT05	1285	**Reimbursable Source Number**		O	AN 1/3
			Number identifying the source of an appropriation or fund reimbursement for a standard accounting classification coding structure			
Not Used	AT06	1286	**Transaction Reference Number**		O	AN 4/20
			Number identifying an original request for goods and services to the matching financial transaction for a standard accounting classification coding structure			
Not Used	AT07	1287	**Accountable Station Number**		O	AN 3/8
			Number identifying an office responsible for entering a financial transaction into the applicable accounting system for a standard accounting classification coding structure			
Not Used	AT08	1288	**Paying Station Number**		O	AN 8/14
			Number identifying an office responsible for making a payment or collection and the corresponding voucher number under which the action was taken for a standard accounting classification coding structure			
Must Use	AT09	352	**Description**		O	AN 1/80
			A free-form description to clarify the related data elements and their content			

	Segment:	**IT1** Baseline Item Data (Invoice)
	Position:	010
	Loop:	IT1 Optional
	Level:	Detail
	Usage:	Optional
	Max Use:	1
	Purpose:	To specify the basic and most frequently used line item data for the invoice and related transactions
	Syntax Notes:	1 If IT106 is present, then IT107 is required.

2	If IT108 is present, then IT109 is required.
3	If IT110 is present, then IT111 is required.
4	If IT112 is present, then IT113 is required.
5	If IT114 is present, then IT115 is required.
6	If IT116 is present, then IT117 is required.
7	If IT118 is present, then IT119 is required.
8	If IT120 is present, then IT121 is required.
9	If IT122 is present, then IT123 is required.
10	If IT124 is present, then IT125 is required.

Semantic Notes: 1   IT101 is the purchase order line item identification.

Comments: 1   Element 235/234 combinations should be interpreted to include products and/or services. See the Data Dictionary for a complete list of ID's.

       2   IT106 through IT125 provides for ten (10) different product/service ID's for each item. For example: Case, Color, Drawing No., UPC No., ISBN No., Model No., SKU.

Notes: *1. Use multiple iterations of this 2/IT1/010 loop to provide invoice data for a specific line item. Allowances or charges identifiable to a line item will be included in that line's 2/SAC/180 loop. Invoice level of allowances or charges, that is, allowances or charges not identifiable to a specific item or line of billing, will be included in the 3/SAC/040 loop.*

2. Use as many 235/234 pairs as necessary to describe the item being invoiced.

3. When billing for metered services, on accounts with more that one meter, each meter charge should be detailed in a separate iteration of the IT1 loop.

Data Element Summary

	Ref. Des.	Data Element	Name		Attributes
	IT101	350	**Assigned Identification**	O	AN 1/11
			Alphanumeric characters assigned for differentiation within a transaction set		
			Use to identify the CLIN, SUBCLIN, or ELIN or other number identifying the line item.		
Must Use	IT102	358	**Quantity Invoiced**	M	R 1/10
			Number of units invoiced (supplier units)		
			When billing for metered services, the quantity invoiced is the number of units of meter usage. (e.g., 1,000 kilowatts).		
Must Use	IT103	355	**Unit or Basis for Measurement Code**	M	ID 2/2
			Code specifying the units in which a value is being expressed, or manner in which a measurement has been taken		
			1. Use to identify the unit of issue for the quantity listed in IT102.		
			2. While any appropriate code. may be used, code SX is preferred		
			SX Shipment		
			Use this code when IT101 is a line item for prepaid transportation charges. Use the 2/SAC/180 segment when not prepaid and add.		
			3. A conversion table may be required to convert agency codes to codes use by ASC X12.		
			Refer to 003040 Data Element Dictionary for acceptable code values.		
Must Use	IT104	212	**Unit Price**	M	R 1/14
			Price per unit of product, service, commodity, etc.		
			Cite the contract or order unit price. In those cases where the line item was purchased without charge, cite the number "0". Use a decimal point to indicate amounts that are not in whole dollars.		
Not Used	IT105	639	**Basis of Unit Price Code**	O	ID 2/2
			Code identifying the type of unit price for an item		
Must Use	IT106	235	**Product/Service ID Qualifier**	O	ID 2/2
			Code identifying the type/source of the descriptive number used in Product/Service ID (234)		

1. Use only codes that were contained in the contract or order. For example, if the item being invoiced was ordered by its National Stock Number, (code FS), use code FS followed by the National Stock Number of the item. Descriptions should be kept to a minimum essential to identify the item for payment purposes. While any code may be used, the following codes are preferred:

A8 Exhibit Line Item Number

AK Refined Product Code

CG Commodity Grouping

Use to indicate a commodity code

CL Color

CN Commodity Name

FS National Stock Number

The NSN shall be transmitted as a continuous set of numbers, and without dashes

FT Federal Supply Classification

See Code Source 27 in the ASC X12 standards for the FSC codes

KA Engineering Data List

KB Data Category Code

LT Lot Number

MF Manufacturer

Use to indicate the manufacturer of the cited line item

MG Manufacturer's Part Number

Use, as applicable, to indicate the manufacturer's part number assigned to the invoiced item

MM Motor Equipment Manufacturing Association (MEMA) Product Type Code

MN Model Number

N1 National Drug Code in 4-4-2 Format

N2 National Drug Code in 5-3-2 Format

N3 National Drug Code in 5-4-1 Format

N4 National Drug Code in 5-4-2 Format

ND National Drug Code (NDC)

PD Part Number Description

Use to indicate a clear text description of an item

PU Part Reference Number

RC Returnable Container No.

SN Serial Number

SV Service Render

Use to indicate a clear text description of a service being invoiced

SW Stock Number

Use to indicate a local stock number

SZ Vendor Alphanumeric Size Code (NRMA)

UK U.P.C./EAN Shipping Code Container Code (1-2-5-5-1)

VP Vendor'r (Selller's) Part Number

ZB Commercial and Government Entity (CAGE) Code

2. IT106 through IT125 are used in pairs. For Example, IT106 will contain a qualifier code and IT107 will contain information related to the qualifying code. So, if IT106 is code FS then IT107 would carry the National Stock Number.

Refer to 003040 Data Element Dictionary for acceptable code values.

Part

IT107	234	**Product/Service ID**	X	AN 1/30

Identifying number for a product or service

IT108	235	**Product/Service ID Qualifier**	O	ID 2/2

Code identifying the type/source of the descriptive number used in Product/Service ID (234)

Refer to 003040 Data Element Dictionary for acceptable code values.

IT109	234	**Product/Service ID**	X	AN 1/30

Identifying number for a product or service

IT110	235	**Product/Service ID Qualifier**	O	ID 2/2

Code identifying the type/source of the descriptive number used in Product/Service ID (234)

Refer to 003040 Data Element Dictionary for acceptable code values.

IT111	234	**Product/Service ID**	X	AN 1/30

Identifying number for a product or service

IT112	235	**Product/Service ID Qualifier**	O	ID 2/2

Code identifying the type/source of the descriptive number used in Product/Service ID (234)

Refer to 003040 Data Element Dictionary for acceptable code values.

IT113	234	**Product/Service ID**	X	AN 1/30

Identifying number for a product or service

IT114	235	**Product/Service ID Qualifier**	O	ID 2/2

Code identifying the type/source of the descriptive number used in Product/Service ID (234)

Refer to 003040 Data Element Dictionary for acceptable code values.

IT115	234	**Product/Service ID**	X	AN 1/30

Identifying number for a product or service

IT116	235	**Product/Service ID Qualifier**	O	ID 2/2

Code identifying the type/source of the descriptive number used in Product/Service ID (234)

Refer to 003040 Data Element Dictionary for acceptable code values.

IT117	234	**Product/Service ID**	X	AN 1/30

Identifying number for a product or service

IT118	235	**Product/Service ID Qualifier**	O	ID 2/2

Code identifying the type/source of the descriptive number used in Product/Service ID (234)

Refer to 003040 Data Element Dictionary for acceptable code values.

IT119	234	**Product/Service ID**	X	AN 1/30

Identifying number for a product or service

IT120	235	**Product/Service ID Qualifier**	O	ID 2/2

Code identifying the type/source of the descriptive number used in Product/Service ID (234)

Refer to 003040 Data Element Dictionary for acceptable code values.

IT121	234	**Product/Service ID**	X	AN 1/30

Identifying number for a product or service

IT122	235	**Product/Service ID Qualifier**	O	ID 2/2

Code identifying the type/source of the descriptive number used in Product/Service ID (234)

Refer to 003040 Data Element Dictionary for acceptable code values.

IT123	234	**Product/Service ID**	X	AN 1/30

Identifying number for a product or service

IT124	235	**Product/Service ID Qualifier**	O	ID 2/2

Code identifying the type/source of the descriptive number used in Product/Service ID (234)

Refer to 003040 Data Element Dictionary for acceptable code values.

IT125	234	**Product/Service ID**	X	AN 1/30

Identifying number for a product or service

Segment:	**TXI** Tax Information	
Position:	040	
Loop:	IT1 Optional	
Level:	Detail	
Usage:	Optional	
Max Use:	10	
Purpose:	To specify tax information	
Syntax Notes:	1	At least one of TXI02 TXI03 or TXI06 is required.
	2	If either TXI04 or TXI05 is present, then the other is required.
	3	If TXI08 is present, then TXI03 is required.
Semantic Notes:		
Comments:	1	TXI02 is the monetary amount of the tax.
	2	TXI03 is the tax percent expressed as a decimal.
	3	If TXI02 is not used, then the application of the percent (TXI03) is between trading partners.
Notes:	*Use this 2/TXI/040 segment only if taxes apply to a line item.*	

Data Element Summary

	Ref. Des.	Data Element	Name		Attributes
Must Use	TXI01	963	**Tax Type Code**	M	ID 2/2
			Code specifying the type of tax		
			Use any code. The following codes are preferred:		
			CA City Tax		
			F1 FICA Tax		
			FD Federal Tax		
			FT Federal Excise Tax		
			GR Gross Receipts Tax		
			LS State and Local Sales Tax		
			Refer to 003040 Data Element Dictionary for acceptable code values.		
	TXI02	782	**Monetary Amount**	X	R 1/15
			Monetary amount		
Not Used	TXI03	954	**Percent**	X	R 1/10
			Percentage expressed as a decimal		
Not Used	TXI04	955	**Tax Jurisdiction Code Qualifier**	X	ID 2/2
			Code identifying the source of the data used in tax jurisdiction code		
Not Used	TXI05	956	**Tax Jurisdiction Code**	X	AN 1/10
			Code identifying the taxing jurisdiction		
Not Used	TXI06	441	**Tax Exempt Code**	X	ID 1/1
			Code identifying exemption status from sales and use tax		
Not Used	TXI07	662	**Relationship Code**	O	ID 1/1
			Code indicating the relationship of the price or amount to the associated segment.		
Not Used	TXI08	828	**Dollar Basis For Percent**	O	R 1/9
			Dollar basis to be used in the percent calculation of the allowance, charge or tax		
Not Used	TXI09	325	**Tax Identification Number**	O	AN 1/20
			Number assigned to a purchaser (buyer, orderer) by a taxing jurisdiction (state, county, etc.); often called a tax exemption number or certificate number		

Segment:	**PID** Product/Item Description	
Position:	060	
Loop:	PID Optional	
Level:	Detail	
Usage:	Optional	
Max Use:	1	
Purpose:	To describe a product or process in coded or free-form format	
Syntax Notes:	1	If PID04 is present, then PID03 is required.
	2	At least one of PID04 or PID05 is required.
	3	If PID07 is present, then PID03 is required.
	4	If PID08 is present, then PID03 is required.
Semantic Notes:	1	Use PID03 to indicate the organization that publishes the code list being referred to.
	2	PID04 should be used for industry-specific product description codes.
	3	PID08 describes the physical characteristics of the product identified in PID04. A "Y" indicates that the specified attribute applies to this item. A "N" indicates it does not apply. Any other value is indeterminate.
Comments:	1	If PID01 = "F", then PID05 is used. If PID01 = "S", then PID04 is used. If PID01 = "X", then both PID04 and PID05 are used.
	2	Use PID06 when necessary to refer to the product surface or layer being described in the segment.
	3	PID07 specifies the individual code list of the agency specified in PID03.
Notes:	*The use of this segment is discouraged. Use only for a clear text description when the product/service identification in 235/234 pairs in the IT1 segment is in sufficient to describe the item or service being invoiced. Do not use when codes in IT106/107 can be used to describe the item or service being invoiced.*	

Data Element Summary

	Ref. Des.	Data Element	Name		Attributes	
Must Use	**PID01**	349	**Item Description Type**		M	ID 1/1
			Code indicating the format of a description			
			F Free-form			
Not Used	**PID02**	750	**Product/Process Characteristic Code**		O	ID 2/3
			Code identifying the general class of a product or process characteristic			
Not Used	**PID03**	559	**Agency Qualifier Code**		X	ID 2/2
			Code identifying the agency assigning the code values			
Not Used	**PID04**	751	**Product Description Code**		X	AN 1/12
			A code from an industry code list which provides specific data about a product characteristic			
	PID05	352	**Description**		X	AN 1/80
			A free-form description to clarify the related data elements and their content			
			Use to identify the item description or job description.			
Not Used	**PID06**	752	**Surface/Layer/Position Code**		O	ID 2/2
			Code indicating the product surface, layer or position that is being described			
Not Used	**PID07**	822	**Source Subqualifier**		O	AN 1/15
			A reference that indicates the table or text maintained by the Source Qualifier			
Not Used	**PID08**	1073	**Yes/No Condition or Response Code**		O	ID 1/1
			Code indicating a Yes or No condition or response			

Segment:	**ITD** Terms of Sale/Deferred Terms of Sale	
Position:	110	
Loop:	IT1 Optional	
Level:	Detail	
Usage:	Optional	
Max Use:	2	
Purpose:	To specify terms of sale	
Syntax Notes:	1	If ITD03 is present, then at least one of ITD04 ITD05 or ITD13 is required.

		2	If ITD08 is present, then at least one of ITD04 ITD05 or ITD13 is required.
		3	If ITD09 is present, then at least one of ITD10 or ITD11 is required.
Semantic Notes:		1	ITD15 is the percentage applied to a base amount used to determine a late payment charge.
Comments:		1	If the code in ITD01 is "04", then ITD07 or ITD09 is required and either ITD10 or ITD11 is required; if the code in ITD01 is "05", then ITD06 or ITD07 is required.

Notes: *1. Use this 2/ITD/110 segment when the discount terms vary by line item. If the discount applies to all of the line items, use the 1/ITD/130 segment.*

2. Use only when a discount is applicable. Do not transmit this segment when a discount is not applicable.

Data Element Summary

	Ref. Des.	Data Element	Name	Attributes	
	ITD01	336	**Terms Type Code**	O	ID 2/2
			Code identifying type of payment terms		
			21 Fast Pay		
			Code indicating that an invoice is subject to accelerated payment		
			Use to indicate FAST PAY procedures are applicable only when that payment procedure is authorized for the contract or order represented by this invoice.		
	ITD02	333	**Terms Basis Date Code**	O	ID 1/2
			Code identifying the beginning of the terms period		
			Use the same code as the one indicated in ITD02 of the Contract Solicitation Response, 843 transaction set. Use of this segment shall not override the terms and conditions of the contract, order, or Prompt Payment Act.		
			Refer to 003040 Data Element Dictionary for acceptable code values.		
	ITD03	338	**Terms Discount Percent**	O	R 1/6
			Terms discount percentage, expressed as a percent, available to the purchaser if an invoice is paid on or before the Terms Discount Due Date		
			The amount shown is a percent, e.g., two and a half percent should be shown as 2.5 (two point five). Do not write the percent as .025.		
Not Used	ITD04	370	**Terms Discount Due Date**	X	DT 6/6
			Date payment is due if discount is to be earned		
	ITD05	351	**Terms Discount Days Due**	X	N0 1/3
			Number of days in the terms discount period by which payment is due if terms discount is earned		
Not Used	ITD06	446	**Terms Net Due Date**	O	DT 6/6
			Date when total invoice amount becomes due		
	ITD07	386	**Terms Net Days**	O	N0 1/3
			Number of days until total invoice amount is due (discount not applicable)		
	ITD08	362	**Terms Discount Amount**	O	N2 1/10
			Total amount of terms discount		
Not Used	ITD09	388	**Terms Deferred Due Date**	O	DT 6/6
			Date deferred payment or percent of invoice payable is due		
Not Used	ITD10	389	**Deferred Amount Due**	X	N2 1/10
			Deferred amount due for payment		
Not Used	ITD11	342	**Percent of Invoice Payable**	X	R 1/5
			Amount of invoice payable expressed in percent		
Not Used	ITD12	352	**Description**	O	AN 1/80
			A free-form description to clarify the related data elements and their content		
Not Used	ITD13	765	**Day of Month**	X	N0 1/2
			The numeric value of the day of the month between 1 and the maximum day of the month being referenced		
Not Used	ITD14	107	**Payment Method Code**	O	ID 1/1

Part 3

Code identifying type of payment procedures

| Not Used | ITD15 | 954 | Percent | | O | R 1/10 |

Percentage expressed as a decimal

Segment:	**REF** Reference Numbers
Position:	120
Loop:	IT1 Optional
Level:	Detail
Usage:	Optional
Max Use:	>1
Purpose:	To specify identifying numbers.
Syntax Notes:	1 At least one of REF02 or REF03 is required.
Semantic Notes:	
Comments:	
Notes:	*Use this 2/REF/120 segment to identify reference numbers that vary by line item. When the reference numbers apply to all the line items in the invoice, use the 1/REF/110 segment.*

Data Element Summary

	Ref. Des.	Data Element	Name		Attributes	
Must Use	REF01	128	**Reference Number Qualifier**		M	ID 2/2

Code qualifying the Reference Number.

			46	Old Meter Number

Identifies meters being removed

| | | | 55 | Sequence Number |

Use to indicate a suffix number associated with a final shipment number (i.e., when transmitting the letter Z to indicate a final shipment). (Applicable to DoD invoices only.)

| | | | AT | Appropriation Number |

Use to identify the accounting/appropriation data of the billed activity when the data is applicable to the cited line item.

| | | | BL | Government Bill of Lading |

Use to indicate the government bill of lading number.

| | | | FS | Final Sequence Number |

Use to indicate the suffix number of a replacement shipment associated with a shipment number (i.e., when transmitting the letter A to indicate the first replacement shipment). (Applicable to DoD invoices only.)

			K5	Task Order
			MG	Meter Number
			RB	Rate code number
			SE	Serial Number

Use to indicate the item's serial number.

| | | | SI | Shipper's Identifying Number for Shipment (SID) |

A unique number (to the shipper) assigned by the shipper to identify the shipment

Use to indicate the vendor shipping number.

| Must Use | REF02 | 127 | **Reference Number** | | X | AN 1/30 |

Reference number or identification number as defined for a particular Transaction Set, or as specified by the Reference Number Qualifier.

| Not Used | REF03 | 352 | **Description** | | X | AN 1/80 |

A free-form description to clarify the related data elements and their content

Segment:		**DTM** Date/Time Reference			
Position:		150			
Loop:		IT1 Optional			
Level:		Detail			
Usage:		Optional			
Max Use:		10			
Purpose:		To specify pertinent dates and times			
Syntax Notes:		1 At least one of DTM02 DTM03 or DTM06 is required.			
		2 If either DTM06 or DTM07 is present, then the other is required.			
Semantic Notes:					
Comments:					
Notes:		*1. Use two iterations of the segment when a range of dates (expressed as period start - period end, is required).*			
		2. Use this 2/DTM/150 segment to specify the dates of the line item data for the invoice. When the date for all items are the same, use the 1/DTM/140 segment.			

Data Element Summary

	Ref. Des.	Data Element	Name		Attributes	
Must Use	DTM01	374	**Date/Time Qualifier**		M	ID 3/3
			Code specifying type of date or time, or both date and time			
			011	Shipped		
				Use to indicate the date the goods were shipped.		
			035	Delivered		
			135	Booking		
				Use to indicate a billing revenue period. When used, cite the last day of the period.		
			150	Service Period Start		
				Use to indicate the performance commencement date for a line item that is ordering a service.		
			151	Service Period End		
				Use to indicate the performance completion date for a line item that is ordering a service.		
			186	Invoice Period Start		
				When the billing period covered by an invoice begins		
			187	Invoice Period End		
				When the billing period covered by an invoice ends		
			266	Base		
				The start of base date for a calendar reference - all dates fall after it		
				Use to indicate a billing demand month. When used, cite the last day of the applicable month.		
	DTM02	373	**Date**		X	DT 6/6
			Date (YYMMDD)			
Not Used	DTM03	337	**Time**		X	TM 4/8
			Time expressed in 24-hour clock time as follows: HHMM, or HHMMSS, or HHMMSSD, or HHMMSSDD, where H = hours (00-23), M = minutes (00-59), S = integer seconds (00-59) and DD = decimal seconds; decimal seconds are expressed as follows: D = tenths (0-9) and DD = hundredths (00-99)			
Not Used	DTM04	623	**Time Code**		O	ID 2/2
			Code identifying the time. In accordance with International Standards Organization standard 8601, time can be specified by a + or - and an indication in hours in relation to Universal Time Coordinate (UTC) time; since + is a restricted character, + and - are substituted by P and M in the codes that follow			

Part 3

Not Used	DTM05	624	Century	O	N0 2/2
			The first two characters in the designation of the year (CCYY)		
Not Used	DTM06	1250	Date Time Period Format Qualifier	X	ID 2/3
			Code indicating the date format, time format, or date and time format		
Not Used	DTM07	1251	Date Time Period	X	AN 1/35
			Expression of a date, a time, or range of dates, times or dates and times		

Segment:	**CAD** Carrier Detail
Position:	160
Loop:	IT1 Optional
Level:	Detail
Usage:	Optional
Max Use:	>1
Purpose:	To specify transportation details for the transaction
Syntax Notes:	1 At least one of CAD05 or CAD04 is required.
	2 If CAD07 is present, then CAD08 is required.
Semantic Notes:	
Comments:	
Notes:	*1. Use only when a different type of transportation method is used than identified in the purchase order.*
	2. Use this 2/CAD/160 segment to identify the transportation data that vary by line item. When the transportation information applies to all line items in the invoice, use the 3/CAD/030 segment.

Data Element Summary

	Ref. Des.	Data Element	Name	Attributes	
	CAD01	91	Transportation Method/Type Code	O	ID 1/2
			Code specifying the method or type of transportation for the shipment		
			1. Use to indicate the transportation method/type code for the line items.		
			2. A conversion table may be required to convert agency codes to codes used by ASC X12.		
			Refer to 003040 Data Element Dictionary for acceptable code values.		
Not Used	CAD02	206	Equipment Initial	O	AN 1/4
			Prefix or alphabetic part of an equipment unit's identifying number		
Not Used	CAD03	207	Equipment Number	O	AN 1/10
			Sequencing or serial part of an equipment unit's identifying number (pure numeric form for equipment number is preferred)		
Not Used	CAD04	140	Standard Carrier Alpha Code	X	ID 2/4
			Standard Carrier Alpha Code		
Must Use	CAD05	387	Routing	X	AN 1/35
			Free-form description of the routing or requested routing for shipment, or the originating carrier's identity		
			Always cite the number 1. This data element is used to satisfy an X12 syntax requirement. The data, (i.e., the number 1), shall not be processed by the receiving application program.		
Not Used	CAD06	368	Shipment/Order Status Code	O	ID 2/2
			Code indicating the status of an order or shipment or the disposition of any difference between the quantity ordered and the quantity shipped for a line item or transaction		
Not Used	CAD07	128	Reference Number Qualifier	O	ID 2/2
			Code qualifying the Reference Number.		
Not Used	CAD08	127	Reference Number	X	AN 1/30
			Reference number or identification number as defined for a particular Transaction Set, or as specified by the Reference Number Qualifier.		
Not Used	CAD09	284	Service Level Code	O	ID 2/2

Code defining service

Segment:	**SAC** Service, Promotion, Allowance, or Charge Information	
Position:	180	
Loop:	SAC Optional	
Level:	Detail	
Usage:	Optional	
Max Use:	1	
Purpose:	To request or identify a service, promotion, allowance, or charge; to specify the amount or percentage for the service, promotion, allowance, or charge	

Syntax Notes:	1	At least one of SAC02 or SAC03 is required.
	2	If either SAC03 or SAC04 is present, then the other is required.
	3	If either SAC06 or SAC07 is present, then the other is required.
	4	If either SAC09 or SAC10 is present, then the other is required.
	5	If SAC11 is present, then SAC10 is required.
	6	If SAC13 is present, then at least one of SAC02 or SAC04 is required.
	7	If SAC14 is present, then SAC13 is required.
Semantic Notes:	1	If SAC01 is "A" or "C", then at least one of SAC05, SAC07, or SAC08 is required.
	2	SAC05 is the total amount for the service, promotion, allowance, or charge. If SAC05 is present with SAC07 or SAC08, then SAC05 takes precedence.
	3	SAC10 alone is used to indicate a specific quantity which could be a dollar amount, that is applicable to service, promotion, allowance or charge. SAC10 and SAC11 used together indicate a quantity range, which could be a dollar amount, that is applicable to service, promotion, allowance, or charge.
	4	SAC13 is used in conjunction with SAC02 or SAC04 to provide a specific reference number as identified by the code used.
	5	SAC14 is used in conjunction with SAC13 to identify an option when there is more than one option of the promotion.
Comments:	1	SAC04 may be used to uniquely identify the service, promotion, allowance, or charge. In addition, it may be used in conjunction to further the code in SAC02.
	2	In some business applications, it is necessary to advise the trading partner of the actual dollar amount that a particular allowance, charge, or promotion was based on to reduce ambiguity. This amount is commonly referred to a "Dollar Basis Amount". It is represented in the SAC segment in SAC10 using the qualifier "DO" - Dollars in SAC09.
Notes:		*Use this 2/SAC/180 segment to identify charges that apply to a line item. If the charges apply to all of the line items, use the 3/SAC/040 segment.*

Data Element Summary

	Ref. Des.	Data Element	Name	Attributes	
Must Use	**SAC01**	**248**	**Allowance or Charge Indicator**	**M**	**ID 1/1**
			Code which indicates an allowance or charge for the service specified		
			A Allowance		
			C Charge		
	SAC02	**1300**	**Service, Promotion, Allowance, or Charge Code**	**X**	**ID 4/4**
			Code identifying the service, promotion, allowance, or charge		
			Any code may be used except those referring to taxes which should be carried in the TX1 segment. Use code F650 to indicate packing, crating and handling.		
			Refer to 003040 Data Element Dictionary for acceptable code values.		
Not Used	**SAC03**	**559**	**Agency Qualifier Code**	**X**	**ID 2/2**
			Code identifying the agency assigning the code values		
Not Used	**SAC04**	**1301**	**Agency Service, Promotion, Allowance, or Charge Code**	**X**	**AN 1/10**
			Agency maintained code identifying the service, promotion, allowance, or charge		

Part

	SAC05	610	**Amount**	O	N2 1/15
			Monetary amount		

Use to identify the amount of the allowance or charge.

	SAC06	378	**Allowance/ Charge Percent Qualifier**	X	ID 1/1
			Code indicating on what basis allowance or charge percent is calculated		
			Refer to 003040 Data Element Dictionary for acceptable code values.		

	SAC07	332	**Allowance or Charge Percent**	X	R 1/6
			Allowance or charge expressed as a percent.		

The amount shown is a percentage, e.g., two and a half percent should be shown as 2.5 (two point five). Do not write as .025.

	SAC08	359	**Allowance or Charge Rate**	O	R 1/9
			Allowance or Charge Rate per Unit		

	SAC09	355	**Unit or Basis for Measurement Code**	X	ID 2/2
			Code specifying the units in which a value is being expressed, or manner in which a measurement has been taken		
			Refer to 003040 Data Element Dictionary for acceptable code values.		

	SAC10	339	**Allowance or Charge Quantity**	X	R 1/10
			Quantity basis when allowance or charge quantity is different from the purchase order or invoice quantity		

	SAC11	339	**Allowance or Charge Quantity**	O	R 1/10
			Quantity basis when allowance or charge quantity is different from the purchase order or invoice quantity		

Not Used	SAC12	331	**Allowance or Charge Method of Handling Code**	O	ID 2/2
			Code indicating method of handling for an allowance or charge		

Not Used	SAC13	127	**Reference Number**	X	AN 1/30
			Reference number or identification number as defined for a particular Transaction Set, or as specified by the Reference Number Qualifier.		

Not Used	SAC14	770	**Option Number**	O	AN 1/20
			A unique number identifying available promotion or allowance options when more than one is offered		

	SAC15	352	**Description**	O	AN 1/80
			A free-form description to clarify the related data elements and their content		

Use only when additional clarification of SAC02 is required.

Segment:	**TXI** Tax Information
Position:	190
Loop:	SAC Optional
Level:	Detail
Usage:	Optional
Max Use:	10
Purpose:	To specify tax information
Syntax Notes:	1 At least one of TXI02 TXI03 or TXI06 is required.
	2 If either TXI04 or TXI05 is present, then the other is required.
	3 If TXI08 is present, then TXI03 is required.
Semantic Notes:	
Comments:	1 TXI02 is the monetary amount of the tax.
	2 TXI03 is the tax percent expressed as a decimal.
	3 If TXI02 is not used, then the application of the percent (TXI03) is between trading partners.
Notes:	*Use this 2/TXI/190 segment only if taxes apply.*

Data Element Summary

	Ref. Des.	Data Element	Name	Attributes	
Must Use	TXI01	963	**Tax Type Code**	M	ID 2/2
			Code specifying the type of tax		
			Use any code. The following codes are preferred:		
			CA City Tax		
			F1 FICA Tax		
			FD Federal Tax		
			FT Federal Excise Tax		
			GR Gross Receipts Tax		
			LS State and Local Sales Tax		
			Refer to 003040 Data Element Dictionary for acceptable code values.		
	TXI02	782	**Monetary Amount**	X	R 1/15
			Monetary amount		
Not Used	TXI03	954	**Percent**	X	R 1/10
			Percentage expressed as a decimal		
Not Used	TXI04	955	**Tax Jurisdiction Code Qualifier**	X	ID 2/2
			Code identifying the source of the data used in tax jurisdiction code		
Not Used	TXI05	956	**Tax Jurisdiction Code**	X	AN 1/10
			Code identifying the taxing jurisdiction		
Not Used	TXI06	441	**Tax Exempt Code**	X	ID 1/1
			Code identifying exemption status from sales and use tax		
Not Used	TXI07	662	**Relationship Code**	O	ID 1/1
			Code indicating the relationship of the price or amount to the associated segment.		
Not Used	TXI08	828	**Dollar Basis For Percent**	O	R 1/9
			Dollar basis to be used in the percent calculation of the allowance, charge or tax		
Not Used	TXI09	325	**Tax Identification Number**	O	AN 1/20
			Number assigned to a purchaser (buyer, orderer) by a taxing jurisdiction (state, county, etc.); often called a tax exemption number or certificate number		

Segment:	**N1** Name
Position:	240
Loop:	N1 Optional
Level:	Detail
Usage:	Optional
Max Use:	1
Purpose:	To identify a party by type of organization, name, and code
Syntax Notes:	1 At least one of N102 or N103 is required.
	2 If either N103 or N104 is present, then the other is required.
Semantic Notes:	
Comments:	1 This segment, used alone, provides the most efficient method of providing organizational identification. To obtain this efficiency the "ID Code" (N104) must provide a key to the table maintained by the transaction processing party.
	2 N105 and N106 further define the type of entity in N101.

Notes:

1. Whenever possible, address information should be transmitted using code values contained in a combination of the N101 and N103/4 data elements. Use N102 and N2-N4 segments only when it is necessary to transmit the full address. For example, if a vendor can be identified by a DUNs number, it is not necessary to transmit the vendor's full address since the relationship between the DUNs number and the vendor's address can be established by accessing a database in which the information is stored, having been put there at the time the vendor electronically registered as a federal government trading partner.

2. Use this 2/N1/240 loop to identify information pertaining to the line item. If the information applies to all of the line items, use the 1/N1/070 loop.

Data Element Summary

	Ref. Des.	Data Element	Name		Attributes
Must Use	N101	98	**Entity Identifier Code**	M	ID 2/2
			Code identifying an organizational entity, a physical location, or an individual		
			MQ Metering Location		
			ST Ship To		
			Use, when the ship-to address differs among line items, to identify the shipped to address.		
			SV Service Performance Site		
			When services are contracted for, this describes the organization for whom or location address at which those services will be performed		
			Use to indicate the location where a service was performed.		
	N102	93	**Name**	X	AN 1/35
			Free-form name		
Must Use	N103	66	**Identification Code Qualifier**	X	ID 1/2
			Code designating the system/method of code structure used for Identification Code (67)		
			1 D-U-N-S Number, Dun & Bradstreet		
			10 Department of Defense Activity Address Code (DODAAC)		
			33 Commercial and Government Entity (CAGE)		
			A2 Military Assistance Program Address Code (MAPAC)		
			Contained in the Military Assistance Program Address Directory (MAPAD); represents the location of an entity		
			FA Facility Identification		
Must Use	N104	67	**Identification Code**	X	AN 2/17
			Code identifying a party or other code		
Not Used	N105	706	**Entity Relationship Code**	O	ID 2/2
			Code describing entity relationship		
Not Used	N106	98	**Entity Identifier Code**	O	ID 2/2
			Code identifying an organizational entity, a physical location, or an individual		

Segment:	**N2** **Additional Name Information**
Position:	250
Loop:	N1 Optional
Level:	Detail
Usage:	Optional
Max Use:	2
Purpose:	To specify additional names or those longer than 35 characters in length
Syntax Notes:	
Semantic Notes:	
Comments:	
Notes:	*1. This segment is not necessary when the cited party can be identified by a code value in N101/03/04.*
	2. Use, as applicable, with codes ST and SV, to provide the necessary identification for the payment.

Data Element Summary

	Ref. Des.	Data Element	Name		Attributes	
Must Use	N201	93	**Name**		M	AN 1/35
			Free-form name			
	N202	93	**Name**		O	AN 1/35
			Free-form name			

Segment:	**N3** Address Information
Position:	260
Loop:	N1 Optional
Level:	Detail
Usage:	Optional
Max Use:	2
Purpose:	To specify the location of the named party
Syntax Notes:	
Semantic Notes:	
Comments:	
Notes:	*1. This segment is not necessary when the cited party can be identified by a code value in N101/03/04.*
	2. Use, as applicable, with codes ST and SV, to provide the necessary identification for the payment.

Data Element Summary

	Ref. Des.	Data Element	Name		Attributes	
Must Use	N301	166	**Address Information**		M	AN 1/35
			Address information			
	N302	166	**Address Information**		O	AN 1/35
			Address information			

Segment:	**N4** Geographic Location	
Position:	270	
Loop:	N1 Optional	
Level:	Detail	
Usage:	Optional	
Max Use:	1	
Purpose:	To specify the geographic place of the named party	
Syntax Notes:	1	If N406 is present, then N405 is required.
Semantic Notes:		
Comments:	1	A combination of either N401 through N404, or N405 and N406 may be adequate to specify a location.
	2	N402 is required only if city name (N401) is in the USA or Canada.
Notes:		*1. This segment is not necessary when the cited party can be identified by a code value in N101/03/04.*
		2. Use, as applicable, with codes ST and SV, to provide the necessary identification for the payment.

Data Element Summary

	Ref. Des.	Data Element	Name		Attributes	
	N401	19	**City Name**		O	AN 2/30
			Free-form text for city name			
	N402	156	**State or Province Code**		O	ID 2/2
			Code (Standard State/Province) as defined by appropriate government agency			
	N403	116	**Postal Code**		O	ID 3/9

Code defining international postal zone code excluding punctuation and blanks (zip code for United States)

| | N404 | 26 | **Country Code** | O | ID 2/3 |

Code identifying the country

A conversion table may be required to convert agency codes to codes used by ASC X12.

| Not Used | N405 | 309 | **Location Qualifier** | X | ID 1/2 |

Code identifying type of location

| Not Used | N406 | 310 | **Location Identifier** | O | AN 1/30 |

Code which identifies a specific location

Segment:	**TDS** Total Monetary Value Summary
Position:	010
Loop:	
Level:	Summary
Usage:	Mandatory
Max Use:	1
Purpose:	To specify the total invoice discounts and amounts
Syntax Notes:	
Semantic Notes:	
Comments:	1 TDS02 is required if the dollar value subject to discount is not equal to the dollar value of TDS01.
Notes:	*There is no need to transmit either the currency symbol (e.g., the dollar sign $), commas separating thousands, or the decimal point because the amount data elements are N2 types which means that there are two decimal places implied in every transmitted number. When using, be sure to follow all whole numbers with two zeros to account for the implied two decimal places.*

Data Element Summary

	Ref. Des.	Data Element	Name	Attributes
Must Use	TDS01	361	**Total Invoice Amount**	M N2 1/10

Amount of invoice (including charges, less allowances) before terms discount (if discount is applicable)

Use to identify the gross total amount of the invoice after addition of charges and deductions for allowances at both the line item and summary levels, (e.g., this amount must equal the sum of IT102 times IT104 plus any amounts in the SAC and TXI segments, in the detail and summary levels, as applicable.

| | TDS02 | 390 | **Amount Subject to Terms Discount** | O N2 1/10 |

Amount upon which the terms discount amount is calculated

Use to identify the total amount of the invoice subject to discounts (which may vary by line). Use is required if the dollar value subject to the terms discount is not equal to the dollar value cited in TDS01.

| | TDS03 | 391 | **Discounted Amount Due** | O N2 1/10 |

Amount of invoice due if paid by terms discount due date (total invoice or installment amount less cash discount)

Use to identify the total amount of the invoice minus allowances and discounts and plus the charges, as applicable.

| | TDS04 | 362 | **Terms Discount Amount** | O N2 1/10 |

Total amount of terms discount

Segment:	**TXI** Tax Information
Position:	020
Loop:	
Level:	Summary
Usage:	Optional
Max Use:	10
Purpose:	To specify tax information
Syntax Notes:	1 At least one of TXI02 TXI03 or TXI06 is required.
	2 If either TXI04 or TXI05 is present, then the other is required.
	3 If TXI08 is present, then TXI03 is required.
Semantic Notes:	
Comments:	1 TXI02 is the monetary amount of the tax.
	2 TXI03 is the tax percent expressed as a decimal.
	3 If TXI02 is not used, then the application of the percent (TXI03) is between trading partners.
Notes:	*Use this 3/TXI/020 segment only if taxes apply.*

Data Element Summary

	Ref. Des.	Data Element	Name		Attributes
Must Use	TXI01	963	**Tax Type Code**	M	ID 2/2

Code specifying the type of tax

Use any code. The following codes are preferred:

CA City Tax
F1 FICA Tax
FD Federal Tax
FT Federal Excise Tax
GR Gross Receipts Tax
LS State and Local Sales Tax

Refer to 003040 Data Element Dictionary for acceptable code values.

	Ref. Des.	Data Element	Name	Attributes	
	TXI02	782	**Monetary Amount**	X	R 1/15
			Monetary amount		
Not Used	TXI03	954	**Percent**	X	R 1/10
			Percentage expressed as a decimal		
Not Used	TXI04	955	**Tax Jurisdiction Code Qualifier**	X	ID 2/2
			Code identifying the source of the data used in tax jurisdiction code		
Not Used	TXI05	956	**Tax Jurisdiction Code**	X	AN 1/10
			Code identifying the taxing jurisdiction		
Not Used	TXI06	441	**Tax Exempt Code**	X	ID 1/1
			Code identifying exemption status from sales and use tax		
Not Used	TXI07	662	**Relationship Code**	O	ID 1/1
			Code indicating the relationship of the price or amount to the associated segment.		
Not Used	TXI08	828	**Dollar Basis For Percent**	O	R 1/9
			Dollar basis to be used in the percent calculation of the allowance, charge or tax		
Not Used	TXI09	325	**Tax Identification Number**	O	AN 1/20

Number assigned to a purchaser (buyer, orderer) by a taxing jurisdiction (state, county, etc.); often called a tax exemption number or certificate number

Segment:	**CAD** Carrier Detail	
Position:	030	
Loop:		
Level:	Summary	
Usage:	Optional	
Max Use:	1	
Purpose:	To specify transportation details for the transaction	
Syntax Notes:	1	At least one of CAD05 or CAD04 is required.
	2	If CAD07 is present, then CAD08 is required.
Semantic Notes:		
Comments:		
Notes:	*1. Use only when a different type of transportation method is used than was identified in the purchase order.*	
	2. Use this 3/CAD/030 segment to identify transportation information that applies to all line items. When the transportation information varies by line item, use the 2/CAD/160 segment.	

Data Element Summary

	Ref. Des.	Data Element	Name		Attributes
	CAD01	91	**Transportation Method/Type Code**	O	**ID 1/2**
			Code specifying the method or type of transportation for the shipment		
			1. Use to indicate the transportation method/type code for the line items.		
			2. A conversion table may be required to convert agency codes to codes used by ASC X12.		
			Refer to 003040 Data Element Dictionary for acceptable code values.		
Not Used	**CAD02**	206	**Equipment Initial**	O	**AN 1/4**
			Prefix or alphabetic part of an equipment unit's identifying number		
Not Used	**CAD03**	207	**Equipment Number**	O	**AN 1/10**
			Sequencing or serial part of an equipment unit's identifying number (pure numeric form for equipment number is preferred)		
Not Used	**CAD04**	140	**Standard Carrier Alpha Code**	X	**ID 2/4**
			Standard Carrier Alpha Code		
Must Use	**CAD05**	387	**Routing**	X	**AN 1/35**
			Free-form description of the routing or requested routing for shipment, or the originating carrier's identity		
			Always cite the number 1. This data element is used to satisfy an X12 syntax requirement. The data shall not be processed by the receiving application program.		
Not Used	**CAD06**	368	**Shipment/Order Status Code**	O	**ID 2/2**
			Code indicating the status of an order or shipment or the disposition of any difference between the quantity ordered and the quantity shipped for a line item or transaction		
Not Used	**CAD07**	128	**Reference Number Qualifier**	O	**ID 2/2**
			Code qualifying the Reference Number.		
Not Used	**CAD08**	127	**Reference Number**	X	**AN 1/30**
			Reference number or identification number as defined for a particular Transaction Set, or as specified by the Reference Number Qualifier.		
Not Used	**CAD09**	284	**Service Level Code**	O	**ID 2/2**
			Code defining service		

Segment:	**SAC** Service, Promotion, Allowance, or Charge Information
Position:	040
Loop:	SAC Optional
Level:	Summary
Usage:	Optional
Max Use:	1
Purpose:	To request or identify a service, promotion, allowance, or charge; to specify the amount or percentage for the service, promotion, allowance, or charge
Syntax Notes:	1 At least one of SAC02 or SAC03 is required.
	2 If either SAC03 or SAC04 is present, then the other is required.
	3 If either SAC06 or SAC07 is present, then the other is required.
	4 If either SAC09 or SAC10 is present, then the other is required.
	5 If SAC11 is present, then SAC10 is required.
	6 If SAC13 is present, then at least one of SAC02 or SAC04 is required.
	7 If SAC14 is present, then SAC13 is required.
Semantic Notes:	1 If SAC01 is "A" or "C", then at least one of SAC05, SAC07, or SAC08 is required.
	2 SAC05 is the total amount for the service, promotion, allowance, or charge.
	If SAC05 is present with SAC07 or SAC08, then SAC05 takes precedence.
	3 SAC10 alone is used to indicate a specific quantity which could be a dollar amount, that is applicable to service, promotion, allowance or charge.
	SAC10 and SAC11 used together indicate a quantity range, which could be a dollar amount, that is applicable to service, promotion, allowance, or charge.
	4 SAC13 is used in conjunction with SAC02 or SAC04 to provide a specific reference number as identified by the code used.
	5 SAC14 is used in conjunction with SAC13 to identify an option when there is more than one option of the promotion.
Comments:	1 SAC04 may be used to uniquely identify the service, promotion, allowance, or charge. In addition, it may be used in conjunction to further the code in SAC02.
	2 In some business applications, it is necessary to advise the trading partner of the actual dollar amount that a particular allowance, charge, or promotion was based on to reduce ambiguity. This amount is commonly referred to a "Dollar Basis Amount". It is represented in the SAC segment in SAC10 using the qualifier "DO" - Dollars in SAC09.
Notes:	*Use the 3/SAC/040 segment to identify charges that apply to all of the line items. If the charges vary by line item, use the 2/SAC/180 segment.*

Data Element Summary

	Ref. Des.	Data Element	Name		Attributes
Must Use	SAC01	248	**Allowance or Charge Indicator**	M	ID 1/1
			Code which indicates an allowance or charge for the service specified		
			A Allowance		
			C Charge		
	SAC02	1300	**Service, Promotion, Allowance, or Charge Code**	X	ID 4/4
			Code identifying the service, promotion, allowance, or charge		
			Use any code except those that are tax related. Those codes should be carried in the TXI segment.		
			Refer to 003040 Data Element Dictionary for acceptable code values.		
Not Used	SAC03	559	**Agency Qualifier Code**	X	ID 2/2
			Code identifying the agency assigning the code values		
Not Used	SAC04	1301	**Agency Service, Promotion, Allowance, or Charge Code**	X	AN 1/10
			Agency maintained code identifying the service, promotion, allowance, or charge		
	SAC05	610	**Amount**	O	N2 1/15
			Monetary amount		
			Use to identify the amount of the allowance or charge.		

	SAC06	378	**Allowance/ Charge Percent Qualifier**	X	ID 1/1

Code indicating on what basis allowance or charge percent is calculated

Refer to 003040 Data Element Dictionary for acceptable code values.

	SAC07	332	**Allowance or Charge Percent**	X	R 1/6

Allowance or charge expressed as a percent.

The amount shown is a percent, e.g., two and a half percent should be shown as 2.5 (two point five). Do not write the percent as .025.

	SAC08	359	**Allowance or Charge Rate**	O	R 1/9

Allowance or Charge Rate per Unit

	SAC09	355	**Unit or Basis for Measurement Code**	X	ID 2/2

Code specifying the units in which a value is being expressed, or manner in which a measurement has been taken

Refer to 003040 Data Element Dictionary for acceptable code values.

	SAC10	339	**Allowance or Charge Quantity**	X	R 1/10

Quantity basis when allowance or charge quantity is different from the purchase order or invoice quantity

	SAC11	339	**Allowance or Charge Quantity**	O	R 1/10

Quantity basis when allowance or charge quantity is different from the purchase order or invoice quantity

Not Used	SAC12	331	**Allowance or Charge Method of Handling Code**	O	ID 2/2

Code indicating method of handling for an allowance or charge

Not Used	SAC13	127	**Reference Number**	X	AN 1/30

Reference number or identification number as defined for a particular Transaction Set, or as specified by the Reference Number Qualifier.

Not Used	SAC14	770	**Option Number**	O	AN 1/20

A unique number identifying available promotion or allowance options when more than one is offered

	SAC15	352	**Description**	O	AN 1/80

A free-form description to clarify the related data elements and their content

Use only when additional clarification of codes in SAC02 is required.

Segment:	**TXI** Tax Information
Position:	050
Loop:	SAC Optional
Level:	Summary
Usage:	Optional
Max Use:	10
Purpose:	To specify tax information
Syntax Notes:	1 At least one of TXI02 TXI03 or TXI06 is required.
	2 If either TXI04 or TXI05 is present, then the other is required.
	3 If TXI08 is present, then TXI03 is required.
Semantic Notes:	
Comments:	1 TXI02 is the monetary amount of the tax.
	2 TXI03 is the tax percent expressed as a decimal.
	3 If TXI02 is not used, then the application of the percent (TXI03) is between trading partners.
Notes:	*Use this 3/TXI/050 segment only if taxes apply at the summary level and they cannot be assigned to a specific line item.*

Data Element Summary

	Ref. Des.	Data Element	Name		Attributes
Must Use	TXI01	963	**Tax Type Code**	M	ID 2/2

Code specifying the type of tax

Use any code. The following codes are preferred:

CA City Tax
F1 FICA Tax
FD Federal Tax
FT Federal Excise Tax
GR Gross Receipts Tax
LS State and Local Sales Tax

Refer to 003040 Data Element Dictionary for acceptable code values.

	Ref. Des.	Data Element	Name		Attributes
	TXI02	782	**Monetary Amount**	X	R 1/15

Monetary amount

Not Used	TXI03	954	**Percent**	X	R 1/10

Percentage expressed as a decimal

Not Used	TXI04	955	**Tax Jurisdiction Code Qualifier**	X	ID 2/2

Code identifying the source of the data used in tax jurisdiction code

Not Used	TXI05	956	**Tax Jurisdiction Code**	X	AN 1/10

Code identifying the taxing jurisdiction

Not Used	TXI06	441	**Tax Exempt Code**	X	ID 1/1

Code identifying exemption status from sales and use tax

Not Used	TXI07	662	**Relationship Code**	O	ID 1/1

Code indicating the relationship of the price or amount to the associated segment.

Not Used	TXI08	828	**Dollar Basis For Percent**	O	R 1/9

Dollar basis to be used in the percent calculation of the allowance, charge or tax

Not Used	TXI09	325	**Tax Identification Number**	O	AN 1/20

Number assigned to a purchaser (buyer, orderer) by a taxing jurisdiction (state, county, etc.); often called a tax exemption number or certificate number

Segment:	**CTT** Transaction Totals
Position:	070
Loop:	
Level:	Summary
Usage:	Mandatory
Max Use:	1
Purpose:	To transmit a hash total for a specific element in the transaction set
Syntax Notes:	1 If CTT03 is present, then CTT04 is required.
	2 If CTT05 is present, then CTT06 is required.
Semantic Notes:	
Comments:	1 This segment is intended to provide hash totals to validate transaction completeness and correctness.

Data Element Summary

	Ref. Des.	Data Element	Name		Attributes
Must Use	CTT01	354	**Number of Line Items**	M	N0 1/6
			Total number of line items in the transaction set		
	CTT02	347	**Hash Total**	O	R 1/10

Sum of values of the specified data element. All values in the data element will be summed without regard to decimal points (explicit or implicit) or signs. Truncation will occur on the left most digits if the sum is greater than the maximum size of the hash total of the data element.

Example:

-.0018 First occurrence of value being hashed. .18 Second occurrence of value being hashed. 1.8 Third occurrence of value being hashed. 18.01 Fourth occurrence of value being hashed. ------- 1855 Hash total prior to truncation. 855 Hash total after truncation to three-digit field.

Not Used	CTT03	81	**Weight**	O	R 1/10
			Numeric value of weight		
Not Used	CTT04	355	**Unit or Basis for Measurement Code**	X	ID 2/2
			Code specifying the units in which a value is being expressed, or manner in which a measurement has been taken		
Not Used	CTT05	183	**Volume**	O	R 1/8
			Value of volumetric measure		
Not Used	CTT06	355	**Unit or Basis for Measurement Code**	X	ID 2/2
			Code specifying the units in which a value is being expressed, or manner in which a measurement has been taken		
Not Used	CTT07	352	**Description**	O	AN 1/80
			A free-form description to clarify the related data elements and their content		

Segment:	**SE** **Transaction Set Trailer**
Position:	080
Loop:	
Level:	Summary
Usage:	Mandatory
Max Use:	1
Purpose:	To indicate the end of the transaction set and provide the count of the transmitted segments (including the beginning (ST) and ending (SE) segments).
Syntax Notes:	
Semantic Notes:	
Comments:	1 SE is the last segment of each transaction set.

Data Element Summary

	Ref. Des.	Data Element	Name	Attributes	
Must Use	SE01	96	**Number of Included Segments**	M	N0 1/10
			Total number of segments included in a transaction set including ST and SE segments		
Must Use	SE02	329	**Transaction Set Control Number**	M	AN 4/9
			Identifying control number that must be unique within the transaction set functional group assigned by the originator for a transaction set		
			Cite the same number that is contained in ST02.		

850 Purchase Order

Functional Group ID=PO

Introduction

This Draft Standard for Trial Use contains the format and establishes the data contents of the Purchase Order Transaction Set (850) for use within the context of an Electronic Data Interchange (EDI) environment. The transaction set can be used to provide for customary and established business and industry practice relative to the placement of purchase orders for goods and services. This transaction set should not be used to convey purchase order changes or purchase order acknowledgment information.

Notes

1. Use this transaction set to issue procurement instruments to include Purchase/Delivery Orders and contracts for federal government purchases.

2. Use, if applicable, segments in Table 1 when the order contains one line item or multiple line items and the data to all the line items. Use the corresponding segments in Table 2 when the order contains multiple line items and the data varies among the line items.

Heading:	Pos. No.	Seg. ID	Name	Req. Des.	Max. Use	Loop Repeat	Notes and Comments
Must Use	010	ST	Transaction Set Header	M	1		
Must Use	020	BEG	Beginning Segment for Purchase Order	M	1		
	030	NTE	Note/Special Instruction	F	100		
	040	CUR	Currency	O	1		
	050	REF	Reference Numbers	O	12		
	060	PER	Administrative Communications Contact	O	3		
Not Used	070	TAX	Tax Reference	O	>1		
	080	FOB	F.O.B. Related Instructions	O	>1		
Not Used	090	CTP	Pricing Information	O	25		
	110	CSH	Header Sale Condition	O	5		
	120	SAC	Service, Promotion, Allowance, or Charge Information	O	25		
	130	ITD	Terms of Sale/Deferred Terms of Sale	O	5		
Not Used	140	DIS	Discount Detail	O	20		
Not Used	145	INC	Installment Information	O	1		
	150	DTM	Date/Time Reference	O	10		
	160	LDT	Lead Time	O	12		
Not Used	180	LIN	Item Identification	O	5		n1
Not Used	185	SI	Service Characteristic Identification	O	2		
	190	PID	Product/Item Description	O	200		
	200	MEA	Measurements	O	40		
	210	PWK	Paperwork	O	25		
	220	PKG	Marking, Packaging, Loading	O	200		

Part 3

	Pos. No.	Seg. ID	Name	Req. Des.	Max. Use	Loop Repeat	Notes and Comments
Not Used	230	TD1	Carrier Details (Quantity and Weight)	O	2		
	240	TD5	Carrier Details (Routing Sequence/Transit Time)	O	12		
Not Used	250	TD3	Carrier Details (Equipment)	O	12		
	260	TD4	Carrier Details (Special Handling or Hazardous Materials or Both)	O	5		
	270	MAN	Marks and Numbers	O	10		
Not Used	280	CTB	Restrictions/ Conditions	O	5		
Not Used	285	TXI	Tax Information	O	>1		
			LOOP ID - N9			1000	
	290	N9	Reference Number	O	1		
	300	MSG	Message Text	O	1000		
			LOOP ID - N1			200	
	310	N1	Name	O	1		
	320	N2	Additional Name Information	O	2		
	330	N3	Address Information	O	2		
	340	N4	Geographic Location	O	1		
Not Used	345	NX2	Real Estate Property ID Component	O	3		
	350	REF	Reference Numbers	O	12		
	360	PER	Administrative Communications Contact	O	3		
Not Used	370	FOB	F.O.B. Related Instructions	O	1		
Not Used	380	TD1	Carrier Details (Quantity and Weight)	O	2		
	390	TD5	Carrier Details (Routing Sequence/Transit Time)	O	12		
Not Used	400	TD3	Carrier Details (Equipment)	O	12		
Not Used	410	TD4	Carrier Details (Special Handling, or Hazardous Materials, or Both)	O	5		
Not Used	420	PKG	Marking, Packaging, Loading	O	200		

Detail:	Pos. No.	Seg. ID	Name	Req. Des.	Max. Use	Loop Repeat	Notes and Comments
			LOOP ID - PO1			100000	
Must Use	010	PO1	Baseline Item Data	M	1		n2
Not Used	018	SI	Service Characteristic Identification	O	5		
Not Used	020	CUR	Currency	O	1		
	030	PO3	Additional Item Detail	O	25		
	040	CTP	Pricing Information	O	25		
	049	MEA	Measurements	O	40		
			LOOP ID - PID			1000	
	050	PID	Product/Item Description	O	1		
Not Used	060	MEA	Measurements	O	10		
	070	PWK	Paperwork	O	25		
	090	PO4	Item Physical Details	O	1		
	100	REF	Reference Numbers	O	12		
	110	PER	Administrative Communications Contact	O	3		
	130	SAC	Service, Promotion, Allowance, or Charge Information	O	25		

	140	IT8	Conditions of Sale	O	1		
	150	ITD	Terms of Sale/Deferred Terms of Sale	O	2		
	160	DIS	Discount Detail	O	20		
Not Used	165	INC	Installment Information	O	1		
Not Used	170	TAX	Tax Reference	O	>1		
	180	FOB	F.O.B. Related Instructions	O	1		
	190	SDQ	Destination Quantity	O	500		
Not Used	200	IT3	Additional Item Data	O	5		
	210	DTM	Date/Time Reference	O	10		
	220	LDT	Lead Time	O	12		
	230	SCH	Line Item Schedule	O	200	n3	
Not Used	235	TC2	Commodity	O	2		
Not Used	240	TD1	Carrier Details (Quantity and Weight)	O	1		
	250	TD5	Carrier Details (Routing Sequence/Transit Time)	O	12		
Not Used	260	TD3	Carrier Details (Equipment)	O	12		
	270	TD4	Carrier Details (Special Handling or Hazardous Materials or Both)	O	5		
	280	MAN	Marks and Numbers	O	10		
	290	AMT	Monetary Amount	O	1	n4	
Not Used	295	TXI	Tax Information	O	>1		

LOOP ID - PKG						200
	300	PKG	Marking, Packaging, Loading	O	1	
Not Used	310	MEA	Measurements	O	>1	

LOOP ID - N9						1000
	330	N9	Reference Number	O	1	
Not Used	335	MEA	Measurements	O	40	
	340	MSG	Message Text	O	1000	

LOOP ID - N1						200
	350	N1	Name	O	1	
	360	N2	Additional Name Information	O	2	
	370	N3	Address Information	O	2	
	380	N4	Geographic Location	O	1	
Not Used	385	NX2	Real Estate Property ID Component	O	3	
	390	REF	Reference Numbers	O	12	
	400	PER	Administrative Communications Contact	O	3	
Not Used	410	FOB	F.O.B. Related Instructions	O	1	
	415	SCH	Line Item Schedule	O	200	
Not Used	420	TD1	Carrier Details (Quantity and Weight)	O	2	
	430	TD5	Carrier Details (Routing Sequence/Transit Time)	O	12	
Not Used	440	TD3	Carrier Details (Equipment)	O	12	
Not Used	450	TD4	Carrier Details (Special Handling, or Hazardous Materials, or Both)	O	5	
Not Used	460	PKG	Marking, Packaging, Loading	O	200	

| LOOP ID - SLN | | | | | | 1000 |
| Not Used | 470 | SLN | Subline Item Detail | O | 1 | |

Not Used	480	SI	Service Characteristic Identification	O	5		
Not Used	490	PID	Product/Item Description	O	1000		
Not Used	500	PO3	Additional Item Detail	O	104		
Not Used	505	TC2	Commodity	O	2		
Not Used	510	SAC	Service, Promotion, Allowance, or Charge Information	O	10		
Not Used	520	DTM	Date/Time/Period	O	10		
Not Used	522	CTP	Pricing Information	O	25		
Not Used	524	PO4	Item Physical Details	O	1		
			LOOP ID - N1			10	
Not Used	530	N1	Name	O	1		
Not Used	540	N2	Additional Name Information	O	2		
Not Used	550	N3	Address Information	O	2		
Not Used	560	N4	Geographic Location	O	1		
Not Used	570	NX2	Real Estate Property ID Component	O	3		
Not Used	580	REF	Reference Numbers	O	12		
Not Used	590	PER	Administrative Communications Contact	O	3		

Summary:	Pos. No.	Seg. ID	Name	Req. Des.	Max. Use	Loop Repeat	Notes and Comments
Must Use	010	CTT	Transaction Totals	M	1		n5
	020	AMT	Monetary Amount	O	1		n6
Must Use	030	SE	Transaction Set Trailer	M	1		

Transaction Set Notes

1. If segment LIN is used, do not use LIN01.

2. PO102 is required.

3. The SCH segment is used to specify various quantities of items ordered that are to be scheduled. When this segment is used the unit of measurement code (SCH02) should always be identical to the unit of measurement code in the associated PO1 segment (PO103) and the sum of values of quantity (SCH01) should always equal the quantity ordered (PO102) in the PO1 segment.

4. If AMT is used in the detail area, then AMT01 will = 1 and AMT02 will indicate total line amount as calculated by the sender.

5. The number of line items (CTT01) is the accumulation of the number of PO1 segments. If used, hash total (CTT02) is the sum of the value of quantities ordered (PO102) for each PO1 segment.

6. If AMT is used in the summary area, then AMT01 will = TT and AMT02 will indicate total transaction amount as calculated by the sender.

Segment:	**ST** Transaction Set Header
Position:	010
Loop:	
Level:	Heading
Usage:	Mandatory
Max Use:	1
Purpose:	To indicate the start of a transaction set and to assign a control number
Syntax Notes:	
Semantic Notes:	1 The transaction set identifier (ST01) used by the translation routines of the interchange partners to select the appropriate transaction set definition (e.g., 810 selects the Invoice Transaction Set).
Comments:	

Data Element Summary

	Ref. Des.	Data Element	Name		Attributes
Must Use	ST01	143	**Transaction Set Identifier Code**		**M** ID 3/3
			Code uniquely identifying a Transaction Set		
			Refer to 003040 Data Element Dictionary for acceptable code values.		
Must Use	ST02	329	**Transaction Set Control Number**		**M** AN 4/9
			Identifying control number that must be unique within the transaction set functional group assigned by the originator for a transaction set		
			Use to transmit a unique number assigned by the originator of the transaction set. This number may be system generated.		

Segment:	**BEG** Beginning Segment for Purchase Order
Position:	020
Loop:	
Level:	Heading
Usage:	Mandatory
Max Use:	1
Purpose:	To indicate the beginning of the Purchase Order Transaction Set and transmit identifying numbers and dates
Syntax Notes:	
Semantic Notes:	
Comments:	
Notes:	*A request has been submitted to ASC X12 to add data elements to the BEG segment that will carry the contract type (in terms of its pricing arrangement, e.g., Firm Fixed Price, Cost Plus Award Fee, etc.), security classification, and type of product or service code. We expect those data elements to be available for use in ASC X12 Version/Release 3050.*

Data Element Summary

	Ref. Des.	Data Element	Name		Attributes
Must Use	BEG01	353	**Transaction Set Purpose Code**		**M** ID 2/2
			Code identifying purpose of transaction set		
			00	Original	
				Use to indicate an original procurement instrument. This code is used only after the contractor has agreed to all terms and conditions to be contained in the procurement instrument transmitted.	
			07	Duplicate	
				Use to indicate the re-transmission of a previously transmitted procurement instrument.	
			22	Information Copy	

Part 3

Use to indicate that this is an information copy of an original procurement instrument. This information copy is sent to addresses other than the selling party, e.g., the Contract Administration Office.

| Must Use | BEG02 | 92 | **Purchase Order Type Code** | | M | ID 2/2 |

Code specifying the type of Purchase Order

Use to identify the type of procurement instrument represented by this transaction set.

| | | | LS | Lease |
| | | | NE | New Order |

Use to indicate a Purchase Order. A request has been submitted to ASC X12 to add a code for Purchase Order. We expect this code will be available for use in ASC X12 Version/Release 3050. In the meantime, use this code.

| | | | RL | Release or Delivery Order |

An order for goods and services placed against a pre-existing contract or blanket order

Use to indicate releases, calls, or delivery orders against existing indefinite procurement instruments.

| | | | RT | Rental |
| | | | ZZ | Mutually Defined |

Use to indicate that a type of procurement instrument other than a lease, purchase order or delivery order is being issued. When used, use the following NTE segment to explain the type of procurement instrument being issued. A request has been submitted to ASC X12 to add codes for Agreement, Blanket Purchase Agreement, Contract, Basic Agreement, Basic Ordering Agreement, Grant, Indefinite Delivery Indefinite Quantity (IDIQ), Indefinite Delivery Definite Quantity (IDDQ), Requirements, Task Order, and Letter Contract. We expect these codes will be available for use in ASC X12 Version/Release 3050. Do not use for releases or delivery orders. When applicable, use code RL.

| Must Use | BEG03 | 324 | **Purchase Order Number** | | M | AN 1/22 |

Identifying number for Purchase Order assigned by the orderer/purchaser

Use to identify the procurement instrument identification number (PIIN) not the order against a basic procurement instrument, e.g., delivery order, release, or call. For purchase orders, cite the order number. For delivery orders, cite the basic procurement instrument identification number (e.g., the contract or schedule number) and cite the delivery order or call number in BEG04. Federal numbers will not exceed 15 characters in length in order to comply with Federal Procurement Data System requirements.

| | BEG04 | 328 | **Release Number** | | O | AN 1/30 |

Number identifying a release against a Purchase Order previously placed by the parties involved in the transaction

Use to identify the delivery order, call or release number, (e.g., the Supplemental PIIN) against the basic procurement instrument cited in BEG03.

| Must Use | BEG05 | 323 | **Purchase Order Date** | | M | DT 6/6 |

Date assigned by the purchaser to Purchase Order

When BEG04 is used, cite the date of the delivery order, call or release. When BEG04 is not used, cite the date of the procurement instrument in BEG03.

| Not Used | BEG06 | 367 | **Contract Number** | | O | AN 1/30 |

Contract number

| | BEG07 | 587 | **Acknowledgment Type** | | O | ID 2/2 |

Code specifying the type of acknowledgment

| | | | AC | Acknowledge - With Detail and Change |

Use to indicate acknowledgment of this 850 is required using the available segments in the 855 and retransmitting the same data in the corresponding segments in the 850. Changes are permitted.

| | | | AD | Acknowledge - With Detail, No Change |

Use to indicate acknowledgment of this 850 is required using the available segments in the 855 and retransmitting the same data in the corresponding segments in the 850 without change.

             AK   Acknowledge - No Detail or Change

Use to indicate acknowledgment by acceptance or rejection of this 850 is required.

Not Used	BEG08	1019	Invoice Type Code	O	ID 3/3

Code defining the method by which invoices are to be processed

Refer to 003040 Data Element Dictionary for acceptable code values.

Segment:	**NTE** Note/Special Instruction
Position:	030
Loop:	
Level:	Heading
Usage:	Floating
Max Use:	100
Purpose:	To transmit information in a free-form format, if necessary, for comment or special instruction
Syntax Notes:	
Semantic Notes:	
Comments:	1 The NTE segment permits free-form information/data which, under ANSI X12 standard implementations, is not machine processable. The use of the NTE segment should therefore be avoided, if at all possible, in an automated environment.
Notes:	*1. Must use when BEG02 is code ZZ, to identify the type of procurement instrument being issued.*
	2. Use of free-form text is discouraged if the information can be provided by some other means within the transaction set.

Data Element Summary

	Ref. Des.	Data Element	Name		Attributes
	NTE01	363	**Note Reference Code**	O	ID 3/3

Code identifying the functional area or purpose for which the note applies

Use any code.

Refer to 003040 Data Element Dictionary for acceptable code values.

	Ref. Des.	Data Element	Name		Attributes
Must Use	NTE02	3	**Free Form Message**	M	AN 1/60

Free-form text

Segment:	**CUR** Currency
Position:	040
Loop:	
Level:	Heading
Usage:	Optional
Max Use:	1
Purpose:	To specify the currency (dollars, pounds, francs, etc.) used in a transaction
Syntax Notes:	1 If CUR08 is present, then CUR07 is required.
	2 If CUR09 is present, then CUR07 is required.
	3 If CUR11 is present, then CUR10 is required.
	4 If CUR12 is present, then CUR10 is required.
	5 If CUR14 is present, then CUR13 is required.
	6 If CUR15 is present, then CUR13 is required.
	7 If CUR17 is present, then CUR16 is required.
	8 If CUR18 is present, then CUR16 is required.
	9 If CUR20 is present, then CUR19 is required.
	10 If CUR21 is present, then CUR19 is required.

Semantic Notes:

Comments: 1   See Figures Appendix for examples detailing the use of the CUR segment.

Notes: *Use to identify the currency in which payment will be made if in other than U.S. Dollars.*

Data Element Summary

	Ref. Des.	Data Element	Name		Attributes
Must Use	CUR01	98	**Entity Identifier Code**	M	ID 2/2
			Code identifying an organizational entity, a physical location, or an individual		
			PR Payer		
			Use to indicate the paying office.		
Must Use	CUR02	100	**Currency Code**	M	ID 3/3
			Code (Standard ISO) for country in whose currency the charges are specified		
			Use the appropriate code to specify the currency that will be used to make payment.		
Not Used	CUR03	280	**Exchange Rate**	O	R 4/6
			Value to be used as a multiplier conversion factor to convert monetary value from one currency to another		
Not Used	CUR04	98	**Entity Identifier Code**	O	ID 2/2
			Code identifying an organizational entity, a physical location, or an individual		
			Refer to 003040 Data Element Dictionary for acceptable code values.		
Not Used	CUR05	100	**Currency Code**	O	ID 3/3
			Code (Standard ISO) for country in whose currency the charges are specified		
Not Used	CUR06	669	**Currency Market/Exchange Code**	O	ID 3/3
			Code identifying the market upon which the currency exchange rate is based		
			Refer to 003040 Data Element Dictionary for acceptable code values.		
Not Used	CUR07	374	**Date/Time Qualifier**	X	ID 3/3
			Code specifying type of date or time, or both date and time		
			Refer to 003040 Data Element Dictionary for acceptable code values.		
Not Used	CUR08	373	**Date**	O	DT 6/6
			Date (YYMMDD)		
Not Used	CUR09	337	**Time**	O	TM 4/8
			Time expressed in 24-hour clock time as follows: HHMM, or HHMMSS, or HHMMSSD, or HHMMSSDD, where H = hours (00-23), M = minutes (00-59), S = integer seconds (00-59) and DD = decimal seconds; decimal seconds are expressed as follows: D = tenths (0-9) and DD = hundredths (00-99)		
Not Used	CUR10	374	**Date/Time Qualifier**	X	ID 3/3
			Code specifying type of date or time, or both date and time		
			Refer to 003040 Data Element Dictionary for acceptable code values.		
Not Used	CUR11	373	**Date**	O	DT 6/6
			Date (YYMMDD)		
Not Used	CUR12	337	**Time**	O	TM 4/8
			Time expressed in 24-hour clock time as follows: HHMM, or HHMMSS, or HHMMSSD, or HHMMSSDD, where H = hours (00-23), M = minutes (00-59), S = integer seconds (00-59) and DD = decimal seconds; decimal seconds are expressed as follows: D = tenths (0-9) and DD = hundredths (00-99)		
Not Used	CUR13	374	**Date/Time Qualifier**	X	ID 3/3
			Code specifying type of date or time, or both date and time		
			Refer to 003040 Data Element Dictionary for acceptable code values.		
Not Used	CUR14	373	**Date**	O	DT 6/6
			Date (YYMMDD)		
Not Used	CUR15	337	**Time**	O	TM 4/8

Time expressed in 24-hour clock time as follows: HHMM, or HHMMSS, or HHMMSSD, or HHMMSSDD, where H = hours (00-23), M = minutes (00-59), S = integer seconds (00-59) and DD = decimal seconds; decimal seconds are expressed as follows: D = tenths (0-9) and DD = hundredths (00-99)

Not Used	CUR16	374	**Date/Time Qualifier**	X	ID 3/3

Code specifying type of date or time, or both date and time

Refer to 003040 Data Element Dictionary for acceptable code values.

Not Used	CUR17	373	**Date**	O	DT 6/6

Date (YYMMDD)

Not Used	CUR18	337	**Time**	O	TM 4/8

Time expressed in 24-hour clock time as follows: HHMM, or HHMMSS, or HHMMSSD, or HHMMSSDD, where H = hours (00-23), M = minutes (00-59), S = integer seconds (00-59) and DD = decimal seconds; decimal seconds are expressed as follows: D = tenths (0-9) and DD = hundredths (00-99)

Not Used	CUR19	374	**Date/Time Qualifier**	X	ID 3/3

Code specifying type of date or time, or both date and time

Refer to 003040 Data Element Dictionary for acceptable code values.

Not Used	CUR20	373	**Date**	O	DT 6/6

Date (YYMMDD)

Not Used	CUR21	337	**Time**	O	TM 4/8

Time expressed in 24-hour clock time as follows: HHMM, or HHMMSS, or HHMMSSD, or HHMMSSDD, where H = hours (00-23), M = minutes (00-59), S = integer seconds (00-59) and DD = decimal seconds; decimal seconds are expressed as follows: D = tenths (0-9) and DD = hundredths (00-99)

Segment:	**REF** Reference Numbers
Position:	050
Loop:	
Level:	Heading
Usage:	Optional
Max Use:	12
Purpose:	To specify identifying numbers.
Syntax Notes:	1 At least one of REF02 or REF03 is required.
Semantic Notes:	
Comments:	
Notes:	*1. Use this 1/REF/050 segment to identify reference numbers that apply to all of the line items. When the reference numbers vary by line item, use the 2/REF/100 segment.*
	2. A request has been submitted to ASC X12 to increase the maximum use of this segment to greater than 1. If approved, the use will be increased in ASC X12 Version/Release 3050. Until approved, there can be no more than 12 iterations of the REF segment at this point in the transaction set.

Data Element Summary

	Ref. Des.	Data Element	Name	Attributes	
Must Use	REF01	128	**Reference Number Qualifier**	M	ID 2/2

Code qualifying the Reference Number.

A request has been submitted to ASC X12 for a code to specify Type of Science and for Catalog number (for Research and Development work). If approved, these codes will be available for use in ASC X12 Version/Release 3050.

16   Military Interdepartmental Purchase Request (MIPR) Number

A specific form used to transmit obligation authority (dollars) and requirements between a service or agency requiring a purchase and a military service or agency responsible for procuring the requirement

2E   Foreign Military Sales Case Number

A reference number designating the foreign military sale records

Use to indicate that the order involves a foreign military sale.

73   Statement of Work (SOW)

Description of a product or service to be procured under a contract; statement of requirements

Use to indicate the statement of work (SOW) number or a number within the statement of work where additional information can be found regarding the line item. If the SOW is a part of the order, the PWK segment can be used to indicate how it is being transmitted to the selling party if not otherwise included in the transaction set.

97   Package Number

A serial number indicating unit shipped

AH   Agreement Number

Use to indicate a Union Agreement number.

AT   Appropriation Number

Use to indicate accounting appropriation data. Cite the data as a literal string in REF03.

AU   Authorization to Meet Competition No.

Use, as applicable, to cite the statutory authority for using other than full and open competition.

BB   Authorization Number

Proves that permission was obtained to provide a service

Use to indicate the statutory authorization under which this order is negotiated.

BM   Bill of Lading Number

Use to indicate a government bill of lading (GBL).

BV   Purchase Order Line Item Identifier (Buyer)

C7   Contract Line Item Number

CH   Customer catalog number

Use to indicate the Catalog of Federal Domestic Assistance where the funding source for a research effort can be found. A request has been submitted to ASC X12 to add a code for the generic term Catalog. We expect this code will be available for use in ASC X12 Version/Release 3050. In the meantime, use this code.

CR   Customer Reference Number

Use to indicate the internal number the contractor assigned to the buying party.

DG   Drawing Number

DS   Defense Priorities Allocation System (DPAS) Priority Rating

IJ   Standard Industry Classification (SIC) Code

Use to indicate the Standard Industrial Classification (SIC) Code applicable to this order.

IL   Internal Order Number

Use to indicate the requisition number (e.g., the MILSTRIP/FEDSTRIP document number).

IX   Item Number

Use to indicate a Federal Supply Class (FSC) special item number.

K4   Criticality Designator

A number assigned to a contract or order that expresses the relative importance of that contract or order and thereby assists the contractor in making performance decisions and assists in making production surveillance decisions

Use to indicate the surveillance criticality designator that will be applicable to the order.

K6   Purchase Description

K7   Paragraph Number

Use to indicate a particular paragraph or section in the order that contains applicable information.

KS   Solicitation

A discreet number assigned by the purchasing activity to differentiate between different solicitations

Use to indicate the solicitation number that resulted in this procurement instrument. If applicable, concatenate the LAST amendment number with the solicitation number.

LT   Lot Number

P4   Project Code

Use to indicate the project number applicable to this order.

PH   Priority Rating

Use to indicate the MILSTRIP/FEDSTRIP priority.

PR   Price Quote Number

Use to indicate the contractor's bid, quote or proposal number.

QC   Product Specification Document Number

Model designation of replacement component

RQ   Purchase Requisition No.

Use, as appropriate, to indicate an internal number such as a purchase request or purchase request order number. When citing a purchase request number, concatenate its line number with the purchase request number if it is necessary to transmit both numbers.

RS   Returnable Container Serial Number

S2   Military Specification Number (MILSPEC)

S3   Specification Number

Use to indicate a specification other than a MILSPEC. When used, identify the specification in REF03.

TG   Transportation Control Number (TCN)

TH   Transportation Account Code (TAC)

TN   Transaction Reference Number

Use to indicate the unique reference number of a related transaction set (e.g., an 84 transaction set carrying a related technical specification or drawing). Each transaction set has a unique number. In the case of the 841 transaction set, that number is carried in SPI02.

TP   Test Specification Number

W2   Weapon System Number

Identifies a weapon system

W6   Federal Supply Schedule Number

Identifies an item with a two-digit group number, two-digit part number, and one-character section letter

XC   Cargo Control Number

Use to indicate the tracking number for bulk fuel being sent by a tanker vessel.

XE   Transportation Priority Number

Number indicating the level of government priority associated with the transportation of a shipment

ZF   Contractor Establishment Code (CEC)

Goverment identifier to designate a contractor; it is nine characters, eight numeric and a final alpha

		ZZ	Mutually Defined		

Use to indicate another type of reference number. When used, identify the nature of the number in REF03. Examples of the numbers that can be included here (for which data maintenance has been submitted to ASC X12) are: Military Standard Number, Technical Document Number, Technical Order Number, Related Contract Line Item Number, and Standard Number. If approved, the codes will be available for use in ASC X12 Version/Release 3050.

REF02	127	Reference Number	X AN 1/30

Reference number or identification number as defined for a particular Transaction Set, or as specified by the Reference Number Qualifier.

If a reference number has an associated revision number, suffix or extension, concatenate the reference and revision/suffix/extension number and carry the resultant number in this data element.

REF03	352	Description	X AN 1/80

A free-form description to clarify the related data elements and their content

1) Use to carry additional information related to the number cited in REF02. Use of free-form text is discouraged.

2) When REF01 is code AT, cite the accounting appropriation as a literal string in this data element.

Segment:	**PER** Administrative Communications Contact
Position:	060
Loop:	
Level:	Heading
Usage:	Optional
Max Use:	3
Purpose:	To identify a person or office to whom administrative communications should be directed
Syntax Notes:	1 If either PER03 or PER04 is present, then the other is required.
	2 If either PER05 or PER06 is present, then the other is required.
Semantic Notes:	
Comments:	
Notes:	*1. Use to identify a contract when that party is not to be associated with an address. When an address is also required, use the 1/PER/360 segment.*
	2. A request has been submitted to ASC X12 to add data element 443, Contact Inquiry Reference, at PER07. This data element will permit citing the title of the party identified in PER02. If approved, this data element will be available for use in ASC X12 Version/Release 3050.

Data Element Summary

	Ref. Des.	Data Element	Name	Attributes
Must Use	PER01	366	**Contact Function Code**	M ID 2/2

Code identifying the major duty or responsibility of the person or group named

	HM	Hazardous Material Contact
	NT	Notification Contact

Use to indicate the party to be contacted for shipping instructions. Use only when LDT01 in the 1/LDT/160 segment cites code AI.

	RE	Receiving Contact

Use to indicate the party to be contacted to schedule a shipment. Use only when LDT01 in the 1/LDT/160 segment cites code AI.

	ZZ	Mutually Defined

Use to indicate an Advisor (the individual who will work with the contractor on a research effort). A request as been submitted to ASC X12 to add a code for ADVISOR. We expect this code will be available for use in ASC X12 Version/Release 3050. In the meantime, use this code.

PER02 93 **Name** O AN 1/35

Free-form name

Cite the last name first, followed by the first name. Do not truncate the last name if the whole name is longer than 35 characters. Instead, truncate or use the initial of the first name.

PER03 365 **Communication Number Qualifier** X ID 2/2

Code identifying the type of communication number

AU	Defense Switched Network	
	Department of Defense telecommunications system and successor of the Automatic Voice Network (AUTOVON)	
EM	Electronic Mail	
FX	Facsimile	
IT	International Telephone	
	Include the country code.	
TE	Telephone	
	Use to indicate the commercial telephone number of the individual cited in PER02.	

PER04 364 **Communication Number** X AN 1/80

Complete communications number including country or area code when applicable

PER05 365 **Communication Number Qualifier** X ID 2/2

Code identifying the type of communication number

Use to specify a second communication number for the party cited in PER02. For example, if PER03/04 cites the commercial telephone number, then PER05/06 can be used to cite an electronic mail number.

AU	Defense Switched Network	
	Department of Defense telecommunications system and successor of the Automatic Voice Network (AUTOVON)	
EM	Electronic Mail	
EX	Telephone Extension	
	Use only if PER03 is used citing either code AU or TE.	
FX	Facsimile	
IT	International Telephone	
	Include the country code.	
TE	Telephone	
	Use to indicate the commercial telephone number of the individual cited in PER02.	

PER06 364 **Communication Number** X AN 1/80

Complete communications number including country or area code when applicable

Segment:	**FOB** F.O.B. Related Instructions
Position:	080
Loop:	
Level:	Heading
Usage:	Optional
Max Use:	>1
Purpose:	To specify transportation instructions relating to shipment
Syntax Notes:	1 If FOB03 is present, then FOB02 is required.
	2 If FOB04 is present, then FOB05 is required.
	3 If FOB07 is present, then FOB06 is required.

Semantic Notes:		
	4	If FOB08 is present, then FOB09 is required.
	1	FOB01 indicates which party will pay the carrier.
	2	FOB02 is the code specifying transportation responsibility location.
	3	FOB06 is the code specifying the title passage location.
	4	FOB08 is the code specifying the point at which the risk of loss transfers. This may be different than the location specified in FOB02/FOB03 and FOB06/FOB07.

Comments:

Notes: *1. Use this 1/FOB/080 segment if the FOB point and the acceptance location apply to all of the line items. When the FOB point or acceptance location vary by line item, use the 2/FOB/180 segment.*

2. This segment is not necessary when the order is for a service.

Data Element Summary

	Ref. Des.	Data Element	Name		Attributes	
Must Use	FOB01	146	**Shipment Method of Payment**		M	ID 2/2
			Code identifying payment terms for transportation charges			
				BP	Paid by Buyer	
					The buyer agrees to the transportation payment term requiring the buyer to pay transportation charges to a specified location (origin or destination location)	
					Use to indicate that the FOB point is origin.	
				PE	Prepaid and Summary Bill	
					Use to indicate that transportation costs are authorized to be prepaid and added to the invoice.	
				PP	Prepaid (by Seller)	
					Use to indicate that the FOB point is destination.	
	FOB02	309	**Location Qualifier**		X	ID 1/2
			Code identifying type of location			
			1. Use to identify the FOB point.			
			2. A request has been submitted to ASC X12 to add codes for Port of Embarkation, Port of Loading, and Government Furnished Property FOB Point. We expect these codes will be available for use in ASC X12 Version/Release 3050.			
				DE	Destination (Shipping)	
				FV	Free Alongside Vessel (Free On Board [F.O.B.] Point)	
				IT	Intermediate FOB Point	
					A location indicating the point of destination is not the origin or final destination but rather at some other point	
					Use to indicate a Freight Forwarder.	
				OR	Origin (Shipping Point)	
				ZZ	Mutually Defined	
					Use to indicate that the FOB point is neither origin nor destination. When used, cite the actual FOB point in FOB03. If the actual FOB point is an address or geographical location, use in conjunction with one iteration of the appropriate N1 loop, using code KX in N101.	
	FOB03	352	**Description**		O	AN 1/80
			A free-form description to clarify the related data elements and their content			
			Use to identify the FOB point only when FOB02 is code ZZ. If necessary, use one iteration of the N1 loop, using code KX in N101, to specify the address of the FOB point. Use is discouraged.			
Not Used	FOB04	334	**Transportation Terms Qualifier Code**		O	ID 2/2
			Code identifying the source of the transportation terms			
			Refer to 003040 Data Element Dictionary for acceptable code values.			
Not Used	FOB05	335	**Transportation Terms Code**		X	ID 3/3
			Code identifying the trade terms which apply to the shipment transportation responsibility			

Refer to 003040 Data Element Dictionary for acceptable code values.

FOB06	309	**Location Qualifier**	X	ID 1/2

Code identifying type of location

Use to identify the acceptance point.

DE	Destination (Shipping)
OR	Origin (Shipping Point)
ZZ	Mutually Defined

> *Use to indicate that the acceptance point is neither origin nor destination. When used, cite the actual acceptance point in FOB07. If the actual acceptance point is an address or geographic location, use in conjunction with one iteration of the N1 loop, using code ZZ in N101.*

FOB07	352	**Description**	O	AN 1/80

A free-form description to clarify the related data elements and their content

> *Use to identify the acceptance point when FOB06 is code ZZ. If necessary, use one iteration of the N1 loop, using code ZZ in N101, to specify the address of the acceptance point. Use is discouraged.*

Not Used	FOB08	54	**Risk of Loss Qualifier**	O	ID 2/2

Code specifying where responsibility for risk of loss passes

Refer to 003040 Data Element Dictionary for acceptable code values.

Not Used	FOB09	352	**Description**	X	AN 1/80

A free-form description to clarify the related data elements and their content

Segment:	**CSH** Header Sale Condition
Position:	110
Loop:	
Level:	Heading
Usage:	Optional
Max Use:	5
Purpose:	To specify general conditions or requirements of the sale
Syntax Notes:	1 If CSH02 is present, then CSH03 is required.
	2 If either CSH06 or CSH07 is present, then the other is required.
Semantic Notes:	1 CSH04 is the account number to which the purchase amount is to be charged.
	2 CSH06 identifies the source of the code value in CSH07.
	3 CSH09 is the percent of the Set-Aside.
Comments:	
Notes:	*Use this 1/CSH/110 segment to specify special services or conditions applicable to all of the line items in the order. When the special services or conditions vary by line item, use the 2/IT8/140 segment.*

Data Element Summary

Ref. Des.	Data Element	Name	Attributes	
CSH01	563	**Sales Requirement Code**	O	ID 1/2

Code to identify a specific requirement or agreement of sale

P2	Ship As Soon As Possible
P4	Do Not Preship
SC	Ship Complete

> *Use to indicate partial shipments will not be accepted.*

SV	Ship Per Release

> *Use to indicate that the ordered item(s) are to be shipped in place.*

CSH02	564	**Do-Not-Exceed Action Code**	O	ID 1/1

Code indicating the action to be taken if the order amount exceeds the value of Do-Not-Exceed Amount (565)

Part 3

Use any code.

Refer to 003040 Data Element Dictionary for acceptable code values.

| | CSH03 | 565 | **Do-Not-Exceed Amount** | X | N2 2/9 |

Maximum monetary amount value which the order must not exceed.

Use to indicate a maximum price that if the vendor would exceed, the order need not be filled.

	CSH04	508	**Account Number**	O	AN 1/35
Not Used					

Account number assigned

| Not Used | CSH05 | 596 | **Required Invoice Date** | O | DT 6/6 |

Date specified by the sender to be shown on the invoice.

| | CSH06 | 559 | **Agency Qualifier Code** | X | ID 2/2 |

Code identifying the agency assigning the code values

     AX   ANSI Accredited Standards Committee, X12

Use this code to comply with the syntax of the CSH segment.

| | CSH07 | 560 | **Special Services Code** | X | ID 2/10 |

Code identifying the special service

Use to identify the inspection location as either at origin or at destination. Data element 560 does not appear in Table 2 of this transaction set. Therefore, if the inspection location varies by line item, code L1 in N101 of the 2/N1/350 loop must be used for this purpose.

     IM   Inspect at Destination

     IO   Inspect at Origin

| Not Used | CSH08 | 566 | **Product/Service Substitution Code** | O | ID 1/2 |

Code indicating product or service substitution conditions

Refer to 003040 Data Element Dictionary for acceptable code values.

| Not Used | CSH09 | 954 | **Percent** | O | R 1/10 |

Percentage expressed as a decimal

Segment:	**SAC** Service, Promotion, Allowance, or Charge Information
Position:	120
Loop:	
Level:	Heading
Usage:	Optional
Max Use:	25
Purpose:	To request or identify a service, promotion, allowance, or charge; to specify the amount or percentage for the service, promotion, allowance, or charge
Syntax Notes:	1 At least one of SAC02 or SAC03 is required.
	2 If either SAC03 or SAC04 is present, then the other is required.
	3 If either SAC06 or SAC07 is present, then the other is required.
	4 If either SAC09 or SAC10 is present, then the other is required.
	5 If SAC11 is present, then SAC10 is required.
	6 If SAC13 is present, then at least one of SAC02 or SAC04 is required.
	7 If SAC14 is present, then SAC13 is required.
Semantic Notes:	1 If SAC01 is "A" or "C", then at least one of SAC05, SAC07, or SAC08 is required.
	2 SAC05 is the total amount for the service, promotion, allowance, or charge.
	If SAC05 is present with SAC07 or SAC08, then SAC05 takes precedence.
	3 SAC10 alone is used to indicate a specific quantity which could be a dollar amount, that is applicable to service, promotion, allowance or charge.
	SAC10 and SAC11 used together indicate a quantity range, which could be a dollar amount, that is applicable to service, promotion, allowance, or charge.
	4 SAC13 is used in conjunction with SAC02 or SAC04 to provide a specific reference number as identified by the code used.
	5 SAC14 is used in conjunction with SAC13 to identify an option when there is more than one option of the promotion.

Comments:	1	SAC04 may be used to uniquely identify the service, promotion, allowance, or charge. In addition, it may be used in conjunction to further the code in SAC02.
	2	In some business applications, it is necessary to advise the trading partner of the actual dollar amount that a particular allowance, charge, or promotion was based on to reduce ambiguity. This amount is commonly referred to a "Dollar Basis Amount". It is represented in the SAC segment in SAC10 using the qualifier "DO" - Dollars in SAC09.

Notes: *Use the 1/SAC/120 segment to identify charges that apply to all of the line items. If the charges vary by line item, use the 2/SAC/130 segment.*

Data Element Summary

	Ref. Des.	Data Element	Name	Attributes	
Must Use	SAC01	248	**Allowance or Charge Indicator**	M	ID 1/1
			Code which indicates an allowance or charge for the service specified		
			C Charge		
			N No Allowance or Charge		
	SAC02	1300	**Service, Promotion, Allowance, or Charge Code**	X	ID 4/4
			Code identifying the service, promotion, allowance, or charge		
			Use any code.		
			Refer to 003040 Data Element Dictionary for acceptable code values.		
Not Used	SAC03	559	**Agency Qualifier Code**	X	ID 2/2
			Code identifying the agency assigning the code values		
			Refer to 003040 Data Element Dictionary for acceptable code values.		
Not Used	SAC04	1301	**Agency Service, Promotion, Allowance, or Charge Code**	X	AN 1/10
			Agency maintained code identifying the service, promotion, allowance, or charge		
	SAC05	610	**Amount**	O	N2 1/15
			Monetary amount		
Not Used	SAC06	378	**Allowance/ Charge Percent Qualifier**	X	ID 1/1
			Code indicating on what basis allowance or charge percent is calculated		
			Refer to 003040 Data Element Dictionary for acceptable code values.		
Not Used	SAC07	332	**Allowance or Charge Percent**	X	R 1/6
			Allowance or charge expressed as a percent.		
Not Used	SAC08	359	**Allowance or Charge Rate**	O	R 1/9
			Allowance or Charge Rate per Unit		
	SAC09	355	**Unit or Basis for Measurement Code**	X	ID 2/2
			Code specifying the units in which a value is being expressed, or manner in which a measurement has been taken		
			A conversion table may be required to convert agency codes to codes used by ASC X12.		
			Refer to 003040 Data Element Dictionary for acceptable code values.		
	SAC10	339	**Allowance or Charge Quantity**	X	R 1/10
			Quantity basis when allowance or charge quantity is different from the purchase order or invoice quantity		
			Use to indicate the quantity to which the amount in SAC05 applies. SAC10/11 can be used together to specify a quantity range to which the amount in SAC05 applies.		
	SAC11	339	**Allowance or Charge Quantity**	O	R 1/10
			Quantity basis when allowance or charge quantity is different from the purchase order or invoice quantity		
Not Used	SAC12	331	**Allowance or Charge Method of Handling Code**	O	ID 2/2
			Code indicating method of handling for an allowance or charge		
			Refer to 003040 Data Element Dictionary for acceptable code values.		
Not Used	SAC13	127	**Reference Number**	X	AN 1/30

Part 3

Reference number or identification number as defined for a particular Transaction Set, or as specified by the Reference Number Qualifier.

| Not Used | SAC14 | 770 | **Option Number** | O | AN 1/20 |

A unique number identifying available promotion or allowance options when more than one is offered

| Not Used | SAC15 | 352 | **Description** | O | AN 1/80 |

A free-form description to clarify the related data elements and their content

Segment:	**ITD** Terms of Sale/Deferred Terms of Sale
Position:	130
Loop:	
Level:	Heading
Usage:	Optional
Max Use:	5
Purpose:	To specify terms of sale
Syntax Notes:	1 If ITD03 is present, then at least one of ITD04 ITD05 or ITD13 is required.
	2 If ITD08 is present, then at least one of ITD04 ITD05 or ITD13 is required.
	3 If ITD09 is present, then at least one of ITD10 or ITD11 is required.
Semantic Notes:	1 ITD15 is the percentage applied to a base amount used to determine a late payment charge.
Comments:	1 If the code in ITD01 is "04", then ITD07 or ITD09 is required and either ITD10 or ITD11 is required; if the code in ITD01 is "05", then ITD06 or ITD07 is required.
Notes:	*1. Use this 1/ITD/130 segment when the discount terms apply to all of the line items. If the discount terms vary by line item, use the 2/ITD/150 segment.*
	2. Payment method was provided at time of registration. Changes to that data must be made by submitting a registration data change using the 838 transaction set.

Data Element Summary

Ref. Des.	Data Element	Name		Attributes	
ITD01	336	**Terms Type Code**		O	ID 2/2
		Code identifying type of payment terms			
		21	Fast Pay		
			Code indicating that an invoice is subject to accelerated payment		
			Use to indicate FAST PAY procedures are applicable.		
ITD02	333	**Terms Basis Date Code**		O	ID 1/2
		Code identifying the beginning of the terms period			
		Use the same code as the one indicated in ITD02 of the Contract Solicitation Response (843 transaction set).			
		Refer to 003040 Data Element Dictionary for acceptable code values.			
ITD03	338	**Terms Discount Percent**		O	R 1/6
		Terms discount percentage, expressed as a percent, available to the purchaser if an invoice is paid on or before the Terms Discount Due Date			
ITD04	370	**Terms Discount Due Date**		X	DT 6/6
		Date payment is due if discount is to be earned			
ITD05	351	**Terms Discount Days Due**		X	N0 1/3
		Number of days in the terms discount period by which payment is due if terms discount is earned			
ITD06	446	**Terms Net Due Date**		O	DT 6/6
		Date when total invoice amount becomes due			
ITD07	386	**Terms Net Days**		O	N0 1/3
		Number of days until total invoice amount is due (discount not applicable)			
ITD08	362	**Terms Discount Amount**		O	N2 1/10
		Total amount of terms discount			

Use, if needed, to prevent differences that can result from rounding off methods.

	ITD09	388	**Terms Deferred Due Date**	O	DT 6/6

Date deferred payment or percent of invoice payable is due

	ITD10	389	**Deferred Amount Due**	X	N2 1/10

Deferred amount due for payment

	ITD11	342	**Percent of Invoice Payable**	X	R 1/5

Amount of invoice payable expressed in percent

Not Used	ITD12	352	**Description**	O	AN 1/80

A free-form description to clarify the related data elements and their content

	ITD13	765	**Day of Month**	X	N0 1/2

The numeric value of the day of the month between 1 and the maximum day of the month being referenced

Not Used	ITD14	107	**Payment Method Code**	O	ID 1/1

Code identifying type of payment procedures

Refer to 003040 Data Element Dictionary for acceptable code values.

	ITD15	954	**Percent**	O	R 1/10

Percentage expressed as a decimal

Segment:	**DTM** Date/Time Reference
Position:	150
Loop:	
Level:	Heading
Usage:	Optional
Max Use:	10
Purpose:	To specify pertinent dates and times
Syntax Notes:	1 At least one of DTM02 DTM03 or DTM06 is required.
	2 If either DTM06 or DTM07 is present, then the other is required.
Semantic Notes:	
Comments:	
Notes:	*1. Use this 1/DTM/150 segment to specify a required delivery date when it is expressed as an actual date. If the delivery schedule is expressed as a set number time period after the occurrence of some event, use the 1/LDT/160 segment. If the 1/LDT/160 segment is used, do not use this segment.*
	2. Use this 1/DTM/150 segment to specify dates (e.g., quote date, transaction set date) if they apply to all of the line items in the order. When the dates vary by line item, use the 2/DTM/200 segment.

Data Element Summary

	Ref. Des.	Data Element	Name	Attributes	
Must Use	DTM01	374	**Date/Time Qualifier**	M	ID 3/3

Code specifying type of date or time, or both date and time

002	Delivery Requested
	Use when an unpriced order is issued. The date cited in DTM02 is assumed to be an estimated date.
037	Ship Not Before
063	Do Not Deliver After
064	Do Not Deliver Before
065	1st Schedule Delivery
066	1st Schedule Ship
077	Requested for Delivery (Week of)
	When this code is used, cite the beginning date of the week.
106	Required By

	Use when delivery is due exactly on the specified date.	
150	Service Period Start	
	Use to specify the performance commencement date for a line item that is ordering a service.	
151	Service Period End	
	Use to specify the performance completion date for a line item that is ordering a service.	
174	Month Ending	
	When used, cite the last date of the applicable month.	
276	Contract Start	
	The start date for a contract	
279	Contract Completion	
	The finish date for a contract	
368	Submittal	
	Date an item was submitted to a customer	
	When the 1/REF/050 segment contains code TN in REF01, use to specify the date of the reference transaction set.	
373	Order Start	
	Use to indicate the start of a period of performance.	
374	Order End	
	Point after which data can no longer be used (or becomes invalid for use)	
	Use to indicate the end of a period of performance.	
994	Quote	
	The date on which a (price) quote was rendered	
	When REF01 is code PR, use to indicate the date of the bid, quote or proposal.	
996	Required Delivery	
	A date on which or before, ordered goods or services must be delivered	
	Use to indicate that delivery is required on or before the specified date.	

DTM02 373	**Date**		X	**DT 6/6**
	Date (YYMMDD)			
DTM03 337	**Time**		X	**TM 4/8**

Time expressed in 24-hour clock time as follows: HHMM, or HHMMSS, or HHMMSSD, or HHMMSSDD, where H = hours (00-23), M = minutes (00-59), S = integer seconds (00-59) and DD = decimal seconds; decimal seconds are expressed as follows: D = tenths (0-9) and DD = hundredths (00-99)

Specify time only in the HHMM format.

DTM04 623	**Time Code**		O	**ID 2/2**

Code identifying the time. In accordance with International Standards Organization standard 8601, time can be specified by a + or - and an indication in hours in relation to Universal Time Coordinate (UTC) time; since + is a restricted character, + and - are substituted by P and M in the codes that follow

Use only when DTM03 is used to express a time.

CD	Central Daylight Time
CS	Central Standard Time
CT	Central Time
ED	Eastern Daylight Time
ES	Eastern Standard Time
ET	Eastern Time
GM	Greenwich Mean Time
LT	Local Time

		MD	Mountain Daylight Time		
		MS	Mountain Standard Time		
		MT	Mountain Time		
		PD	Pacific Daylight Time		
		PS	Pacific Standard Time		
		PT	Pacific Time		

Not Used	DTM05	624	**Century**	O	N0 2/2

The first two characters in the designation of the year (CCYY)

	DTM06	1250	**Date Time Period Format Qualifier**	X	ID 2/3

Code indicating the date format, time format, or date and time format

Use only when the date cannot be expressed in YYMMDD format. In that case, use any code and carry the date and/or time in DTM07.

Refer to 003040 Data Element Dictionary for acceptable code values.

	DTM07	1251	**Date Time Period**	X	AN 1/35

Expression of a date, a time, or range of dates, times or dates and times

When delivery is specified as a range of time for a given date, e.g., use code RTM in DTM06 to qualify a range of times for a delivery on March 30, 1994 between 1:00 PM and 4:00 PM local time. Use DTM01/02 to convey the March 30, 1994 date.

Segment:	**LDT** Lead Time
Position:	160
Loop:	
Level:	Heading
Usage:	Optional
Max Use:	12
Purpose:	To specify lead time for availability of products and services
Syntax Notes:	
Semantic Notes:	1 LDT04 is the effective date of lead time information.
Comments:	1 LDT02 is the quantity of unit of time periods.
Notes:	*1. Use this 1/LDT/160 segment when the required delivery schedule is expressed as a specified time period from a stated event. The 1/DTM/150 segment is used when the required delivery date is an actual date. If the DTM segment is used to provide a date, this segment is not used.*
	2. Use this 1/LDT/160 segment if the delivery schedule applies to all of the line items. If the delivery schedule varies by line item, use the 2/LDT/220 segment.

Data Element Summary

	Ref. Des.	Data Element	Name	Attributes	
Must Use	LDT01	345	**Lead Time Code**	M	ID 2/2

Code indicating the time range

A request has been submitted to ASC X12 to add code AY - From Date of Award to Date of Delivery. We expect this code will be available for use in ASC X12 Version/Release 3050.

		AA	From date of PO receipt to sample ready
		AD	From date of sample approval to first product shipment
		AE	From date of PO receipt to shipment
		AF	From date of PO receipt to delivery
		AH	From Date of Receipt of First Article to First Article Approval
		AI	From Date of a Specified Event to Delivery

Use to indicate that the consignee or other contact must be notified within the time period cited to schedule a shipment. When used, cite the contract communications number in the 1/PER/060 segment.

		AZ	From Date of Receipt of Item to Date of Approval of Item

Must Use	LDT02	380	Quantity		M	R 1/15

Numeric value of quantity

Must Use	LDT03	344	Unit of Time Period or Interval		M	ID 2/2

Code indicating the time period or interval

			CY	Calendar Year
			DA	Calendar Days
			KK	Maximum Calendar Days

Use to indicate a flexible time period, e.g., X number of days or less.

			MO	Month
			QY	Quarter of a Year
			SA	Semiannual
			WK	Weeks

	LDT04	373	Date		O	DT 6/6

Date (YYMMDD)

Use to cite a date relevant to lead time code, for example, the start of the cited activity.

Segment:	**PID** Product/Item Description
Position:	190
Loop:	
Level:	Heading
Usage:	Optional
Max Use:	200
Purpose:	To describe a product or process in coded or free-form format
Syntax Notes:	1 If PID04 is present, then PID03 is required.
	2 At least one of PID04 or PID05 is required.
	3 If PID07 is present, then PID03 is required.
	4 If PID08 is present, then PID03 is required.
Semantic Notes:	1 Use PID03 to indicate the organization that publishes the code list being referred to.
	2 PID04 should be used for industry-specific product description codes.
	3 PID08 describes the physical characteristics of the product identified in PID04. A "Y" indicates that the specified attribute applies to this item. A "N" indicates it does not apply. Any other value is indeterminate.
Comments:	1 If PID01 = "F", then PID05 is used. If PID01 = "S", then PID04 is used. If PID01 = "X", then both PID04 and PID05 are used.
	2 Use PID06 when necessary to refer to the product surface or layer being described in the segment.
	3 PID07 specifies the individual code list of the agency specified in PID03.
Notes:	*1. Use to provide a brief description of the supplies or services being ordered.*
	2. Use is discouraged. Whenever possible, items should be described by successive iterations of 235/234 pairs in the PO1 segment or by a reference number. Use coded data whenever possible.
	3. Use this 1/PID/190 segment to provide an overall description of the order that applies to all the line items. When descriptions vary by line item, transmit a general description in this segment and use the 2/PID/050 segment to transmit the varying descriptions.

Data Element Summary

	Ref. Des.	Data Element	Name	Attributes	
Must Use	PID01	349	**Item Description Type**	M	ID 1/1
			Code indicating the format of a description		
			F Free-form		
Not Used	PID02	750	**Product/Process Characteristic Code**	O	ID 2/3
			Code identifying the general class of a product or process characteristic		
			Refer to 003040 Data Element Dictionary for acceptable code values.		

Not Used	PID03	559	**Agency Qualifier Code**	X	ID 2/2

Code identifying the agency assigning the code values

Refer to 003040 Data Element Dictionary for acceptable code values.

Not Used	PID04	751	**Product Description Code**	X	AN 1/12

A code from an industry code list which provides specific data about a product characteristic

	PID05	352	**Description**	X	AN 1/80

A free-form description to clarify the related data elements and their content

Use is discouraged.

Not Used	PID06	752	**Surface/Layer/Position Code**	O	ID 2/2

Code indicating the product surface, layer or position that is being described

Refer to 003040 Data Element Dictionary for acceptable code values.

Not Used	PID07	822	**Source Subqualifier**	O	AN 1/15

A reference that indicates the table or text maintained by the Source Qualifier

Not Used	PID08	1073	**Yes/No Condition or Response Code**	O	ID 1/1

Code indicating a Yes or No condition or response

Refer to 003040 Data Element Dictionary for acceptable code values.

Segment:	**MEA** Measurements
Position:	200
Loop:	
Level:	Heading
Usage:	Optional
Max Use:	40
Purpose:	To specify physical measurements or counts, including dimensions, tolerances, variances, and weights (See Figures Appendix for example of use of C001)
Syntax Notes:	1 At least one of MEA03 MEA05 MEA06 or MEA08 is required.
	2 If MEA03 is present, then MEA04 is required.
	3 If MEA05 is present, then MEA04 is required.
	4 If MEA06 is present, then MEA04 is required.
	5 If MEA07 is present, then at least one of MEA03 MEA05 or MEA06 is required.
	6 Only one of MEA08 or MEA03 may be present.
Semantic Notes:	1 MEA04 defines the unit of measure for MEA03, MEA05, and MEA06.
Comments:	1 When citing dimensional tolerances, any measurement requiring a sign (+ or -), or any measurement where a positive (+) value cannot be assumed, use MEA05 as the negative (-) value and MEA06 as the positive (+) value.
Notes:	*1. Use the 1/MEA/200 segment to provide measurements that apply to all of the line items. If measurements vary by line item, use the 2/MEA/049 segment.*
	2. This segment can be used to provide any measurement applicable to the order including the variations in quantity; warranty periods; and for a requirements or indefinite quantity procurement instrument, the minimum/maximum quantity per order, the maximum that may be ordered during a specified time period, and the maximum obligations of the government and contractor.

Data Element Summary

Ref. Des.	Data Element	Name		Attributes
MEA01	737	**Measurement Reference ID Code**	O	ID 2/2

Code identifying the broad category to which a measurement applies

Use any code.

	BT	Batch Limits

Limits set on test results from all product made for one unit or period of production

> *Use to indicate the limits of the government's obligation to order under a requirements or indefinite quantity procurement instrument. Do not use for a purchase order or delivery order.*

      CT   Counts

> *Use to indicate variations in quantity when expressed as a discrete quantity. Use MEA05/06 to provide the quantity over and under.*

      DE   Defects

> *Use to indicate a warranty period.*

      LT   Lot Limits

Limits set on test results from all product contained in a single shipment (which may involve any multiple or fraction of transportation carrier units) to one customer

> *Use to indicate the limits of the contractor's obligation to deliver under a requirements or indefinite quantity procurement instrument. Do not use for a purchase order or delivery order.*

      PM   Permitted

The condition or activity approved by the appropriate regulatory agency

> *Use to indicate that measurement values are applicable to the minimum and maximum quantity or dollar value permitted per order against an indefinite instrument. Use MEA05/06 to cite the minimum and maximum.*

      RG   Regulatory Limit

> *Use to specify the maximum the government may order from a requirements or indefinite quantity procurement instrument in a specified time period. A request has been submitted to ASC X12 to add a code for Order Limits. We expect this code to be available for use in ASC X12 Version/Release 3050. In the meantime, use this code. Do not use for purchase order or delivery order.*

MEA02 738   **Measurement Qualifier**   O   ID 1/3

Code identifying a specific product or process characteristic to which a measurement applies

Use any code but the listed codes are preferred.

      MX   Maximum

> *Use when MEA01 is either code BT or LT, use to indicate the maximum limit of the government's obligation to order or the contractor's obligation to deliver under a requirements or an indefinite quantity contract. When MEA01 is code RG, use to indicate the maximum amount that can be ordered from a requirements or indefinite quantity contract in a specified period of time.*

      PO   Percent of Order (-, +)

Expression of allowable variance of order expressed either as absolute (for example 92% to 110%) or relative percent (for example - 8% to + 10%)

> *Use to indicate the percent variation in quantity permitted for the line items. Use MEA0/06 to indicate the percent over and under.*

      TT   Time

> *Use to indicate the length of a warranty period. Specify the length of the time period in MEA03 and the time period in MEA04-1.*

MEA03 739   **Measurement Value**   X   R 1/10

The value of the measurement

MEA04 C001   **Composite Unit of Measure**   C

To identify a composite unit of measure (See Figures Appendix for examples of use)

> *This composite data element can be used to specify the maximum amount that may be ordered during a specified period of time from a requirements or indefinite quantity contract. For example: if the maximum that can be ordered in a quarter is 10,000 each, then MEA01 would cite code RG, MEA02 would cite code MX, MEA03 would cite 10,000, MEA04-1 would cite code EA, and MEA04-4 would cite Q1.*

Must Use   C00101 355   **Unit or Basis for Measurement Code**   M   ID 2/2

Code specifying the units in which a value is being expressed, or manner in which a measurement has been taken

1. Use any code.

2. A conversion table may be required to convert agency codes to codes used by ASC X12.

Refer to 003040 Data Element Dictionary for acceptable code values.

Not Used	C00102	1018	**Exponent**	O	R 1/15

Power to which a unit is raised

Not Used	C00103	649	**Multiplier**	O	R 1/10

Value to be used as a multiplier to obtain a new value

	C00104	355	**Unit or Basis for Measurement Code**	O	ID 2/2

Code specifying the units in which a value is being expressed, or manner in which a measurement has been taken

1. Use any code.

2. A conversion table may be required to convert agency codes to codes used by ASC X12.

Refer to 003040 Data Element Dictionary for acceptable code values.

Not Used	C00105	1018	**Exponent**	O	R 1/15

Power to which a unit is raised

Not Used	C00106	649	**Multiplier**	O	R 1/10

Value to be used as a multiplier to obtain a new value

Not Used	C00107	355	**Unit or Basis for Measurement Code**	O	ID 2/2

Code specifying the units in which a value is being expressed, or manner in which a measurement has been taken

Refer to 003040 Data Element Dictionary for acceptable code values.

Not Used	C00108	1018	**Exponent**	O	R 1/15

Power to which a unit is raised

Not Used	C00109	649	**Multiplier**	O	R 1/10

Value to be used as a multiplier to obtain a new value

Not Used	C00110	355	**Unit or Basis for Measurement Code**	O	ID 2/2

Code specifying the units in which a value is being expressed, or manner in which a measurement has been taken

Refer to 003040 Data Element Dictionary for acceptable code values.

Not Used	C00111	1018	**Exponent**	O	R 1/15

Power to which a unit is raised

Not Used	C00112	649	**Multiplier**	O	R 1/10

Value to be used as a multiplier to obtain a new value

Not Used	C00113	355	**Unit or Basis for Measurement Code**	O	ID 2/2

Code specifying the units in which a value is being expressed, or manner in which a measurement has been taken

Refer to 003040 Data Element Dictionary for acceptable code values.

Not Used	C00114	1018	**Exponent**	O	R 1/15

Power to which a unit is raised

Not Used	C00115	649	**Multiplier**	O	R 1/10

Value to be used as a multiplier to obtain a new value

	MEA05	740	**Range Minimum**	X	R 1/10

The value specifying the minimum of the measurement range

1. When MEA01 is code CT or MEA02 is code PO, use to specify the variation in quantity under.

2. When MEA01 is code PM, use to indicate the minimum quantity or dollar value for an order that can be placed against a requirements or indefinite quantity instrument.

	MEA06	741	**Range Maximum**	X	R 1/10

The value specifying the maximum of the measurement range

1. When MEA01 is code CT or MEA02 is code PO, use to specify the variation in quantity over.

2. When MEA01 is code PM, use to indicate the maximum quantity or dollar value for an order that can be placed against a requirements or indefinite quantity instrument.

Not Used	MEA07 935	**Measurement Significance Code**		O	ID 2/2

Code used to benchmark, qualify or further define a measurement value

Refer to 003040 Data Element Dictionary for acceptable code values.

Not Used	MEA08 936	**Measurement Attribute Code**		X	ID 2/2

Code used to express an attribute response when a numeric measurement value cannot be determined

Refer to 003040 Data Element Dictionary for acceptable code values.

Not Used	MEA09 752	**Surface/Layer/Position Code**		O	ID 2/2

Code indicating the product surface, layer or position that is being described

Refer to 003040 Data Element Dictionary for acceptable code values.

Not Used	MEA10 1373	**Measurement Method or Device**		O	ID 2/4

The method or device used to record the measurement

Refer to 003040 Data Element Dictionary for acceptable code values.

Segment:	**PWK** Paperwork
Position:	210
Loop:	
Level:	Heading
Usage:	Optional
Max Use:	25
Purpose:	To identify the type and transmission of paperwork or supporting information
Syntax Notes:	1 If either PWK05 or PWK06 is present, then the other is required.
Semantic Notes:	
Comments:	1 PWK05 and PWK06 may be used to identify the addressee by a code number.
	2 PWK07 may be used to indicate special information to be shown on the specified report.
	3 PWK08 may be used to indicate action pertaining to a report.
Notes:	*1. Use, as applicable, to indicate how technical documentation, drawings or specifications are being provided by the buying party or required by the buying party or required to be provided by the contractor and how that paperwork will be provided.*
	2. Use this 1/PWK/210 segment when the information applies to all the line items. If the information varies by line item, use the 2/PWK/070 segment.

Data Element Summary

	Ref. Des.	Data Element	Name		Attributes
Must Use	PWK01 755		**Report Type Code**	M	ID 2/2

Code indicating the title or contents of a document, report or supporting item

A request has been submitted to ASC X12 to add codes for: Certified Cost and Price Data, Wage Determination, Union Agreement, Attachment, and Contract Security Classification Specification. We expect these codes to be available for use in ASC X12 Version/Release 3050.

	23	Contractual Plan

Use to indicate a proposal. A request has been submitted to ASC X12 to add a code for Proposal. We expect this code will be available for use in ASC X12 Version/Release 3050. In the meantime, use this code.

	25	Purchase Plan

Use to indicate a make or buy plan.

	35	Subcontractor Plan
	C1	Cost Data Summary

Use to indicate cost and price data must be provided.

	CP	Certificate of Compliance (Material Certification)

Use to indicate a Certificate of Conformance. When used, PWK04 should cite code PC.

CX	Cost/Schedule Status Report (C/SSR)	

Contract status report showing budget, performance, actual, cost variance, schedule variance, budget at complete, estimate at complete, and variance at complete at specified levels of the work breakdown structure

CY   Contract Funds Status Report (CFSR)

Status report for funds appropriation including commitments, actual cost, forecast of billings, and estimated termination costs

DW   Drawing(s)

F1   Cost Performance Report (CPR) Format 1

Detailed contract status report including current reporting month values at specified levels of the work breakdown structure

F2   Cost Performance Report (CPR) Format 2

Detailed contract status report at specified levels of the organization breakdown structure

F3   Cost Performance Report (CPR) Format 3

Contract baseline report that summarizes changes to the contract over a given reporting period with beginning and ending values

F4   Cost Performance Report (CPR) Format 4

Contract resource summary report that forecasts labor requirements for the remainder of a contract

F5   Cost Performance Report (CPR) Format 5

Contract summary or detail report explaining significant cost or schedule variances

IT   Certified Inspection and Test Results

MR   Material Inspection and Receiving Report

MS   Material Safety Data Sheet

PD   Proof of Delivery

PJ   Purchasing Specification

Specifications, generated by a customer, setting acceptance limits on the properties or performance of the product being purchased; purchasing specifications may additionally supply instructions for packaging, transportation, delivery, and payments

SN   Shipping Notice

SP   Specification

US   "BUY AMERICA" Certification of Compliance

PWK02 756   **Report Transmission Code**   O   ID 2/2

Code defining timing, transmission method or format by which reports are to be sent

While any code can be used, Code EL is preferred when the indicated paperwork can be provided electronically using one of the ASC X12 transaction sets specifically designed for the purpose.

BM   By Mail

EL   Electronically Only

FX   By Fax

WS   With Shipment (With Package)

PWK03 757   **Report Copies Needed**   O   N0 1/2

The number of copies of a report that should be sent to the addressee

PWK04 98   **Entity Identifier Code**   O   ID 2/2

Code identifying an organizational entity, a physical location, or an individual

Part

1. Use to indicate the recipient of the paperwork if there is only one recipient and provide the address, if necessary, in the N1 loop. If there is more than one recipient, identify all recipients and their addresses in the N1 loop.

2. A request has been submitted to ASC X12 to add codes for Contracting Officer Representative, and Party to Receive Proposal. We expect these codes will be available for use in ASC X12 Version/Release 3050.

BY	Buying Party (Purchaser)	
	Use to indicate the Contracting Officer.	
C4	Contract Administration Office	
	Established at either a contractor facility or in a geographic area, and responsible for administering on behalf of the buying activities that assigned contracts for administration and all contracts awarded to either the specific contractor or all contractors in the geographic area	
IS	Party to Receive Certified Inspection Report	
KF	Audit Office	
	The office performing the audit	
KG	Project Manager	
	The address of the person responsible for the management of a designated project	
KY	Technical Office	
PA	Party to Receive Inspection Report	
PC	Party to Receive Cert. of Conformance (C.A.A.)	
SM	Party to Receive Shipping Manifest	
ZD	Party to Receive Reports	
	The organization designated to receive reports	

PWK05	66	**Identification Code Qualifier**	X	ID 1/2

Code designating the system/method of code structure used for Identification Code (67)

1	D-U-N-S Number, Dun & Bradstreet	
10	Department of Defense Activity Address Code (DODAAC)	
	Includes Civilian Agency Activity Address Code.	
33	Commercial and Government Entity (CAGE)	

PWK06	67	**Identification Code**	X	AN 2/17

Code identifying a party or other code

PWK07	352	**Description**	O	AN 1/80

A free-form description to clarify the related data elements and their content

Use only if necessary to provide additional information or instructions related to a specified paperwork item. Use is discouraged.

PWK08	C002	**Actions Indicated**	O	

Actions to be performed on the piece of paperwork identified

Must Use	C00201	704	**Paperwork/Report Action Code**	M	ID 1/2

Code specifying how the paperwork or report that is identified in the PWK segment relates to the transaction set or to identify the action that is required

2	Report to be Filed	
	Use to indicate that the specified paperwork is required to be provided by the contractor.	
3	Complete	
	Use the information provided, add additional required data, distribute as indicated	
	Use to indicate that the specified paperwork is being provided by the buying activity in a separate medium or transaction set, but is a part of the order. Data maintenance has been submitted to ASC X12 asking for a code for Provided. If approved, that code will be available for use in ASC X12 Version/Release 3050. In the meantime, use this code.	

Not Used	C00202	704	**Paperwork/Report Action Code**	O	ID 1/2

Code specifying how the paperwork or report that is identified in the PWK segment relates to the transaction set or to identify the action that is required

Refer to 003040 Data Element Dictionary for acceptable code values.

Not Used	C00203	704	**Paperwork/Report Action Code**	O	ID 1/2

Code specifying how the paperwork or report that is identified in the PWK segment relates to the transaction set or to identify the action that is required

Refer to 003040 Data Element Dictionary for acceptable code values.

Not Used	C00204	704	**Paperwork/Report Action Code**	O	ID 1/2

Code specifying how the paperwork or report that is identified in the PWK segment relates to the transaction set or to identify the action that is required

Refer to 003040 Data Element Dictionary for acceptable code values.

Not Used	C00205	704	**Paperwork/Report Action Code**	O	ID 1/2

Code specifying how the paperwork or report that is identified in the PWK segment relates to the transaction set or to identify the action that is required

Refer to 003040 Data Element Dictionary for acceptable code values.

Segment:	**PKG** Marking, Packaging, Loading
Position:	220
Loop:	
Level:	Heading
Usage:	Optional
Max Use:	200
Purpose:	To describe marking, packaging, loading, and unloading requirements
Syntax Notes:	1 At least one of PKG04 PKG05 or PKG06 is required.
	2 If PKG04 is present, then PKG01 is required.
	3 If PKG05 is present, then PKG01 is required.
Semantic Notes:	1 PKG04 should be used for industry-specific packaging description codes.
Comments:	1 Use the MEA (Measurements) Segment to define dimensions, tolerances, weights, counts, physical restrictions, etc.
	2 If PKG01 = "F", then PKG05 is used. If PKG01 = "S", then PKG04 is used. If PKG01 = "X", then both PKG04 and PKG05 are used.
	3 Use PKG03 to indicate the organization that publishes the code list being referred to.
	4 Special marking or tagging data can be given in PKG05 (description).
Notes:	*1. Use this 1/PKG/220 segment to identify packaging requirements that apply to all of the line items. When the packaging requirements vary by line item, use the 2/PKG/300 segment.*
	2. A request has been submitted to ASC X12 to add MIL-STD 2073-2C codes to ASC X12 standards. If approved, those codes will be available for use in ASC X12 Version/Release 3050 and they will be carried in PKG02/03/04. Until those codes are available, packaging information can be transmitted as a MIL-STD 2073-2C code string (as is currently done in a paper instrument) in PKG05. If additional packaging information is required to be provided to prospective bidders the N9 loop (code K7) can be used.
	3. Do not use when standard commercial packaging is acceptable.

Data Element Summary

Ref. Des.	Data Element	Name		Attributes	
PKG01	**349**	**Item Description Type**		X	ID 1/1

Code indicating the format of a description

F   Free-form

Use when the packaging information is provided in free-form text.

S   Structured (From Industry Code List)

Use when the packaging information is provided as a MIL-STD 2073-2C code string.

Part

		X	Semi-structured (Code and Text)		

Use when the packaging information is provided as both free-form text and a MIL-STD 2073-2C code string.

PKG02	753	**Packaging Characteristic Code**	O	ID 1/5

Code specifying the marking, packaging, loading and related characteristics being described

A request has been submitted to ASC X12 to add MIL-STD 2073-2C packaging characteristic codes, e.g., CD - Cleaning/Drying Procedures, CT - Cushioning Thickness, etc. We expect those codes to be available in ASC X12 Version/Release 3050. In the meantime, use code 65 when providing MIL-STD 2073-2C code string in PKG05.

		65	Core Characteristics

Use to indicate MIL-STD 2073-2C packaging codes. Cite the code string in PKG05.

PKG03	559	**Agency Qualifier Code**	O	ID 2/2

Code identifying the agency assigning the code values

	DD	Department of Defense
		Responsible for Military Specification
	GS	General Services Administration (GSA)
		Responsible for Federal Specification
	ZZ	Mutually Defined

Use to indicate an activity other than DoD or GSA. Data maintenance has been submitted to ASC X12. If approved, a code for Federal Government will be available in ASC X12 Version/Release 3060.

Not Used	PKG04	754	**Packaging Description Code**	X	AN 1/7

A code from an industry code list which provides specific data about the marking, packaging or loading and unloading of a product

PKG05	352	**Description**	X	AN 1/80

A free-form description to clarify the related data elements and their content

Use to identify a string of MIL-STD 2073-2C packaging codes or to provide packaging information in free-form text. The MIL-STD 2073-2C code string uses a positional and sequential system. Coded data must appear in the sequence and the number of positions specified in Appendix F of MIL-STD 2073-1. Zeros shall be inserted in the code string for data that is not being provided. A comma (,) will be used as a delimiter between the data in the code string. Use of this data element is discouraged.

Not Used	PKG06	400	**Unit Load Option Code**	X	ID 2/2

Code identifying loading or unloading a shipment

Refer to 003040 Data Element Dictionary for acceptable code values.

Segment:	**TD5** Carrier Details (Routing Sequence/Transit Time)
Position:	240
Loop:	
Level:	Heading
Usage:	Optional
Max Use:	12
Purpose:	To specify the carrier and sequence of routing and provide transit time information
Syntax Notes:	1 At least one of TD502 TD504 TD505 TD506 or TD512 is required.
	2 If TD502 is present, then TD503 is required.
	3 If TD507 is present, then TD508 is required.
	4 If TD510 is present, then TD511 is required.
Semantic Notes:	
Comments:	1 When specifying a routing sequence to be used for the shipment movement in lieu of specifying each carrier within the movement, use TD502 to identify the party responsible for defining the routing sequence, and use TD503 to identify the actual routing sequence, specified by the party identified in TD502.

Notes: *1. Use this 1/TD5/240 segment to specify the transportation method that is applicable to all of the line items. If the transportation method varies by line item, use the 2/TD5/250 segment.*

2. Use the 1/TD5/390 when the transportation method code is the same for all the line items but is dependent upon the citing of a named party.

Data Element Summary

	Ref. Des.	Data Element	Name	Attributes	
Not Used	TD501	133	**Routing Sequence Code**	O	ID 1/2

Code describing the relationship of a carrier to a specific shipment movement

Refer to 003040 Data Element Dictionary for acceptable code values.

	TD502	66	**Identification Code Qualifier**	X	ID 1/2

Code designating the system/method of code structure used for Identification Code (67)

    10   Department of Defense Activity Address Code (DODAAC)

When TD504 is code PL, use code 10 to indicate the number in TD503 is the DoDAAC of the pipeline.

	TD503	67	**Identification Code**	X	AN 2/17

Code identifying a party or other code

	TD504	91	**Transportation Method/Type Code**	X	ID 1/2

Code specifying the method or type of transportation for the shipment

1. Use any code.

2. A conversion table may be required to convert agency codes to codes used by ASC X12.

    D   Parcel Post

Use to indicate the U.S. Postal Service and not a private carrier.

Not Used	TD505	387	**Routing**	X	AN 1/35

Free-form description of the routing or requested routing for shipment, or the originating carrier's identity

Not Used	TD506	368	**Shipment/Order Status Code**	X	ID 2/2

Code indicating the status of an order or shipment or the disposition of any difference between the quantity ordered and the quantity shipped for a line item or transaction

Refer to 003040 Data Element Dictionary for acceptable code values.

Not Used	TD507	309	**Location Qualifier**	O	ID 1/2

Code identifying type of location

Refer to 003040 Data Element Dictionary for acceptable code values.

Not Used	TD508	310	**Location Identifier**	X	AN 1/30

Code which identifies a specific location

Not Used	TD509	731	**Transit Direction Code**	O	ID 2/2

The point of origin and point of direction

Refer to 003040 Data Element Dictionary for acceptable code values.

Not Used	TD510	732	**Transit Time Direction Qualifier**	O	ID 2/2

Code specifying the value of time used to measure the transit time

Refer to 003040 Data Element Dictionary for acceptable code values.

Not Used	TD511	733	**Transit Time**	X	R 1/4

The numeric amount of transit time

Not Used	TD512	284	**Service Level Code**	X	ID 2/2

Code defining service

Refer to 003040 Data Element Dictionary for acceptable code values.

Segment:	**TD4** Carrier Details (Special Handling or Hazardous Materials or Both)
Position:	260
Loop:	
Level:	Heading
Usage:	Optional
Max Use:	5
Purpose:	To specify transportation special handling requirements, or hazardous materials information, or both
Syntax Notes:	1 At least one of TD401 TD402 or TD404 is required.
	2 If TD402 is present, then TD403 is required.
Semantic Notes:	
Comments:	
Notes:	*Use this 1/TD4/260 segment to provide hazardous material information that applies to all the line items. If the hazardous material varies by line items, use the 2/TD4/270 segment.*

Data Element Summary

Ref. Des.	Data Element	Name		Attributes
TD401	152	**Special Handling Code**	X	**ID 2/3**
		Code specifying special transportation handling instructions		
		HM Endorsed as Hazardous Material		
		NC Notify Consignee Before Delivery		
TD402	208	**Hazardous Material Code Qualifier**	X	**ID 1/1**
		Code which qualifies the Hazardous Material Class Code (209)		
		A request for the following codes has been submitted to ASC X12: Storage Compatibility Group and Hazard Class or Division. We expect these codes to be available in ASC X12 Version/Release 3050.		
		D Hazardous Materials ID, DOT		
TD403	209	**Hazardous Material Class Code**	X	**AN 2/4**
		Code specifying the kind of hazard for a material		
TD404	352	**Description**	X	**AN 1/80**
		A free-form description to clarify the related data elements and their content		
		Use is discouraged.		

Segment:	**MAN** Marks and Numbers
Position:	270
Loop:	
Level:	Heading
Usage:	Optional
Max Use:	10
Purpose:	To indicate identifying marks and numbers for shipping containers
Syntax Notes:	
Semantic Notes:	1 When both MAN02 and MAN03 are used, MAN02 is the starting number of a sequential range and MAN03 is the ending number of that range.
	2 When both MAN05 and MAN06 are used, MAN05 is the starting number of a sequential range, and MAN06 is the ending number of that range.
Comments:	
Notes:	*1. Use this 1/MAN/270 segment when marks and numbers apply to all of the line items. Use the 2/MAN/280 segment when the marks and numbers vary by line item.*
	2. Use to identify such data as MILSTRIP/FEDSTRIP number, Transportation Control number, Project Priority number, and consignee related codes.

Data Element Summary

	Ref. Des.	Data Element	Name		Attributes	
Must Use	MAN01	88	**Marks and Numbers Qualifier**		M	ID 1/2

Code specifying the application or source of Marks and Numbers (87)

       S   Entire Shipment

Use to indicate that the marks and numbers are applicable to all line items in the order.

	Ref. Des.	Data Element	Name		Attributes	
Must Use	MAN02	87	**Marks and Numbers**		M	AN 1/45

Marks and numbers used to identify a shipment or parts of a shipment

	MAN03	87	**Marks and Numbers**		O	AN 1/45

Marks and numbers used to identify a shipment or parts of a shipment

	MAN04	88	**Marks and Numbers Qualifier**		O	ID 1/2

Code specifying the application or source of Marks and Numbers (87)

       S   Entire Shipment

Use to indicate that the marks and numbers are applicable to all line items in the order.

	MAN05	87	**Marks and Numbers**		O	AN 1/45

Marks and numbers used to identify a shipment or parts of a shipment

	MAN06	87	**Marks and Numbers**		O	AN 1/45

Marks and numbers used to identify a shipment or parts of a shipment

Segment:	**N9** Reference Number
Position:	290
Loop:	N9 Optional
Level:	Heading
Usage:	Optional
Max Use:	1
Purpose:	To transmit identifying numbers and descriptive information as specified by the reference number qualifier
Syntax Notes:	1 At least one of N902 or N903 is required.
	2 If N906 is present, then N905 is required.
Semantic Notes:	1 N906 reflects the time zone which the time reflects.
Comments:	
Notes:	*1. Use the 1/N9/290 segment to specify clauses, special instructions or other references which are applicable to all of the line items. Use the 2/N9/330 segment to specify similar information applicable to a line item.*
	2. When an alternate section is relevant for a cited clause, concatenate the alpha/numeric alternate cite with the clause number in N902.

Data Element Summary

	Ref. Des.	Data Element	Name		Attributes	
Must Use	N901	128	**Reference Number Qualifier**		M	ID 2/2

Code qualifying the Reference Number.

A request has been submitted to ASC X12 to add codes for Circular number, which will be used to specify an OMB Circular number, Special Instruction, and Federal Information Resources Management Regulation. We expect these codes to be available for use in ASC X12 Version/Release 3050.

       73   Statement of Work (SOW)

                    Description of a product or service to be procured under a contract; statement of requirements

       CJ   Clause Number

Part 3

Use to indicate a purchasing activity generated clause or special provision not found in the FAR, DFARS, Agency acquisition regulation supplement, or FIRMR. Identify the source of the clause in N903.

DD   Document Identification Code

Use to identify a Department of Labor wage determination.

DF   Defense Federal Acquisition Regulations (DFAR)

Use to indicate a clause found in the DFARS.

DX   Department/Agency Number

Use to indicate an agency clause and specify the agency in N903.

FA   Federal Acquisition Regulations (FAR)

GS   General Services Administration Regulations (GSAR)

K7   Paragraph Number

Use to identify information for contractors, e.g., packaging information. Cite an applicable number in N902 and provide the information in the following MSG segment. The numbering system can be based on the uniform contract format, e.g., H-1 for special requirements, or any other numbering system the originator desires. The 2/REF/100 segment can then be used to cite the reference when it is applicable to a line item.

KY   Site Specific Procedures, Terms, and Conditions

A set of procedures, terms, and conditions, applicable to a category of procurement emanating from a specific location, which will be incorporated into all procurement actions in that category by referencing its unique number rather than by incorporating the lengthy details it represents

KZ   Master Solicitation Procedures, Terms, and Conditions

A set of standard procedures, terms, and conditions, applicable to a category of procurement, which will be incorporated into all procurement actions in that category by referencing its unique number rather than by incorporating the lengthy details it represents

Use, if applicable, to indicate the master solicitation that contains applicable terms and conditions.

VB   Department of Veterans Affairs Acquisition Regulations (VAAR)

ZZ   Mutually Defined

Use to identify any other reference that cannot use a specific qualifier code. Indicate in N903 the source of the reference and use the following MSG segment for text, if necessary.

	N902	127	**Reference Number**	X	AN 1/30

Reference number or identification number as defined for a particular Transaction Set, or as specified by the Reference Number Qualifier.

	N903	369	**Free-form Description**	X	AN 1/45

Free-form descriptive text

Use is discouraged.

	N904	373	**Date**	O	DT 6/6

Date (YYMMDD)

Use to indicate the date of a clause, wage determination, or other reference. When the date is used it will be in YYMMDD format so a clause date should always end with the numeric 01 indicating the first day of the month. This rule is necessary to comply with ASC X12 syntax.

Not Used	N905	337	**Time**	X	TM 4/8

Time expressed in 24-hour clock time as follows: HHMM, or HHMMSS, or HHMMSSD, or HHMMSSDD, where H = hours (00-23), M = minutes (00-59), S = integer seconds (00-59) and DD = decimal seconds; decimal seconds are expressed as follows: D = tenths (0-9) and DD = hundredths (00-99)

Not Used	N906	623	**Time Code**	O	ID 2/2

Code identifying the time. In accordance with International Standards Organization standard 8601, time can be specified by a + or - and an indication in hours in relation to Universal Time Coordinate (UTC) time; since + is a restricted character, + and - are substituted by P and M in the codes that follow

Refer to 003040 Data Element Dictionary for acceptable code values.

Segment:	**MSG** Message Text
Position:	300
Loop:	N9 Optional
Level:	Heading
Usage:	Optional
Max Use:	1000
Purpose:	To provide a free form format that would allow the transmission of text information.
Syntax Notes:	
Semantic Notes:	
Comments:	1 MSG02 is not related to the specific characteristics of a printer, but identifies top of page, advance a line, etc.
Notes:	*1. Use this segment to carry the title and full text, if required, a special instruction, or other information associated with the number cited in N902.*
	2. Use of this segment is discouraged.

Data Element Summary

	Ref. Des.	Data Element	Name	Attributes	
Must Use	MSG01	933	**Free-Form Message Text**	M	AN 1/264
			Free-form message text		
Not Used	MSG02	934	**Printer Carriage Control Code**	O	ID 2/2
			A field to be used for the control of the line feed of the receiving printer		
			Refer to 003040 Data Element Dictionary for acceptable code values.		

Segment:	**N1** Name
Position:	310
Loop:	N1 Optional
Level:	Heading
Usage:	Optional
Max Use:	1
Purpose:	To identify a party by type of organization, name, and code
Syntax Notes:	1 At least one of N102 or N103 is required.
	2 If either N103 or N104 is present, then the other is required.
Semantic Notes:	
Comments:	1 This segment, used alone, provides the most efficient method of providing organizational identification. To obtain this efficiency the "ID Code" (N104) must provide a key to the table maintained by the transaction processing party.
	2 N105 and N106 further define the type of entity in N101.
Notes:	*1. Whenever possible, address information should be transmitted using code values contained in a combination of the N101, N103/04 data elements. Use N102 and the N2-N4 segments only when it is necessary to transmit the full address. For example, if a vendor can be identified by a DUNs number, it is not necessary to transmit the vendor's full address since the relationship between the DUNs number and the vendor's address can be established by accessing a data base in which the information is stored, having been put there at the time the vendor electronically registered as a federal government trading partner.*
	2. Use the 1/N1/310 loop to identify organizations or people that apply to all of the line items, or are not applicable at the line item level (e.g., ordering party, etc.). When the addresses vary by line item, use the 2/N1/350 loop.
	3. At least three iterations of this segment are required using codes BY, PO and SE.

Part 3

Data Element Summary

	Ref. Des.	Data Element	Name		Attributes
Must Use	N101	98	**Entity Identifier Code**	M	ID 2/2

Code identifying an organizational entity, a physical location, or an individual

A request has been submitted to ASC X12 to add additional codes for Contracting Officer Representative, Party Authorized to Definitize Contract Action, Government Furnished Property FOB Point, Party to Receive Proposal, and Transportation Office. We expect these codes will be available for use in ASC X12 Version/Release 3050.

28	Subcontractor
31	Postal Mailing Address

Use only when an actual mailing address is required, and is different from the address provided for any other qualifier code. Do not use if another qualifier code can be used to pass this address. When used, cite the name of the party in N102 and N2 segment, if necessary.

54	Order Writer

Individual who receives the product from the customer and prepares the repair order describing work to be performed

Use to indicate activities authorized to place orders against basic contracts, e.g., requirements, indefinite quantity, BPAs, BOAs, etc. Do not use for purchase orders or delivery orders.

88	Approver

Manufacturer's representative approving claim for payment

Use to indicate the party approving a Contract Data Requirements List (CDRL).

AE	Additional Delivery Address

Use to indicate a shipment in-place location.

AG	Agent/Agency
BT	Bill-to-Party

Use to indicate the party who will provide reimbursement for the payment of a contractor's invoice. This is an internal government billed party and not the party the contractor bills. Use is discouraged. Use only when the vendor receiving the order or other party receiving the order or a copy of the order, needs to receive this information.

BY	Buying Party (Purchaser)

Use to indicate the purchasing office or activity.

C4	Contract Administration Office

Established at either a contractor facility or in a geographic area, and responsible for administering on behalf of the buying activities that assigned contracts for administration and all contracts awarded to either the specific contractor or all contractors in the geographic area

CP	Party to Receive Cert. of Compliance

Use to indicate the party to receive a Certificate of Conformance.

IC	Intermediate Consignee

Use to indicate a freight forwarder.

KE	Place of Performance

Use to specify a manufacturing facility other than the contractor's facility.

KX	Free on Board Point

Use to indicate the FOB point when it has to be described by a specific address rather than as a code value indicating either origin or destination.

KY	Technical Office

Use to indicate the technical office that has cognizance over the technical portion of the order, if different than the office originating the order. Do not use unless it is intended for the vendor to deal directly with the cited party.

L1 Inspection Location

Place where the item was viewed or inspected

Use to indicate the inspection location when it has to be described as a specific address rather than a location such as origin or destination.

MF Manufacturer of Goods

MP Manufacturing Plant

Use to indicate that the manufacturing facility is different from the contractor or contractor's mailing address.

OB Ordered By

Use to identify the activity placing an order against a basic contract.

OH Other Departments

Use to indicate the Hazardous Materials Office. A request has been submitted to ASC X12 to add a code for this location. If approved it will be available for use in ASC X12 Version/Release 3050. Until that time, use this code.

OI Outside Inspection Agency

Use to indicate the inspection agency is other than the Contract Administration Office.

PK Party to Receive Copy

Use this code to indicate the party receiving a solicitation. A request has been submitted to ASC X12 to add a code for this purpose. We expect it to be available for use in ASC X12 Version/Release 3050. Until that time, use this code.

PL Party to Receive Purchase Order

Use to indicate entities other than the contractor that are to receive copies of the order.

PO Party to Receive Invoice for Goods or Services

Use to indicate where the invoice should be mailed.

PR Payer

Use to indicate the paying office.

PZ Party to Receive Equipment

Name a party to receive the transfer of equipment

Use to indicate the requesting agency/activity. A request has been submitted to ASC X12 to add a code for Requestor. We expect this code will be available for use in ASC X12 Version/Release 3060. In the meantime, use this code.

RC Receiving Location

Use to indicate a location where the material will be both inspected and accepted. A request has been submitted to ASC X12 to add a code for Inspection and Acceptance. We expect this code to be available for use in ASC X12 Version/Release 3050. Until that time, use this code.

RI Remit To

Use to indicate the address to which payment should be sent if it is different from the contractor's mailing address, e.g., a bank, financial office location, etc.

SE Selling Party

SK Secondary Location Address (SLA)

Identifies a physical address location in which a telecommunications circuit terminates; this address is in addition to a main service address

Use to indicate a preliminary inspection location for a first article. A request has been submitted to ASC X12 to add a code for Preliminary Inspection Location. We expect this code will be available for use in ASC X12 Version/Release 3050. In the meantime, use this code.

	ST		Ship To		

Use to indicate the address to which an item must be shipped. If the ship-to address is an FPO or APO, identify the FPO or APO in the N4 segment using N401 and N403.

	SV		Service Performance Site		

When services are contracted for, this describes the organization for whom or location address at which those services will be performed

Use to indicate a location where a service, e.g., grass cutting, will be performed.

	X2		Party to Perform Packaging		

A party responsible for packaging an item after it has been produced

	Z7		Mark-for Party		

The party for whom the needed material is intended

	ZZ		Mutually Defined		

Use to identify the acceptance location when it cannot be described using a point such as origin or destination. Data maintenance has been submitted to ASC X12 asking for a code for Acceptance Point. If approved, the code will be available in ASC X12 Version/Release 3050.

	N102	**93**	**Name**	**X**	**AN 1/35**

Free-form name

	N103	**66**	**Identification Code Qualifier**	**X**	**ID 1/2**

Code designating the system/method of code structure used for Identification Code (67)

1. Use, when applicable, to identify the named party.

2. A request has been submitted to ASC X12 to add a code for Contractor Establishment Code. We expect this code to be available for use in the ASC X12 Version/Release 3050.

3. While Federal EDI will use the DUNS number, other numbers may be required for a period of transition in order to cross-reference existing data bases with new procurement actions.

			1	D-U-N-S Number, Dun & Bradstreet	

Use of the DUNs number is preferred over any other coded number to identify a named party.

			10	Department of Defense Activity Address Code (DODAAC)	

Use to indicate either a Department of Defense Activity Address Code or a Civilian Agency Activity Address Code.

			33	Commercial and Government Entity (CAGE)	

Use to indicate vendors with CAGE codes.

			A2	Military Assistance Program Address Code (MAPAC)	

Contained in the Military Assistance Program Address Directory (MAPAD); represents the location of an entity

Use to indicate a MAPAC address.

			FA	Facility Identification	

Use to indicate a vendor facility that cannot be identified by either a CAGE code or a DUNS number.

		N104	**67**	**Identification Code**	**X**	**AN 2/17**

Code identifying a party or other code

Not Used	**N105**	**706**	**Entity Relationship Code**	**O**	**ID 2/2**

Code describing entity relationship

Refer to 003040 Data Element Dictionary for acceptable code values.

Not Used	**N106**	**98**	**Entity Identifier Code**	**O**	**ID 2/2**

Code identifying an organizational entity, a physical location, or an individual

Refer to 003040 Data Element Dictionary for acceptable code values.

Segment:	**N2** Additional Name Information
Position:	320
Loop:	N1 Optional
Level:	Heading
Usage:	Optional
Max Use:	2
Purpose:	To specify additional names or those longer than 35 characters in length
Syntax Notes:	
Semantic Notes:	
Comments:	
Notes:	*This segment is not necessary when the cited party can be identified by a code value in N101/03/04.*

Data Element Summary

	Ref. Des.	Data Element	Name		Attributes	
Must Use	N201	93	Name		M	AN 1/35
			Free-form name			
	N202	93	Name		O	AN 1/35
			Free-form name			

Segment:	**N3** Address Information
Position:	330
Loop:	N1 Optional
Level:	Heading
Usage:	Optional
Max Use:	2
Purpose:	To specify the location of the named party
Syntax Notes:	
Semantic Notes:	
Comments:	
Notes:	*This segment is not necessary when the party can be identified by a code value in N101/03/04.*

Data Element Summary

	Ref. Des.	Data Element	Name		Attributes	
Must Use	N301	166	**Address Information**		M	AN 1/35
			Address information			
	N302	166	**Address Information**		O	AN 1/35
			Address information			

Segment:	**N4** Geographic Location
Position:	340
Loop:	N1 Optional
Level:	Heading
Usage:	Optional
Max Use:	1
Purpose:	To specify the geographic place of the named party
Syntax Notes:	1 If N406 is present, then N405 is required.
Semantic Notes:	
Comments:	1 A combination of either N401 through N404, or N405 and N406 may be adequate to specify a location.
	2 N402 is required only if city name (N401) is in the USA or Canada.

Notes: *1. This segment is not necessary when the party can be identified by a code value in N101/03/04.*

2. When identifying an APO/FPO, N401 carries the APO/FPO city name and N403 carries the ZIP code of the city.

Data Element Summary

	Ref. Des.	Data Element	Name		Attributes	
	N401	19	**City Name**		O	AN 2/30
			Free-form text for city name			
	N402	156	**State or Province Code**		O	ID 2/2
			Code (Standard State/Province) as defined by appropriate government agency			
	N403	116	**Postal Code**		O	ID 3/9
			Code defining international postal zone code excluding punctuation and blanks (zip code for United States)			
	N404	26	**Country Code**		O	ID 2/3
			Code identifying the country			
			A conversion table may be required to convert agency codes to ASC X12 codes.			
Not Used	N405	309	**Location Qualifier**		X	ID 1/2
			Code identifying type of location			
			Refer to 003040 Data Element Dictionary for acceptable code values.			
Not Used	N406	310	**Location Identifier**		O	AN 1/30
			Code which identifies a specific location			

Segment:	**REF** Reference Numbers
Position:	350
Loop:	N1 Optional
Level:	Heading
Usage:	Optional
Max Use:	12
Purpose:	To specify identifying numbers.
Syntax Notes:	1 At least one of REF02 or REF03 is required.
Semantic Notes:	
Comments:	

Notes: *1. This 1/REF/350 segment can be used to establish distribution lists for named parties when applicable. Use of distribution lists reduces the need to repeat addresses in table 2.*

2. Use this segment also to provide reference numbers associated with a delivery, i.e., when N101 is code ST.

Data Element Summary

	Ref. Des.	Data Element	Name		Attributes	
Must Use	REF01	128	**Reference Number Qualifier**		M	ID 2/2
			Code qualifying the Reference Number.			
			BM	Bill of Lading Number		
				Use to indicate a government bill of lading (GBL).		
			KC	Exhibit Distribution List		
				Qualifies a list of addressees to which the distribution of a cited contract exhibit must be made		
				Use to indicate a CDRL distribution list. Cite the distribution list number in REF02.		
			KK	Delivery Reference		

Use to indicate a delivery (i.e., shipment) distribution list when there are multiple ship-to addresses but the list is the same for all line items. Cite the distribution list number in REF02.

| | REF02 | 127 | Reference Number | X | AN 1/30 |

Reference number or identification number as defined for a particular Transaction Set, or as specified by the Reference Number Qualifier.

| Not Used | REF03 | 352 | Description | X | AN 1/80 |

A free-form description to clarify the related data elements and their content

Segment:	**PER** Administrative Communications Contact
Position:	360
Loop:	N1 Optional
Level:	Heading
Usage:	Optional
Max Use:	3
Purpose:	To identify a person or office to whom administrative communications should be directed
Syntax Notes:	1 If either PER03 or PER04 is present, then the other is required.
	2 If either PER05 or PER06 is present, then the other is required.
Semantic Notes:	
Comments:	
Notes:	*1. Use this 1/PER/360 segment to identify contacts not associated with an address.*
	2. A request has been submitted to ASC X12 to add data element 443, Contact Inquiry Reference, at PER07. This data element will permit citing the title of the party identified in PER02. If approved, this data element will be available for use in ASC X12 Version/Release 3050.

Data Element Summary

	Ref. Des.	Data Element	Name	Attributes	
Must Use	PER01	366	**Contact Function Code**	M	ID 2/2

Code identifying the major duty or responsibility of the person or group named

Use to identify individuals who can be contacted regarding the order.

BD	Buyer Name or Department
CN	General Contact

When N101 is code ST, use to indicate the accepting official at destination.

HM	Hazardous Material Contact
PC	Purchasing Contracting Officer (PCO)

Person to whom a warrant has been issued authorizing that person to obligate funds on behalf of the government

PD	Project Director

Use to indicate the Investigator, i.e., the principal party working on a research effort. A request has been submitted to ASC X12 to add a code for Investigator (for research and development work). We expect this code will be available for use in ASC X12 Version/Release 3050. In the meantime, use this code.

RP	Responsible Person

When N101 is code C4, use to indicate the accepting official at origin.

SU	Supplier Contact

Use to indicate the selling party's point of contact.

| | PER02 | 93 | Name | O | AN 1/35 |

Free-form name

Cite the last name first, followed by the first name. Do not truncate the last name if whole name is longer than 35 characters. Instead, truncate the first name or use the initial of the first name.

Part 3

PER03	365	**Communication Number Qualifier**		X	ID 2/2

Code identifying the type of communication number

AU	Defense Switched Network
	Department of Defense telecommunications system and successor of the Automatic Voice Network (AUTOVON)
EM	Electronic Mail
FX	Facsimile
IT	International Telephone
TE	Telephone
	Use to indicate the commercial telephone number of the individual cited in PER02.

PER04	364	**Communication Number**		X	AN 1/80

Complete communications number including country or area code when applicable

When PER03 is code TE, include the area code.

PER05	365	**Communication Number Qualifier**		X	ID 2/2

Code identifying the type of communication number

Use to identify a second communications number for the party cited in PER02. For example, if PER03/04 cites a commercial telephone number, PER05/06 can be used to cite an Electronic Mail address.

AU	Defense Switched Network
	Department of Defense telecommunications system and successor of the Automatic Voice Network (AUTOVON)
EM	Electronic Mail
EX	Telephone Extension
	Use only if PER03 is used citing either code AU or TE.
FX	Facsimile
IT	International Telephone
	Include the country code.
TE	Telephone
	Use to indicate the commercial telephone number of the individual cited in PER02.

PER06	364	**Communication Number**		X	AN 1/80

Complete communications number including country or area code when applicable

When PER05 is code TE, include the area code.

Segment:	**TD5** Carrier Details (Routing Sequence/Transit Time)
Position:	390
Loop:	N1 Optional
Level:	Heading
Usage:	Optional
Max Use:	12
Purpose:	To specify the carrier and sequence of routing and provide transit time information
Syntax Notes:	1 At least one of TD502 TD504 TD505 TD506 or TD512 is required.
	2 If TD502 is present, then TD503 is required.
	3 If TD507 is present, then TD508 is required.
	4 If TD510 is present, then TD511 is required.
Semantic Notes:	
Comments:	1 When specifying a routing sequence to be used for the shipment movement in lieu of specifying each carrier within the movement, use TD502 to identify the party responsible for defining the routing sequence, and use TD503 to identify the actual routing sequence, specified by the party identified in TD502.

Notes: *Use this 1/TD5/390 segment when the shipment method is applicable to a named entity and is the same for all the line items that will be shipped to that named entity. If the shipment method for the named entity varies by line item, use the 2/TD5/430 segment.*

Data Element Summary

	Ref. Des.	Data Element	Name		Attributes	
Not Used	TD501	133	**Routing Sequence Code**		O	ID 1/2
			Code describing the relationship of a carrier to a specific shipment movement			
			Refer to 003040 Data Element Dictionary for acceptable code values.			
	TD502	66	**Identification Code Qualifier**		X	ID 1/2
			Code designating the system/method of code structure used for Identification Code (67)			
			10	Department of Defense Activity Address Code (DODAAC)		
				When TD504 is code PL, use code 10 to identify the number in TD503 as the DoDAAC of the pipeline.		
	TD503	67	**Identification Code**		X	AN 2/17
			Code identifying a party or other code			
	TD504	91	**Transportation Method/Type Code**		X	ID 1/2
			Code specifying the method or type of transportation for the shipment			
			1. Use any code.			
			2. A conversion table may be required to convert agency codes to codes used by ASC X12.			
			D	Parcel Post		
				Use to indicate the U.S. Postal Service and not a private carrier.		
Not Used	TD505	387	**Routing**		X	AN 1/35
			Free-form description of the routing or requested routing for shipment, or the originating carrier's identity			
Not Used	TD506	368	**Shipment/Order Status Code**		X	ID 2/2
			Code indicating the status of an order or shipment or the disposition of any difference between the quantity ordered and the quantity shipped for a line item or transaction			
			Refer to 003040 Data Element Dictionary for acceptable code values.			
Not Used	TD507	309	**Location Qualifier**		O	ID 1/2
			Code identifying type of location			
			Refer to 003040 Data Element Dictionary for acceptable code values.			
Not Used	TD508	310	**Location Identifier**		X	AN 1/30
			Code which identifies a specific location			
Not Used	TD509	731	**Transit Direction Code**		O	ID 2/2
			The point of origin and point of direction			
			Refer to 003040 Data Element Dictionary for acceptable code values.			
Not Used	TD510	732	**Transit Time Direction Qualifier**		O	ID 2/2
			Code specifying the value of time used to measure the transit time			
			Refer to 003040 Data Element Dictionary for acceptable code values.			
Not Used	TD511	733	**Transit Time**		X	R 1/4
			The numeric amount of transit time			
Not Used	TD512	284	**Service Level Code**		X	ID 2/2
			Code defining service			
			Refer to 003040 Data Element Dictionary for acceptable code values.			

Part 3

Segment:	**PO1** Baseline Item Data
Position:	010
Loop:	PO1 Mandatory
Level:	Detail
Usage:	Mandatory
Max Use:	1
Purpose:	To specify basic and most frequently used line item data
Syntax Notes:	1 If PO103 is present, then PO102 is required.
	2 If PO105 is present, then PO104 is required.
	3 If PO106 is present, then PO107 is required.
	4 If PO108 is present, then PO109 is required.
	5 If PO110 is present, then PO111 is required.
	6 If PO112 is present, then PO113 is required.
	7 If PO114 is present, then PO115 is required.
	8 If PO116 is present, then PO117 is required.
	9 If PO118 is present, then PO119 is required.
	10 If PO120 is present, then PO121 is required.
	11 If PO122 is present, then PO123 is required.
	12 If PO124 is present, then PO125 is required.
Semantic Notes:	
Comments:	1 See the Data Dictionary for a complete list of IDs.
	2 PO101 is the line item identification.
	3 PO106 through PO125 provide for ten (10) different product/service ID's per each item. For example: Case, Color, Drawing No., UPC No., ISBN No., Model No., SKU.
Notes:	*Use the 2/PO1/010 loop to specify all information related to a CLIN, SUBCLIN or ELIN. Each iteration of the PO1 loop will carry all the information related to the CLIN, SUBCLIN or ELIN cited in PO101.*

Data Element Summary

Ref. Des.	Data Element	Name	Attributes	
PO101	350	**Assigned Identification**	O	AN 1/11
		Alphanumeric characters assigned for differentiation within a transaction set		
		Use to identify the CLIN, SUBCLIN, or ELIN or other number identifying the line item.		
PO102	330	**Quantity Ordered**	X	R 1/9
		Quantity ordered		
		1. Use to specify the quantity of the item being ordered. Step ladder quantities and related prices will be cited in the 2/CTP/040 segment.		
		2. Do not use this data element when quantities are specified at the SUBCLIN level.		
PO103	355	**Unit or Basis for Measurement Code**	O	ID 2/2
		Code specifying the units in which a value is being expressed, or manner in which a measurement has been taken		
		1. Use any code.		
		2. A conversion table may be required to convert agency codes to codes used by ASC X12.		
		SX Shipment		
		Use this code when PO101 is a line item for prepaid transportation charges. Use the 2/SAC/130 segment when no prepaid and add.		
PO104	212	**Unit Price**	X	R 1/14
		Price per unit of product, service, commodity, etc.		
		When PO105 is code TB, enter the number 0.		
PO105	639	**Basis of Unit Price Code**	O	ID 2/2
		Code identifying the type of unit price for an item		
		Use any code.		
		TB To be negotiated.		

Use to indicate the cost of the item cited in PO101 is included in the cost of another, related item. For example, if this line item is for data or documentation, it might be "not separately priced." The cost of the data or documentation in that case could be included in the cost of the item itself. Data maintenance has been submitted to ASC X12 asking for a code value indicating Not Separately Priced. If approved, that code will be available for use in ASC X12 Version/Release 3050. Until a new code is approved, use this code.

PO106   235   **Product/Service ID Qualifier**   O   ID 2/2

Code identifying the type/source of the descriptive number used in Product/Service ID (234)

1. PO106 through PO125 are used in pairs. For example, PO106 will contain a qualifier code and PO107 will contain information related to the qualifying code. So, if PO106 is code FS then PO107 would carry the National Stock Number.

2. Any code can be used but listed codes are preferred.

3. Use as many codes as necessary to describe the ordered item. There is no need to use all the codes or even all of the applicable codes. Select from the code list the minimum set of codes and code values necessary to describe the item.

4. Data maintenance has been submitted to ASC X12 for the following additional codes: Exhibit Identifier, Data Category Code, Replacement National Stock Number, Item Type Number, Time Compliant Technical Order, Cognizance Symbol, Material Control code, Special Material Identification code, Item Management code, Shelf-Life code, and Shelf-Life Action code. If approved, these codes will be available for use in ASC X12 Version/Release 3050.

A8   Exhibit Line Item Number

The line item of a document referenced in and appended to a procurement instrument which establishes a delivery requirement

AK   Refined Product Code

CG   Commodity Grouping

Use to indicate a commodity code.

CH   Country of Origin Code

CL   Color

CN   Commodity Name

F7   End-Item Description

Item identifier describes an end-item associated with the use of the required material

Use to identify the end item, if applicable, to which the ordered item applies.

F8   Next Higher Used Assembly

Item identifier describes the next higher assembly associated with the use of the required material

Use to identify, if applicable, the next higher assembly to which the ordered item applies.

FS   National Stock Number

The NSN shall be transmitted as a continuous set of numbers, and without the dashes.

FT   Federal Supply Classification

See Code Source 27 for the FSCs associated with this code.

KA   Engineering Data List

Use, if applicable, to indicate the list that contains the technical information related to the line item cited in PO101.

KB   Data Category Code

When PO101 is a CLIN or a SUBCLIN related to an exhibit, use to specify the data category of a CDRL.

LT   Lot Number

MF   Manufacturer

	Use to identify a manufacturer (by name) who does not have a CAGE code. Use code ZB for a CAGE code.
MG	Manufacturer's Part Number
	Use to specify the manufacturer's part number assigned to the ordered item.
MN	Model Number
MS	Military Specification (MILSPEC) Number
N1	National Drug Code in 4-4-2 Format
	4-digit manufacturer ID, 4-digit product ID, 2-digit trade package size
N2	National Drug Code in 5-3-2 Format
	5-digit manufacturer ID, 3-digit product ID, 2-digit trade package size
N3	National Drug Code in 5-4-1 Format
	5-digit manufacturer ID, 4-digit product ID, 1-digit trade package size
N4	National Drug Code in 5-4-2 Format
	5-digit manufacturer ID, 4-digit product ID, 2-digit trade package size
ND	National Drug Code (NDC)
PD	Part Number Description
	Use to provide a text description of an item.
PI	Purchaser's Item Code
	Use to provide a text description of an item that has no other assigned identification number.
PN	Company Part Number
PU	Part Reference Number
	Often on a part or subassembly drawing there is a reference number shown that is not a part number but may refer to a set of notes for use in fabrication, assembly, or in repairing the item; it may refer to a physical location within the product, such as location of a particular part on a truck engine, or to a reference to a circuit location on an electronic assembly
	Use to indicate a part number assigned by an industry (not tied to a specific manufacturer). Do not use for National Drug Codes.
PW	Part Drawing
RC	Returnable Container No.
	Use to indicate an NSN, manufacturer's part number or other identifying number (except a serial number) of a returnable container. The serial number of a returnable container will be carried in an REF segment using qualifier code RS.
SH	Service Requested
	A numeric or alphanumeric code from a list of services available to the customer
SN	Serial Number
	Use to identify, if applicable, the serial number of the item cited in PO101. For example, if the solicitation is for the repair of a serial numbered aircraft engine.
SR	Substitute Product Number
SV	Service Rendered
	Use to specify in text, the service being ordered.
SW	Stock Number
	Use to indicate a local stock number.
SZ	Vendor Alphanumeric Size Code (NRMA)
	Use to indicate the size of the item being ordered.
UK	U.P.C./EAN Shipping Container Code (1-2-5-5-1)

		A 14-digit code that uniquely identifies the manufacturer's shipping unit, including the packaging indicator and check digit; the first digit is the packaging indicator, the next two digits are the number system characters, the next five digits are the manufacturer ID number, the second five digits are the item code, and the final digit is the check digit

VP   Vendor's (Seller's) Part Number

Use to identify a part number assigned by a selling party other than the manufacturer.

ZB   Commercial and Government Entity (CAGE) Code

A code that identifies a commercial contrator authorized to do business with the U.S. government

Use to identify a manufacturer.

PO107	234	**Product/Service ID**	X	AN 1/30
		Identifying number for a product or service		
PO108	235	**Product/Service ID Qualifier**	O	ID 2/2
		Code identifying the type/source of the descriptive number used in Product/Service ID (234)		
		Refer to 003040 Data Element Dictionary for acceptable code values.		
PO109	234	**Product/Service ID**	X	AN 1/30
		Identifying number for a product or service		
PO110	235	**Product/Service ID Qualifier**	O	ID 2/2
		Code identifying the type/source of the descriptive number used in Product/Service ID (234)		
		Refer to 003040 Data Element Dictionary for acceptable code values.		
PO111	234	**Product/Service ID**	X	AN 1/30
		Identifying number for a product or service		
PO112	235	**Product/Service ID Qualifier**	O	ID 2/2
		Code identifying the type/source of the descriptive number used in Product/Service ID (234)		
		Refer to 003040 Data Element Dictionary for acceptable code values.		
PO113	234	**Product/Service ID**	X	AN 1/30
		Identifying number for a product or service		
PO114	235	**Product/Service ID Qualifier**	O	ID 2/2
		Code identifying the type/source of the descriptive number used in Product/Service ID (234)		
		Refer to 003040 Data Element Dictionary for acceptable code values.		
PO115	234	**Product/Service ID**	X	AN 1/30
		Identifying number for a product or service		
PO116	235	**Product/Service ID Qualifier**	O	ID 2/2
		Code identifying the type/source of the descriptive number used in Product/Service ID (234)		
		Refer to 003040 Data Element Dictionary for acceptable code values.		
PO117	234	**Product/Service ID**	X	AN 1/30
		Identifying number for a product or service		
PO118	235	**Product/Service ID Qualifier**	O	ID 2/2
		Code identifying the type/source of the descriptive number used in Product/Service ID (234)		
		Refer to 003040 Data Element Dictionary for acceptable code values.		
PO119	234	**Product/Service ID**	X	AN 1/30
		Identifying number for a product or service		
PO120	235	**Product/Service ID Qualifier**	O	ID 2/2
		Code identifying the type/source of the descriptive number used in Product/Service ID (234)		
		Refer to 003040 Data Element Dictionary for acceptable code values.		
PO121	234	**Product/Service ID**	X	AN 1/30
		Identifying number for a product or service		
PO122	235	**Product/Service ID Qualifier**	O	ID 2/2
		Code identifying the type/source of the descriptive number used in Product/Service ID (234)		

Part 3

Refer to 003040 Data Element Dictionary for acceptable code values.

PO123	234	**Product/Service ID**		X	AN 1/30

Identifying number for a product or service

PO124	235	**Product/Service ID Qualifier**		O	ID 2/2

Code identifying the type/source of the descriptive number used in Product/Service ID (234)

Refer to 003040 Data Element Dictionary for acceptable code values.

PO125	234	**Product/Service ID**		X	AN 1/30

Identifying number for a product or service

Segment:	**PO3** Additional Item Detail
Position:	030
Loop:	PO1 Mandatory
Level:	Detail
Usage:	Optional
Max Use:	25
Purpose:	To specify additional item-related data involving variations in normal price/quantity structure
Syntax Notes:	1 If PO304 is present, then at least one of PO303 or PO305 is required.
Semantic Notes:	
Comments:	1 Some examples of price/quantity variations are: price in different units from the PO1 segment, price changes by date, or price changes by quantity (break and level).
	2 PO307 defines the unit of measure for PO306.
Notes:	*Use this segment to provide additional information relative to the item indicated in PO101.*

Data Element Summary

	Ref. Des.	Data Element	Name	Attributes	
Must Use	PO301	371	**Change Reason Code**	M	ID 2/2

Code specifying the reason for price or quantity change

	AQ	Alternate Quantity and Unit of Measure

Use to indicate that an item has an alternate quantity and unit of measurement with both being applicable to the solicited item. For example, the requirement might be for 10 sheets of steel of a certain dimension. Another way of describing the item could be in terms of its weight, such as 10,000 pounds of steel. This issue is related to the difference in order and billing units of measurement.

	EV	Estimated Quantity

Use to indicate the estimated quantity for a requirement or indefinite quantity instrument.

Not Used	PO302	373	**Date**	O	DT 6/6

Date (YYMMDD)

Not Used	PO303	236	**Price Identifier Code**	X	ID 3/3

Code identifying pricing specification

Refer to 003040 Data Element Dictionary for acceptable code values.

Not Used	PO304	212	**Unit Price**	O	R 1/14

Price per unit of product, service, commodity, etc.

Not Used	PO305	639	**Basis of Unit Price Code**	X	ID 2/2

Code identifying the type of unit price for an item

Refer to 003040 Data Element Dictionary for acceptable code values.

Must Use	PO306	380	**Quantity**	M	R 1/15

Numeric value of quantity

Must Use	PO307	355	**Unit or Basis for Measurement Code**	M	ID 2/2

Code specifying the units in which a value is being expressed, or manner in which a measurement has been taken

1. Use any code.

2. A conversion table may be required to convert agency codes used by ASC X12.

Refer to 003040 Data Element Dictionary for acceptable code values.

Not Used	PO308	352	**Description**		O	AN 1/80

A free-form description to clarify the related data elements and their content

Segment:	**CTP** Pricing Information
Position:	040
Loop:	PO1 Mandatory
Level:	Detail
Usage:	Optional
Max Use:	25
Purpose:	To specify pricing information
Syntax Notes:	1 If CTP04 is present, then CTP05 is required.
	2 If CTP06 is present, then CTP07 is required.
	3 If CTP09 is present, then CTP02 is required.
Semantic Notes:	1 CTP07 is a multiplier factor to arrive at a final discounted price. A multiplier of .90 would be the factor if a 10% discount is given.
	2 CTP08 is the rebate amount.
Comments:	1 See Figures Appendix for an example detailing the use of CTP03 and CTP04.
	See Figures Appendix for an example detailing the use of CTP03, CTP04 and CTP07.
Notes:	*1. Use this 2/CTP/040 segment to specify prices for step-ladder quantities of the line item cited in PO101 for a basic procurement instrument, e.g., a requirements or indefinite quantity contract.*
	2. Example of step-ladder pricing for ranges 1-10, 11-20, 21-30, 31-50:
	*CTP**PBQ**1*EA n/l*
	*CTP**ICL*25.00*10*EA n/l*
	*CTP**ICL*24.50*20*EA n/l*
	*CTP**ICL*23.50*30*EA n/l*
	*CTP**MAX*22.00*50*EA n/l*
	3. A request has been submitted to ASC X12 asking that the maximum use of this segment be increased from 25 to greater than 1 and to add data element 499, Condition Code, in order to specify a packaging level, protection level or delivery zone. If approved, these changes will be available for use in ASC X12 Version/Release 3050.

Data Element Summary

	Ref. Des.	Data Element	Name		Attributes	
Not Used	CTP01	687	**Class of Trade Code**		O	ID 2/2
			Code indicating class of trade			
			Refer to 003040 Data Element Dictionary for acceptable code values.			
	CTP02	236	**Price Identifier Code**		X	ID 3/3

Code identifying pricing specification

1. Use to indicate the type of prices included in the order.

2. Data maintenance has been submitted to ASC X12 asking for the addition of codes for: packaging protection levels and packing levels. If approved, these codes will be available for use in ASC X12 Version/Release 3050.

ALT   Alternate Price

Use to indicate a lease-to-purchase price. Data maintenance has been submitted to ASC X12.

GOV   Government Price

			Use to indicate the sale price to the government.	
	ICL		Unit Price Through Quantity	
			When specifying prices for different quantities, use to indicate the end of a quantity range.	
	MAX		Maximum Order Quantity Price	
			When specifying prices for different quantities, use to indicate the quantity above which the price will not change.	
	PBQ		Unit Price Beginning Quantity	
			When specifying prices for different quantities, use to indicate the beginning of a quantity range.	
	SPC		Special Price	
			Use to indicate a lease price. Data maintenance has been submitted to ASC X12.	

	CTP03	212	**Unit Price**	O	R 1/14
			Price per unit of product, service, commodity, etc.		
	CTP04	380	**Quantity**	O	R 1/15
			Numeric value of quantity		
	CTP05	355	**Unit or Basis for Measurement Code**	X	ID 2/2
			Code specifying the units in which a value is being expressed, or manner in which a measurement has been taken		
			1. Use any code.		
			2. A conversion table may be required to convert agency codes to codes used by ASC X12.		
			Refer to 003040 Data Element Dictionary for acceptable code values.		
Not Used	CTP06	648	**Price Multiplier Qualifier**	O	ID 3/3
			Code indicating the type of price multiplier		
			Refer to 003040 Data Element Dictionary for acceptable code values.		
Not Used	CTP07	649	**Multiplier**	X	R 1/10
			Value to be used as a multiplier to obtain a new value		
Not Used	CTP08	782	**Monetary Amount**	O	R 1/15
			Monetary amount		
Not Used	CTP09	639	**Basis of Unit Price Code**	O	ID 2/2
			Code identifying the type of unit price for an item		
			Refer to 003040 Data Element Dictionary for acceptable code values.		

Segment:	**MEA** Measurements
Position:	049
Loop:	PO1 Mandatory
Level:	Detail
Usage:	Optional
Max Use:	40
Purpose:	To specify physical measurements or counts, including dimensions, tolerances, variances, and weights (See Figures Appendix for example of use of C001)
Syntax Notes:	1 At least one of MEA03 MEA05 MEA06 or MEA08 is required.
	2 If MEA03 is present, then MEA04 is required.
	3 If MEA05 is present, then MEA04 is required.
	4 If MEA06 is present, then MEA04 is required.
	5 If MEA07 is present, then at least one of MEA03 MEA05 or MEA06 is required.
	6 Only one of MEA08 or MEA03 may be present.
Semantic Notes:	1 MEA04 defines the unit of measure for MEA03, MEA05, and MEA06.
Comments:	1 When citing dimensional tolerances, any measurement requiring a sign (+ or -), or any measurement where a positive (+) value cannot be assumed, use MEA05 as the negative (-) value and MEA06 as the positive (+) value.

Notes: *1. Use the 2/MEA/049 segment when measurements vary by line item. When measurements apply to all of the line items, use the 1/MEA/200 segment.*

2. This segment can be used to provide any measurement applicable to the order including the variations in quantity; warranty periods; and for a requirements or indefinite quantity procurement instrument, the minimum/maximum quantity per order, the maximum that may be ordered during a specified time period, and the maximum obligations of the government and contractor.

Data Element Summary

Ref. Des.	Data Element	Name	Attributes
MEA01	737	**Measurement Reference ID Code**	O ID 2/2

Code identifying the broad category to which a measurement applies

Use any code. Listed codes are preferred.

BT   Batch Limits

Limits set on test results from all product made for one unit or period of production

Use to indicate the limits of the government's obligation to order under requirements or indefinite quantity procurement instrument. Do not use for a purchase order or delivery order.

CT   Counts

Use to indicate variations in quantity when expressed as a discrete quantity. Use MEA05/06 to provide the quantity over and under.

DE   Defects

Use to indicate a warranty period.

LT   Lot Limits

Limits set on test results from all product contained in a single shipment (which may involve any multiple or fraction of transportation carrier units) to one customer

Use to indicate the limits of the contractor's obligation to deliver under a requirements or indefinite quantity procurement instrument. Do not use for a purchase order or delivery order.

PM   Permitted

The condition or activity approved by the appropriate regulatory agency

Use to indicate that measurement values are applicable to the minimum and maximum quantity or dollar value permitted per order against an indefinite instrument. Use MEA05/06 to cite the minimum and maximum.

RG   Regulatory Limit

Use to specify the maximum the government may order from a requirements or indefinite quantity procurement instrument in a specified time period. A request has been submitted to ASC X12 to add a code for Order Limits. We expect this code to be available for use in ASC X12 Version/Release 3050. In the meantime, use this code. Do not use for purchase order or delivery order.

| MEA02 | 738 | **Measurement Qualifier** | O   ID 1/3 |

Code identifying a specific product or process characteristic to which a measurement applies

Use any code. Listed codes are to be used in accordance with their accompanying notes.

MX   Maximum

Use when MEA01 is either code BT or LT, use to indicate the maximum limit of the government's obligation to order or the contractor's obligation to deliver under a requirements or an indefinite quantity contract. When MEA01 is code RG, use to indicate the maximum amount that can be ordered from a requirements or indefinite quantity contract in a specified period of time.

PO   Percent of Order (-, +)

Part 3

Expression of allowable variance of order expressed either as absolute (for example 92% to 110%) or relative percent (for example - 8% to + 10%)

Use to indicate the percent variation in quantity permitted for the line items. Use MEA05/06 to indicate the percent over and under.

		TT	Time		

Use to indicate the length of a warranty period. Specify the length of the time period in MEA03 and the time period in MEA04-1.

	MEA03	739	**Measurement Value**	X	R 1/10

The value of the measurement

	MEA04	C001	**Composite Unit of Measure**	C	

To identify a composite unit of measure (See Figures Appendix for examples of use)

This composite data element can be used to specify the maximum amount that may be ordered during a specified period of time from a requirements or indefinite quantity contract. For example: if the maximum that can be ordered in a quarter is 10,000 each, then MEA01 would cite code RG, MEA02 would cite code MX, MEA03 would cite 10,000, MEA04-1 would cite code EA, and MEA04-4 would cite Q1.

Must Use	C00101	355	**Unit or Basis for Measurement Code**	M	ID 2/2

Code specifying the units in which a value is being expressed, or manner in which a measurement has been taken

1. Use any code.

2. A conversion table may be required to convert agency codes to codes used by ASC X12.

Refer to 003040 Data Element Dictionary for acceptable code values.

Not Used	C00102	1018	**Exponent**	O	R 1/15

Power to which a unit is raised

Not Used	C00103	649	**Multiplier**	O	R 1/10

Value to be used as a multiplier to obtain a new value

	C00104	355	**Unit or Basis for Measurement Code**	O	ID 2/2

Code specifying the units in which a value is being expressed, or manner in which a measurement has been taken

A conversion table may be required to convert agency codes to codes used by ASC X12.

Refer to 003040 Data Element Dictionary for acceptable code values.

Not Used	C00105	1018	**Exponent**	O	R 1/15

Power to which a unit is raised

Not Used	C00106	649	**Multiplier**	O	R 1/10

Value to be used as a multiplier to obtain a new value

Not Used	C00107	355	**Unit or Basis for Measurement Code**	O	ID 2/2

Code specifying the units in which a value is being expressed, or manner in which a measurement has been taken

Refer to 003040 Data Element Dictionary for acceptable code values.

Not Used	C00108	1018	**Exponent**	O	R 1/15

Power to which a unit is raised

Not Used	C00109	649	**Multiplier**	O	R 1/10

Value to be used as a multiplier to obtain a new value

Not Used	C00110	355	**Unit or Basis for Measurement Code**	O	ID 2/2

Code specifying the units in which a value is being expressed, or manner in which a measurement has been taken

Refer to 003040 Data Element Dictionary for acceptable code values.

Not Used	C00111	1018	**Exponent**	O	R 1/15

Power to which a unit is raised

Not Used	C00112	649	**Multiplier**	O	R 1/10

Value to be used as a multiplier to obtain a new value

Not Used	C00113	355	**Unit or Basis for Measurement Code**	O	ID 2/2

Code specifying the units in which a value is being expressed, or manner in which a measurement has been taken

Refer to 003040 Data Element Dictionary for acceptable code values.

Not Used	C00114	1018	**Exponent**	O	R 1/15

Power to which a unit is raised

Not Used	C00115	649	**Multiplier**	O	R 1/10

Value to be used as a multiplier to obtain a new value

	MEA05	740	**Range Minimum**	X	R 1/10

The value specifying the minimum of the measurement range

1. When MEA01 is code CT or MEA02 is code PO, use to specify the variation in quantity under.
2. When MEA01 is code PM, use to indicate the minimum quantity or dollar value for an order that can be placed against a requirements or indefinite quantity instrument.

	MEA06	741	**Range Maximum**	X	R 1/10

The value specifying the maximum of the measurement range

1. When MEA01 is code CT or MEA02 is code PO, use to specify the variation in quantity over.
2. When MEA01 is code PM, use to indicate the maximum quantity or dollar value for an order that can be placed against a requirements or indefinite quantity instrument.

Not Used	MEA07	935	**Measurement Significance Code**	O	ID 2/2

Code used to benchmark, qualify or further define a measurement value

Refer to 003040 Data Element Dictionary for acceptable code values.

Not Used	MEA08	936	**Measurement Attribute Code**	X	ID 2/2

Code used to express an attribute response when a numeric measurement value cannot be determined

Refer to 003040 Data Element Dictionary for acceptable code values.

Not Used	MEA09	752	**Surface/Layer/Position Code**	O	ID 2/2

Code indicating the product surface, layer or position that is being described

Refer to 003040 Data Element Dictionary for acceptable code values.

Not Used	MEA10	1373	**Measurement Method or Device**	O	ID 2/4

The method or device used to record the measurement

Refer to 003040 Data Element Dictionary for acceptable code values.

Segment:	**PID** Product/Item Description
Position:	050
Loop:	PID Optional
Level:	Detail
Usage:	Optional
Max Use:	1
Purpose:	To describe a product or process in coded or free-form format
Syntax Notes:	1 If PID04 is present, then PID03 is required.
	2 At least one of PID04 or PID05 is required.
	3 If PID07 is present, then PID03 is required.
	4 If PID08 is present, then PID03 is required.
Semantic Notes:	1 Use PID03 to indicate the organization that publishes the code list being referred to.
	2 PID04 should be used for industry-specific product description codes.
	3 PID08 describes the physical characteristics of the product identified in PID04. A "Y" indicates that the specified attribute applies to this item. A "N" indicates it does not apply. Any other value is indeterminate.
Comments:	1 If PID01 = "F", then PID05 is used. If PID01 = "S", then PID04 is used. If PID01 = "X", then both PID04 and PID05 are used.
	2 Use PID06 when necessary to refer to the product surface or layer being described in the segment.
	3 PID07 specifies the individual code list of the agency specified in PID03.
Notes:	*Use the 2/PID/050 segment when the information applies to a specific line item. Use the 1/PID/190 segment when the information applies to all the line items. Use is discouraged.*

Data Element Summary

	Ref. Des.	Data Element	Name	Attributes	
Must Use	PID01	349	**Item Description Type**	M	ID 1/1
			Code indicating the format of a description		
			F Free-form		
Not Used	PID02	750	**Product/Process Characteristic Code**	O	ID 2/3
			Code identifying the general class of a product or process characteristic		
			Refer to 003040 Data Element Dictionary for acceptable code values.		
Not Used	PID03	559	**Agency Qualifier Code**	X	ID 2/2
			Code identifying the agency assigning the code values		
			Refer to 003040 Data Element Dictionary for acceptable code values.		
Not Used	PID04	751	**Product Description Code**	X	AN 1/12
			A code from an industry code list which provides specific data about a product characteristic		
	PID05	352	**Description**	X	AN 1/80
			A free-form description to clarify the related data elements and their content		
			Use, if necessary, to provide a brief description of the line item being ordered. Use is discouraged.		
Not Used	PID06	752	**Surface/Layer/Position Code**	O	ID 2/2
			Code indicating the product surface, layer or position that is being described		
			Refer to 003040 Data Element Dictionary for acceptable code values.		
Not Used	PID07	822	**Source Subqualifier**	O	AN 1/15
			A reference that indicates the table or text maintained by the Source Qualifier		
Not Used	PID08	1073	**Yes/No Condition or Response Code**	O	ID 1/1
			Code indicating a Yes or No condition or response		
			Refer to 003040 Data Element Dictionary for acceptable code values.		

Segment:	**PWK** Paperwork
Position:	070
Loop:	PO1 Mandatory
Level:	Detail
Usage:	Optional
Max Use:	25
Purpose:	To identify the type and transmission of paperwork or supporting information
Syntax Notes:	1 If either PWK05 or PWK06 is present, then the other is required.
Semantic Notes:	
Comments:	1 PWK05 and PWK06 may be used to identify the addressee by a code number.
	2 PWK07 may be used to indicate special information to be shown on the specified report.
	3 PWK08 may be used to indicate action pertaining to a report.
Notes:	*1. Use to indicate how technical documentation, drawings or specifications, etc., applicable to a specific line item, are being provided by the buying party or required to be provided by the selling party. The segment also indicates how the paperwork is to be provided.*
	2. Use the 2/PWK/070 segment to provide paperwork information that applies to a line item. If the paperwork information applies to all of the line items, use the 1/PWK/210 segment.

Data Element Summary

	Ref. Des.	Data Element	Name	Attributes	
Must Use	PWK01	755	**Report Type Code**	M	ID 2/2
			Code indicating the title or contents of a document, report or supporting item		
			A request has been submitted to ASC X12 to add codes for: Certified Cost and Price Data, Wage Determination, Union Agreement, Attachment, and Contract Security Classification Specification. We expect these codes to be available for use in ASC X12 Version/Release 3050.		

C1	Cost Data Summary	

Use to indicate that the cost and price data is required.

CP	Certificate of Compliance (Material Certification)	

Use to indicate a Certificate of Conformance. When used, PWK04 should cite code PC.

CX	Cost/Schedule Status Report (C/SSR)

Contract status report showing budget, performance, actual, cost variance, schedule variance, budget at complete, estimate at complete, and variance at complete at specified levels of the work breakdown structure

CY	Contract Funds Status Report (CFSR)

Status report for funds appropriation including commitments, actual cost, forecast of billings, and estimated termination costs

DW	Drawing(s)
F1	Cost Performance Report (CPR) Format 1

Detailed contract status report including current reporting month values at specified levels of the work breakdown structure

F2	Cost Performance Report (CPR) Format 2

Detailed contract status report at specified levels of the organization breakdown structure

F3	Cost Performance Report (CPR) Format 3

Contract baseline report that summarizes changes to the contract over a given reporting period with beginning and ending values

F4	Cost Performance Report (CPR) Format 4

Contract resource summary report that forecasts labor requirements for the remainder of a contract

F5	Cost Performance Report (CPR) Format 5

Contract summary or detail report explaining significant cost or schedule variances

KA	Contract Data Requirements List (CDRL)

Use to indicate that additional information will be provided relative to a CDRL being transmitted in this order.

MR	Material Inspection and Receiving Report
MS	Material Safety Data Sheet
PD	Proof of Delivery
PJ	Purchasing Specification

Specifications, generated by a customer, setting acceptance limits on the properties or performance of the product being purchased; purchasing specifications may additionally supply instructions for packaging, transportation, delivery, and payments

SD	Support Data for a Request for Quote

Use to indicate that supporting technical documentation is either being provided by the buying party or required of the selling party.

US	"BUY AMERICA" Certification of Compliance

PWK02 756   Report Transmission Code   O   ID 2/2

Code defining timing, transmission method or format by which reports are to be sent

While any code can be used, code EL is preferred when the indicated paperwork can be provided electronically using one of the transaction sets specifically designed for the purpose.

BM	By Mail
EL	Electronically Only
FX	By Fax
WS	With Shipment (With Package)

PWK03 757   Report Copies Needed   O   N0 1/2

			The number of copies of a report that should be sent to the addressee		
	PWK04	98	**Entity Identifier Code**	O	**ID 2/2**
			Code identifying an organizational entity, a physical location, or an individual		
			BY	Buying Party (Purchaser)	
				Use to indicate the Contracting Officer.	
			C4	Contract Administration Office	
				Established at either a contractor facility or in a geographic area, and responsible for administering on behalf of the buying activities that assigned contracts for administration and all contracts awarded to either the specific contractor or all contractors in the geographic area	
			IS	Party to Receive Certified Inspection Report	
			KF	Audit Office	
				The office performing the audit	
			KG	Project Manager	
				The address of the person responsible for the management of a designated project	
			KY	Technical Office	
			PA	Party to Receive Inspection Report	
			PC	Party to Receive Cert. of Conformance (C.A.A.)	
			SM	Party to Receive Shipping Manifest	
			ZD	Party to Receive Reports	
				The organization designated to receive reports	
	PWK05	66	**Identification Code Qualifier**	X	**ID 1/2**
			Code designating the system/method of code structure used for Identification Code (67)		
			Use to indicate the recipient of the paperwork if there is only one recipient and provide the address, if necessary, in the N1 loop. If there is more than one recipient, identify all recipients and their addresses in the N1 loop.		
			1	D-U-N-S Number, Dun & Bradstreet	
			10	Department of Defense Activity Address Code (DODAAC)	
			33	Commercial and Government Entity (CAGE)	
	PWK06	67	**Identification Code**	X	**AN 2/17**
			Code identifying a party or other code		
	PWK07	352	**Description**	O	**AN 1/80**
			A free-form description to clarify the related data elements and their content		
			Use only if necessary to provide additional information or instructions related to a specific paperwork item. Use is discouraged.		
	PWK08	C002	**Actions Indicated**	O	
			Actions to be performed on the piece of paperwork identified		
Must Use	C00201	704	**Paperwork/Report Action Code**	M	**ID 1/2**
			Code specifying how the paperwork or report that is identified in the PWK segment relates to the transaction set or to identify the action that is required		
			2	Report to be Filed	
				Use to indicate the identified paperwork is required to be provided by the contractor.	
			3	Complete	
				Use the information provided, add additional required data, distribute as indicated	
				Use to indicate the specified paperwork will be provided by the buying activity. A request has been submitted to ASC X12 to add a code for Provided. We expect this code will be available for use in ASC X12 Version/Release 3050. In the meantime, use this code.	
Not Used	C00202	704	**Paperwork/Report Action Code**	O	**ID 1/2**

Code specifying how the paperwork or report that is identified in the PWK segment relates to the transaction set or to identify the action that is required

Refer to 003040 Data Element Dictionary for acceptable code values.

| Not Used | C00203 | 704 | **Paperwork/Report Action Code** | O | ID 1/2 |

Code specifying how the paperwork or report that is identified in the PWK segment relates to the transaction set or to identify the action that is required

Refer to 003040 Data Element Dictionary for acceptable code values.

| Not Used | C00204 | 704 | **Paperwork/Report Action Code** | O | ID 1/2 |

Code specifying how the paperwork or report that is identified in the PWK segment relates to the transaction set or to identify the action that is required

Refer to 003040 Data Element Dictionary for acceptable code values.

| Not Used | C00205 | 704 | **Paperwork/Report Action Code** | O | ID 1/2 |

Code specifying how the paperwork or report that is identified in the PWK segment relates to the transaction set or to identify the action that is required

Refer to 003040 Data Element Dictionary for acceptable code values.

Segment:	**PO4** Item Physical Details
Position:	090
Loop:	PO1 Mandatory
Level:	Detail
Usage:	Optional
Max Use:	1
Purpose:	To specify the physical qualities, packaging, weights, and dimensions relating to the item
Syntax Notes:	1 If PO402 is present, then PO403 is required.
	2 If PO405 is present, then PO406 is required.
	3 If PO406 is present, then PO407 is required.
	4 If either PO408 or PO409 is present, then the other is required.
	5 If PO410 is present, then PO413 is required.
	6 If PO411 is present, then PO413 is required.
	7 If PO412 is present, then PO413 is required.
	8 If PO413 is present, then at least one of PO410 PO411 or PO412 is required.
Semantic Notes:	
Comments:	1 PO403 - The "Unit of Measure Code" (Element #355) in this segment position is for purposes of defining the pack (PO401) /size (PO402) measure which indicates the quantity in the inner pack unit. Example: If the carton contains 24 12-Ounce packages, it would be described as follows: Element 356 = 24; Element 357 = 12; Element 355 = OZ.
	2 PO413 defines the unit of measure for PO410, PO411, and PO412.
Notes:	*1. Use this segment to specify the dimensions of the unit or intermediate container. In ASC X12 Version/Release 3050, this segment will be used to specify the number of items in a unit container, the number of unit containers in an intermediate container and the gross weight and cube of these containers. Until then, that information is contained in the MIL-STD 2073-2C code string at either the header or detail level.*
	2. A request has been submitted to ASC X12 to increase the maximum use of this segment to greater than one in order to pass dimensions of both a unit and intermediate container. If approved, this increase will be available in ASC X12 Version/Release 3050. In the meantime, dimensions of either a unit of intermediate container can be provided.

Data Element Summary

	Ref. Des.	Data Element	Name	Attributes	
Not Used	PO401	356	**Pack**	O	N0 1/6
			Number of inner pack units per outer pack unit		
Not Used	PO402	357	**Size**	O	R 1/8
			Size of supplier units in pack		

| Not Used | PO403 | 355 | **Unit or Basis for Measurement Code** | X | ID 2/2 |

Code specifying the units in which a value is being expressed, or manner in which a measurement has been taken

Refer to 003040 Data Element Dictionary for acceptable code values.

| | PO404 | 103 | **Packaging Code** | O | AN 5/5 |

Code identifying the type of packaging; Part 1: Packaging Form, Part 2: Packaging Material

PKG	Package

Use to indicate an intermediate container. A request has been submitted to ASC X12 to add a code for Intermediate container. If approved, this code will be available in ASC X12 Version/Release 3050. In the meantime, use this code.

UNT	Unit

Use to indicate a unit container.

01	Aluminum
04	As Specified by the DOT
07	Burlap
10	Chemically Hardened Fibre
13	Cloth
16	Cloth Top
19	Cloth or Fabric
22	Compressed
25	Corrugated or Solid
28	Double-wall Paper
31	Fiber
34	Fiber (Paperboard)
37	Fiberboard
40	Fiberboard Metal
43	Glass
46	In Inner Containers
48	Wire/Cord

Something that binds, ties, or encircles the package/container to secure and maintain unit integrity

49	Insulated
50	Steel - Vinyl Coated

Steel that has been covered with a plastic material

51	Wire Mesh
52	Iron or Steel
53	Jumbo
54	Special Jumbo
55	Lead
58	Metal
59	Metal Cans
61	Moisture Resistant
64	Molded Plastic
67	Multiple-wall Paper (2 or more walls)
70	Multiple-wall Paper (3 or more walls)
71	Not Otherwise Specified
72	Paper - VCI

Water-resistent paper that is treated by the addition of materials to provide resistence to damage or deterioration by water in liquid form

73	Other than Glass

74	Other than Metal or Plastic Tubes, or Glass		
75	Plastic - Vacuum Formed		

Packaging material that is formed by heating plastic sheet and drawing it against the mold surface by evacuating the air between the sheet and the mold

76	Paper
77	Plastic - Structural Foam

A method of manufacturing containers and shipping devices by mixing plastic resins with a foaming agent, heating it and injecting the mix into a two-piece machined aluminum mold

78	Plastic - Injection Molded

Packaging material that is formed by melting the material and then forcing it under pressure into a cavity of a closed mold

79	Plastic
80	Polyethylene Lined
81	Plastic - Virgin

Plastic in the form of pellets, granules, powder, floc, or liquid that has not been subjected to use or processing other than for its initial manufacture

82	Pulpboard
83	Plastic - Regrind

A plastic prepared from discarded articles that have been reprocessed, often changing some of its original properties

84	Polystyrene

A polymer prepared by the polymerization of styrene as the sole monomer

85	Rubber
86	Foam

In packaging, a cushioning material used to reduce shock and vibration or abrasion

88	Rubber and Fabric
89	Special
90	Standard
91	Stainless Steel
92	Tubes, Metal, or Plastic
94	Wood
95	Single Wall Corrugated Board

The structure formed by one corrugated inner member between two flat facings; also known as double face

96	Double Wall Corrugated Board

The structure formed by three flat facings and two intermediate corrugated members

97	Triple Wall Corrugated Board

The structure formed by four flat facings and three intermediate corrugated members

Not Used	PO405	187	**Weight Qualifier**	O	ID 1/2

Code defining the type of weight

Refer to 003040 Data Element Dictionary for acceptable code values.

Not Used	PO406	384	**Gross Weight per Pack**	X	R 1/9

Numeric value of gross weight per pack

Not Used	PO407	355	**Unit or Basis for Measurement Code**	X	ID 2/2

Code specifying the units in which a value is being expressed, or manner in which a measurement has been taken

Refer to 003040 Data Element Dictionary for acceptable code values.

Not Used	PO408	385	**Gross Volume per Pack**	X	R 1/9

Part 3

Numeric value of gross volume per pack

| Not Used | PO409 | 355 | **Unit or Basis for Measurement Code** | X | ID 2/2 |

Code specifying the units in which a value is being expressed, or manner in which a measurement has been taken

Refer to 003040 Data Element Dictionary for acceptable code values.

| | PO410 | 82 | **Length** | X | R 1/8 |

Largest horizontal dimension of an object measured when the object is in the upright position

| | PO411 | 189 | **Width** | X | R 1/8 |

Shorter measurement of the two horizontal dimensions measured with the object in the upright position

| | PO412 | 65 | **Height** | X | R 1/8 |

Vertical dimension of an object measured when the object is in the upright position

Use to indicate the interior depth of a container.

| | PO413 | 355 | **Unit or Basis for Measurement Code** | X | ID 2/2 |

Code specifying the units in which a value is being expressed, or manner in which a measurement has been taken

1. Use any code.

2. A conversion table may be required to convert agency codes to codes used by ASC X12.

Refer to 003040 Data Element Dictionary for acceptable code values.

Segment:	**REF** Reference Numbers
Position:	100
Loop:	PO1 Mandatory
Level:	Detail
Usage:	Optional
Max Use:	12
Purpose:	To specify identifying numbers.
Syntax Notes:	1 At least one of REF02 or REF03 is required.
Semantic Notes:	
Comments:	
Notes:	*Use this 2/REF/100 segment to identify reference numbers that vary by line item. When the reference numbers apply to all the line items in the order, use the 1/REF/050 segment.*

Data Element Summary

	Ref. Des.	Data Element	Name		Attributes
Must Use	REF01	128	**Reference Number Qualifier**	M	ID 2/2

Code qualifying the Reference Number.

Use any code. Listed codes are preferred.

| | 16 | Military Interdepartmental Purchase Request (MIPR) Number |

A specific form used to transmit obligation authority (dollars) and requirements between a service or agency requiring a purchase and a military service or agency responsible for procuring the requirement

| | 2E | Foreign Military Sales Case Number |

A reference number designating the foreign military sale records

Use to indicate that the item is being solicited as part of a foreign military sale.

| | 73 | Statement of Work (SOW) |

Description of a product or service to be procured under a contract; statement of requirements

Use to indicate the statement of work (SOW) number or a number within the statement of work where additional information can be found regarding the line item. If the SOW is a part of the order, the PWK segment can be used to indicate how it is being transmitted to the selling party if not otherwise included in the transaction set.

82   Data Item Description (DID) Reference

Specific data elements that the government will ask a contractor to provide and are spelled out in specific requirement documents

83   Extended (or Exhibit) Line Item Number (ELIN)

Identifies specific line items to be delivered for a contract

97   Package Number

A serial number indicating unit shipped

AH   Agreement Number

Use to indicate a Union Agreement number.

AT   Appropriation Number

Use to indicate accounting appropriation data. Cite the data as a literal string in REF03.

BL   Government Bill of Lading

BV   Purchase Order Line Item Identifier (Buyer)

C7   Contract Line Item Number

CT   Contract Number

DG   Drawing Number

EV   Receiver Identification Number

A unique number identifying the organization/site location designated to receive the current transmitted transaction set

Use to indicate the office or other symbol of the requiring office responsible for ensuring the adequacy of the technical data.

IJ   Standard Industry Classification (SIC) Code

Use to identify the SIC code of the cited line item.

IL   Internal Order Number

Use to indicate the requisition number (e.g., the MILSTRIP/FEDSTRIP document number).

IX   Item Number

Use to indicate a Federal Supply Class (FSC) special item number.

K0   Approval Code

Use to indicate the approval code on a CDRL. Codes associated with code K0 are found in code source 329.

K4   Criticality Designator

A number assigned to a contract or order that expresses the relative importance of that contract or order and thereby assists the contractor in making performance decisions and assists in making production surveillance decisions

Use to indicate the surveillance criticality designator applicable to the line item.

K6   Purchase Description

K7   Paragraph Number

Use to indicate a particular paragraph or section in an order that contains information applicable to a line item.

KC   Exhibit Distribution List

Qualifies a list of addressees to which the distribution of a cited contract exhibit must be made

Use to indicate an exhibit distribution list to which data items on the CDRL are to be delivered.

KK   Delivery Reference

Use to indicate a Ship-To address list.

KS   Solicitation

A discreet number assigned by the purchasing activity to differentiate between different solicitations

Use to cite the solicitation number from which this line item was awarded.

KV   Distribution Statement Code

Use to indicate the code on a Contract Data Requirements List that specifies the distribution statement a contractor is to mark on a data item.

LT   Lot Number

P4   Project Code

Use to indicate the project number applicable to this line item.

PH   Priority Rating

Use to indicate the MILSTRIP/FEDSTRIP priority rating.

PR   Price Quote Number

QC   Product Specification Document Number

Model designation of replacement component

RQ   Purchase Requisition No.

Use, as appropriate, to indicate an internal number such as a purchase request or purchase request order number. When citing a purchase request number, concatenate its line item number with the purchase request number if it is necessary to transmit both numbers.

RS   Returnable Container Serial Number

S2   Military Specification Number (MILSPEC)

S3   Specification Number

Use to indicate a specification other than a MILSPEC.

TG   Transportation Control Number (TCN)

TH   Transportation Account Code (TAC)

TN   Transaction Reference Number

Use to indicate the unique reference number of a related transaction set (e.g., an 841 transaction set carrying a related technical specification or drawing). Each transaction set has a unique number. In the case of the 841 transaction set, that number is carried in SPI02.

TP   Test Specification Number

W2   Weapon System Number

Identifies a weapon system

XC   Cargo Control Number

Use to indicate the tracking number for bulk fuel being sent by a tanker vessel.

XE   Transportation Priority Number

Number indicating the level of government priority associated with the transportation of a shipment

ZF   Contractor Establishment Code (CEC)

Goverment identifier to designate a contractor; it is nine characters, eight numeric and a final alpha

ZZ   Mutually Defined

Use to indicate another type of reference number. When used, identify the nature of the number in REF03. Examples of the numbers that can be included here (for which data maintenance has been requested from ASC X12) is: DD Form 250 Requirement Code, Military Standard Number, Technical Document Number, Technical Order Number, Related Contract Line Item Number and Standard Number. If approved, these codes will be available in ASC X12 Version/Release 3050.

REF02   127   Reference Number   X   AN 1/30

Reference number or identification number as defined for a particular Transaction Set, or as specified by the Reference Number Qualifier.

If a reference number has an associated revision number, suffix or extension, concatenate the reference and revision/suffix/extension number and carry the resultant number in this data element.

REF03	352	Description	X	AN 1/80

A free-form description to clarify the related data elements and their content

1. Use to carry additional information related to the cited reference number.

2. Use is discouraged.

Segment:	**PER** Administrative Communications Contact
Position:	110
Loop:	PO1 Mandatory
Level:	Detail
Usage:	Optional
Max Use:	3
Purpose:	To identify a person or office to whom administrative communications should be directed
Syntax Notes:	1 If either PER03 or PER04 is present, then the other is required.
	2 If either PER05 or PER06 is present, then the other is required.
Semantic Notes:	
Comments:	
Notes:	*1. Use this 1/PER/360 segment to identify contacts not associated with an address.*
	2. A request has been submitted to ASC X12 to add data element 443, Contact Inquiry Reference, at PER07. This data element will permit citing the title of the party identified in PER02. If approved, this data element will be available for use in ASC X12 Version/Release 3050.

Data Element Summary

	Ref. Des.	Data Element	Name		Attributes	
Must Use	PER01	366	**Contact Function Code**		M	ID 2/2

Code identifying the major duty or responsibility of the person or group named

AU	Report Authorizer	

Use to indicate the party approving the Contract Data Requirements List.

NT	Notification Contact

Use to indicate the party to be contacted for shipping instructions. Use only when LDT01 in the 220 segment cites code AI.

PI	Preparer

A firm, organization, or individual who determines the tax liability from information supplied by the taxpayer

Use to indicate the preparer of the Contract Data Requirements List.

RE	Receiving Contact

Use to indicate the party to be contacted to schedule a shipment. Use only when LDT01 in the 2/LDT/220 segment cites code AI.

PER02	93	**Name**		O	AN 1/35

Free-form name

Cite the last name first, followed by the first name. Do not truncate the last name if the whole name is longer than 35 characters. Instead, truncate or use the initial of the first name.

PER03	365	**Communication Number Qualifier**		X	ID 2/2

Code identifying the type of communication number

AU	Defense Switched Network

Department of Defense telecommunications system and successor of the Automatic Voice Network (AUTOVON)

EM		Electronic Mail		
FX		Facsimile		
IT		International Telephone		
		Include the country code.		
TE		Telephone		

PER04	364	**Communication Number**	X	AN 1/80

Complete communications number including country or area code when applicable

PER05	365	**Communication Number Qualifier**	X	ID 2/2

Code identifying the type of communication number

Use to identify a second communications number for the party cited in PER02. For example, if PER03/04 cites a commercial telephone number, PER05/06 can be used to cite an Electronic Mail address.

AU		Defense Switched Network
		Department of Defense telecommunications system and successor of the Automatic Voice Network (AUTOVON)
EM		Electronic Mail
EX		Telephone Extension
		Use only if PER03 is used citing either code AU or TE.
FX		Facsimile
IT		International Telephone
		Include the country code.
TE		Telephone
		Use to indicate the commercial telephone number of the named party.

PER06	364	**Communication Number**	X	AN 1/80

Complete communications number including country or area code when applicable

Segment:	**SAC** Service, Promotion, Allowance, or Charge Information
Position:	130
Loop:	PO1 Mandatory
Level:	Detail
Usage:	Optional
Max Use:	25
Purpose:	To request or identify a service, promotion, allowance, or charge; to specify the amount or percentage for the service, promotion, allowance, or charge
Syntax Notes:	1 At least one of SAC02 or SAC03 is required.
	2 If either SAC03 or SAC04 is present, then the other is required.
	3 If either SAC06 or SAC07 is present, then the other is required.
	4 If either SAC09 or SAC10 is present, then the other is required.
	5 If SAC11 is present, then SAC10 is required.
	6 If SAC13 is present, then at least one of SAC02 or SAC04 is required.
	7 If SAC14 is present, then SAC13 is required.
Semantic Notes:	1 If SAC01 is "A" or "C", then at least one of SAC05, SAC07, or SAC08 is required.
	2 SAC05 is the total amount for the service, promotion, allowance, or charge. If SAC05 is present with SAC07 or SAC08, then SAC05 takes precedence.
	3 SAC10 alone is used to indicate a specific quantity which could be a dollar amount, that is applicable to service, promotion, allowance or charge. SAC10 and SAC11 used together indicate a quantity range, which could be a dollar amount, that is applicable to service, promotion, allowance, or charge.
	4 SAC13 is used in conjunction with SAC02 or SAC04 to provide a specific reference number as identified by the code used.
	5 SAC14 is used in conjunction with SAC13 to identify an option when there is more than one option of the promotion.

Comments:	1	SAC04 may be used to uniquely identify the service, promotion, allowance, or charge. In addition, it may be used in conjunction to further the code in SAC02.	
	2	In some business applications, it is necessary to advise the trading partner of the actual dollar amount that a particular allowance, charge, or promotion was based on to reduce ambiguity. This amount is commonly referred to a "Dollar Basis Amount". It is represented in the SAC segment in SAC10 using the qualifier "DO" - Dollars in SAC09.	
Notes:		*Use the 2/SAC/130 segment to identify charges that apply to a line item. If the charges apply to all of the line items, use the 1/SAC/120 segment.*	

Data Element Summary

	Ref. Des.	Data Element	Name		Attributes	
Must Use	SAC01	248	**Allowance or Charge Indicator**		M	ID 1/1
			Code which indicates an allowance or charge for the service specified			
			C	Charge		
			N	No Allowance or Charge		
	SAC02	1300	**Service, Promotion, Allowance, or Charge Code**		X	ID 4/4
			Code identifying the service, promotion, allowance, or charge			
			Use any code.			
			Refer to 003040 Data Element Dictionary for acceptable code values.			
Not Used	SAC03	559	**Agency Qualifier Code**		X	ID 2/2
			Code identifying the agency assigning the code values			
			Refer to 003040 Data Element Dictionary for acceptable code values.			
Not Used	SAC04	1301	**Agency Service, Promotion, Allowance, or Charge Code**		X	AN 1/10
			Agency maintained code identifying the service, promotion, allowance, or charge			
	SAC05	610	**Amount**		O	N2 1/15
			Monetary amount			
Not Used	SAC06	378	**Allowance/ Charge Percent Qualifier**		X	ID 1/1
			Code indicating on what basis allowance or charge percent is calculated			
			Refer to 003040 Data Element Dictionary for acceptable code values.			
Not Used	SAC07	332	**Allowance or Charge Percent**		X	R 1/6
			Allowance or charge expressed as a percent.			
Not Used	SAC08	359	**Allowance or Charge Rate**		O	R 1/9
			Allowance or Charge Rate per Unit			
	SAC09	355	**Unit or Basis for Measurement Code**		X	ID 2/2
			Code specifying the units in which a value is being expressed, or manner in which a measurement has been taken			
			A conversion table may be required to convert agency codes used by ASC X12.			
			Refer to 003040 Data Element Dictionary for acceptable code values.			
	SAC10	339	**Allowance or Charge Quantity**		X	R 1/10
			Quantity basis when allowance or charge quantity is different from the purchase order or invoice quantity			
			Use to indicate the quantity to which the amount in SAC05 applies. SAC10/11 can be used together to specify a quantity range to which the amount in SAC05 applies.			
	SAC11	339	**Allowance or Charge Quantity**		O	R 1/10
			Quantity basis when allowance or charge quantity is different from the purchase order or invoice quantity			
Not Used	SAC12	331	**Allowance or Charge Method of Handling Code**		O	ID 2/2
			Code indicating method of handling for an allowance or charge			
			Refer to 003040 Data Element Dictionary for acceptable code values.			
Not Used	SAC13	127	**Reference Number**		X	AN 1/30

Reference number or identification number as defined for a particular Transaction Set, or as specified by the Reference Number Qualifier.

Not Used	SAC14	770	**Option Number**	O	**AN 1/20**

A unique number identifying available promotion or allowance options when more than one is offered

Not Used	SAC15	352	**Description**	O	**AN 1/80**

A free-form description to clarify the related data elements and their content

Segment:	**IT8** Conditions of Sale
Position:	140
Loop:	PO1 Mandatory
Level:	Detail
Usage:	Optional
Max Use:	1
Purpose:	To specify general conditions or requirements and to detail conditions for substitution of alternate products
Syntax Notes:	1 At least one of IT801 IT802 IT803 IT805 or IT807 is required.
	2 If IT808 is present, then IT809 is required.
	3 If IT810 is present, then IT811 is required.
	4 If IT812 is present, then IT813 is required.
	5 If IT814 is present, then IT815 is required.
	6 If IT816 is present, then IT817 is required.
	7 If IT818 is present, then IT819 is required.
	8 If IT820 is present, then IT821 is required.
	9 If IT822 is present, then IT823 is required.
	10 If IT824 is present, then IT825 is required.
	11 If IT826 is present, then IT827 is required.
Semantic Notes:	1 IT804 is the account number to which the purchase amount is to be charged.
Comments:	1 Element 235/234 combinations should be interpreted to include products and/or services. See the Data Dictionary for a complete list of IDs.
	2 IT808 through IT827 provides for ten (10) different product/service IDs for each item. Example: Case, Color, Drawing No., UPC No., ISBN No., Model No., SKU.
Notes:	*Use the 2/IT8/140 segment to specify special services/conditions that vary by line item. Use the 1/CSH/110 segment when the special services/conditions apply to all the line items.*

Data Element Summary

Ref. Des.	Data Element	Name		Attributes
IT801	563	**Sales Requirement Code**	X	**ID 1/2**

Code to identify a specific requirement or agreement of sale

Data maintenance has been sent to ASC X12 asking for the addition of codes for: Restricted to Historically Black Colleges and Universities or Minority Institutions, Restricted to Educational Institutions, Restricted to Industrial Preparedness Program Participants, Restricted to Qualified Bidders List, Restricted to Qualified Manufacturers List, Restricted to Qualified Products List (QPL) Products, Restricted to U.S. and Canadian Sources, Other Unlisted Sales Condition, Unrestricted Procurement, and Restricted to Young Investigator Program. If approved, those codes will be available for use in ASC X12 Version/Release 3050.

P2	Ship As Soon As Possible
P4	Do Not Preship
SC	Ship Complete

Use to indicate partial shipments will not be accepted.

SV	Ship Per Release

Use to indicate that the line item is to be shipped in place.

IT802	564	**Do-Not-Exceed Action Code**	X	**ID 1/1**

Code indicating the action to be taken if the order amount exceeds the value of Do-Not-Exceed Amount (565)

Use any code.

Refer to 003040 Data Element Dictionary for acceptable code values.

	IT803	565	**Do-Not-Exceed Amount**	X	N2 2/9

Maximum monetary amount value which the order must not exceed.

Use to indicate a maximum amount to be paid, that if the vendor cannot sell for that price, the order need not be filled.

Not Used	IT804	508	**Account Number**	O	AN 1/35

Account number assigned

Not Used	IT805	596	**Required Invoice Date**	X	DT 6/6

Date specified by the sender to be shown on the invoice.

Not Used	IT806	559	**Agency Qualifier Code**	O	ID 2/2

Code identifying the agency assigning the code values

Refer to 003040 Data Element Dictionary for acceptable code values.

Not Used	IT807	566	**Product/Service Substitution Code**	X	ID 1/2

Code indicating product or service substitution conditions

Refer to 003040 Data Element Dictionary for acceptable code values.

Not Used	IT808	235	**Product/Service ID Qualifier**	O	ID 2/2

Code identifying the type/source of the descriptive number used in Product/Service ID (234)

Refer to 003040 Data Element Dictionary for acceptable code values.

Not Used	IT809	234	**Product/Service ID**	X	AN 1/30

Identifying number for a product or service

Not Used	IT810	235	**Product/Service ID Qualifier**	O	ID 2/2

Code identifying the type/source of the descriptive number used in Product/Service ID (234)

Refer to 003040 Data Element Dictionary for acceptable code values.

Not Used	IT811	234	**Product/Service ID**	X	AN 1/30

Identifying number for a product or service

Not Used	IT812	235	**Product/Service ID Qualifier**	O	ID 2/2

Code identifying the type/source of the descriptive number used in Product/Service ID (234)

Refer to 003040 Data Element Dictionary for acceptable code values.

Not Used	IT813	234	**Product/Service ID**	X	AN 1/30

Identifying number for a product or service

Not Used	IT814	235	**Product/Service ID Qualifier**	O	ID 2/2

Code identifying the type/source of the descriptive number used in Product/Service ID (234)

Refer to 003040 Data Element Dictionary for acceptable code values.

Not Used	IT815	234	**Product/Service ID**	X	AN 1/30

Identifying number for a product or service

Not Used	IT816	235	**Product/Service ID Qualifier**	O	ID 2/2

Code identifying the type/source of the descriptive number used in Product/Service ID (234)

Refer to 003040 Data Element Dictionary for acceptable code values.

Not Used	IT817	234	**Product/Service ID**	X	AN 1/30

Identifying number for a product or service

Not Used	IT818	235	**Product/Service ID Qualifier**	O	ID 2/2

Code identifying the type/source of the descriptive number used in Product/Service ID (234)

Refer to 003040 Data Element Dictionary for acceptable code values.

Not Used	IT819	234	**Product/Service ID**	X	AN 1/30

Identifying number for a product or service

Not Used	IT820	235	**Product/Service ID Qualifier**	O	ID 2/2

Code identifying the type/source of the descriptive number used in Product/Service ID (234)

Part 3

Refer to 003040 Data Element Dictionary for acceptable code values.

Not Used	IT821	234	**Product/Service ID**	X	AN 1/30

Identifying number for a product or service

Not Used	IT822	235	**Product/Service ID Qualifier**	O	ID 2/2

Code identifying the type/source of the descriptive number used in Product/Service ID (234)

Refer to 003040 Data Element Dictionary for acceptable code values.

Not Used	IT823	234	**Product/Service ID**	X	AN 1/30

Identifying number for a product or service

Not Used	IT824	235	**Product/Service ID Qualifier**	O	ID 2/2

Code identifying the type/source of the descriptive number used in Product/Service ID (234)

Refer to 003040 Data Element Dictionary for acceptable code values.

Not Used	IT825	234	**Product/Service ID**	X	AN 1/30

Identifying number for a product or service

Not Used	IT826	235	**Product/Service ID Qualifier**	O	ID 2/2

Code identifying the type/source of the descriptive number used in Product/Service ID (234)

Refer to 003040 Data Element Dictionary for acceptable code values.

Not Used	IT827	234	**Product/Service ID**	X	AN 1/30

Identifying number for a product or service

Segment:	**ITD** Terms of Sale/Deferred Terms of Sale
Position:	150
Loop:	PO1 Mandatory
Level:	Detail
Usage:	Optional
Max Use:	2
Purpose:	To specify terms of sale
Syntax Notes:	1 If ITD03 is present, then at least one of ITD04 ITD05 or ITD13 is required.
	2 If ITD08 is present, then at least one of ITD04 ITD05 or ITD13 is required.
	3 If ITD09 is present, then at least one of ITD10 or ITD11 is required.
Semantic Notes:	1 ITD15 is the percentage applied to a base amount used to determine a late payment charge.
Comments:	1 If the code in ITD01 is "04", then ITD07 or ITD09 is required and either ITD10 or ITD11 is required; if the code in ITD01 is "05", then ITD06 or ITD07 is required.
Notes:	*Use this 2/ITD/150 segment when the discount terms vary by line item. If the discount applies to all of the line items, use the 1/ITD/130 segment.*

Data Element Summary

Ref. Des.	Data Element	Name		Attributes
ITD01	336	**Terms Type Code**	O	ID 2/2

Code identifying type of payment terms

    21   Fast Pay

Code indicating that an invoice is subject to accelerated payment

Use to indicate FAST PAY procedures are applicable.

ITD02	333	**Terms Basis Date Code**	O	ID 1/2

Code identifying the beginning of the terms period

Use the same code as the one indicated in ITD02 of the Contract Solicitation Response, 843 transaction set.

Refer to 003040 Data Element Dictionary for acceptable code values.

ITD03	338	**Terms Discount Percent**	O	R 1/6

Terms discount percentage, expressed as a percent, available to the purchaser if an invoice is paid on or before the Terms Discount Due Date

	ITD04	370	**Terms Discount Due Date**	X	DT 6/6
			Date payment is due if discount is to be earned		
	ITD05	351	**Terms Discount Days Due**	X	N0 1/3
			Number of days in the terms discount period by which payment is due if terms discount is earned		
	ITD06	446	**Terms Net Due Date**	O	DT 6/6
			Date when total invoice amount becomes due		
	ITD07	386	**Terms Net Days**	O	N0 1/3
			Number of days until total invoice amount is due (discount not applicable)		
	ITD08	362	**Terms Discount Amount**	O	N2 1/10
			Total amount of terms discount		
			Use, if needed, to prevent differences that can result from rounding off methods.		
	ITD09	388	**Terms Deferred Due Date**	O	DT 6/6
			Date deferred payment or percent of invoice payable is due		
	ITD10	389	**Deferred Amount Due**	X	N2 1/10
			Deferred amount due for payment		
	ITD11	342	**Percent of Invoice Payable**	X	R 1/5
			Amount of invoice payable expressed in percent		
Not Used	ITD12	352	**Description**	O	AN 1/80
			A free-form description to clarify the related data elements and their content		
	ITD13	765	**Day of Month**	X	N0 1/2
			The numeric value of the day of the month between 1 and the maximum day of the month being referenced		
Not Used	ITD14	107	**Payment Method Code**	O	ID 1/1
			Code identifying type of payment procedures		
			Refer to 003040 Data Element Dictionary for acceptable code values.		
	ITD15	954	**Percent**	O	R 1/10
			Percentage expressed as a decimal		

Segment:	**DIS** Discount Detail
Position:	160
Loop:	PO1 Mandatory
Level:	Detail
Usage:	Optional
Max Use:	20
Purpose:	To specify the exact type and terms of various discount information
Syntax Notes:	
Semantic Notes:	
Comments:	
Notes:	*Use this segment to identify promotional quantity or volume discount information applicable to the line item.*

Data Element Summary

	Ref. Des.	Data Element	Name	Attributes	
Must Use	DIS01	653	**Discount Terms Type Code**	M	ID 3/3
			Code to define the units in which the discount will be determined, i.e., dollars, case, truckload, etc.		
			Use the same code as provided in the Contract Solicitation Response, 843 transaction set.		
			Refer to 003040 Data Element Dictionary for acceptable code values.		
Must Use	DIS02	654	**Discount Base Qualifier**	M	ID 2/2
			Code to define unit of discount, i.e., dollars, cases, alternate products, etc.		
			Use the same code as provided in the Contract Solicitation Response, 843 transaction set.		

Refer to 003040 Data Element Dictionary for acceptable code values.

Must Use	DIS03	655	**Discount Base Value**	M	R 1/10

A multiplier amount used in conjunction with discount base qualifier to determine the value of the discount

Must Use	DIS04	656	**Discount Control Limit Qualifier**	M	ID 2/3

Code to define the units of the limits for determining discount

Use the same code as provided in the Contract Solicitation Response, 843 transaction set.

Refer to 003040 Data Element Dictionary for acceptable code values.

Must Use	DIS05	657	**Discount Control Limit**	M	N0 1/10

Amount or time minimum for application of the discount.

	DIS06	658	**Upper Discount Control Limit**	O	N0 1/10

Amount or time maximum for application of the discount.

Segment:	**FOB** F.O.B. Related Instructions
Position:	180
Loop:	PO1 Mandatory
Level:	Detail
Usage:	Optional
Max Use:	1
Purpose:	To specify transportation instructions relating to shipment
Syntax Notes:	1 If FOB03 is present, then FOB02 is required.
	2 If FOB04 is present, then FOB05 is required.
	3 If FOB07 is present, then FOB06 is required.
	4 If FOB08 is present, then FOB09 is required.
Semantic Notes:	1 FOB01 indicates which party will pay the carrier.
	2 FOB02 is the code specifying transportation responsibility location.
	3 FOB06 is the code specifying the title passage location.
	4 FOB08 is the code specifying the point at which the risk of loss transfers. This may be different than the location specified in FOB02/FOB03 and FOB06/FOB07.
Comments:	
Notes:	*1. Use this 2/FOB/180 segment to identify the FOB point and acceptance location when they vary by line item. If the FOB point and acceptance location apply to all the line items, use the 1/FOB/080 segment.*
	2. Do not use when the line item is for a service.

Data Element Summary

	Ref. Des.	Data Element	Name		Attributes
Must Use	FOB01	146	**Shipment Method of Payment**	M	ID 2/2

Code identifying payment terms for transportation charges

BP	Paid by Buyer	

The buyer agrees to the transportation payment term requiring the buyer to pay transportation charges to a specified location (origin or destination location)

Use to indicate that the FOB point is origin.

PE	Prepaid and Summary Bill

Use to indicate that the shipping costs are authorized to be prepaid and added to an invoice.

PP	Prepaid (by Seller)

Use to indicate that the FOB point is destination.

	FOB02	309	**Location Qualifier**	X	ID 1/2

Code identifying type of location

1. Use to identify the FOB point.

2. A request has been submitted to ASC X12 to add codes for Port of Embarkation, Port of Loading, and Government Furnished Property FOB Point. We expect these codes will be available for use in ASC X12 Version/Release 3050.

DE	Destination (Shipping)
FV	Free Alongside Vessel (Free On Board [F.O.B.] Point)
IT	Intermediate FOB Point

A location indicating the point of destination is not the origin or final destination but rather at some other point

Use to indicate a freight forwarder.

OR	Origin (Shipping Point)
ZZ	Mutually Defined

Use to indicate that the FOB point is neither origin nor destination. When used, cite the actual FOB point in FOB03. If the actual FOB point is an address or geographical location, use in conjunction with one iteration of the appropriate N1 loop, using code KX in N101.

	FOB03	352	**Description**		O	AN 1/80

A free-form description to clarify the related data elements and their content

Use to identify the FOB point only when FOB02 is code ZZ. If necessary, use one iteration of the N1 loop, using code KX in N101, to specify the address of the FOB point. Use is discouraged.

Not Used	FOB04	334	**Transportation Terms Qualifier Code**		O	ID 2/2

Code identifying the source of the transportation terms

Refer to 003040 Data Element Dictionary for acceptable code values.

Not Used	FOB05	335	**Transportation Terms Code**		X	ID 3/3

Code identifying the trade terms which apply to the shipment transportation responsibility

Refer to 003040 Data Element Dictionary for acceptable code values.

	FOB06	309	**Location Qualifier**		X	ID 1/2

Code identifying type of location

Use to identify the acceptance point.

DE	Destination (Shipping)
OR	Origin (Shipping Point)
ZZ	Mutually Defined

Use to identify the acceptance point when it is neither origin nor destination. When used, cite the actual acceptance point in FOB07. If the actual acceptance point is an address or geographic location, use in conjunction with the appropriate N1 loop, using code ZZ in N101.

	FOB07	352	**Description**		O	AN 1/80

A free-form description to clarify the related data elements and their content

Use to identify the acceptance point when FOB06 is code ZZ. If necessary, use one iteration of the N1 loop, using code ZZ in N101, to specify the address of the acceptance point. Use is discouraged.

Not Used	FOB08	54	**Risk of Loss Qualifier**		O	ID 2/2

Code specifying where responsibility for risk of loss passes

Refer to 003040 Data Element Dictionary for acceptable code values.

Not Used	FOB09	352	**Description**		X	AN 1/80

A free-form description to clarify the related data elements and their content

Segment:	**SDQ** Destination Quantity	
Position:	190	
Loop:	PO1 Mandatory	
Level:	Detail	
Usage:	Optional	
Max Use:	500	
Purpose:	To specify destination and quantity detail	
Syntax Notes:	1	If SDQ05 is present, then SDQ06 is required.
	2	If SDQ07 is present, then SDQ08 is required.
	3	If SDQ09 is present, then SDQ10 is required.
	4	If SDQ11 is present, then SDQ12 is required.
	5	If SDQ13 is present, then SDQ14 is required.
	6	If SDQ15 is present, then SDQ16 is required.
	7	If SDQ17 is present, then SDQ18 is required.
	8	If SDQ19 is present, then SDQ20 is required.
	9	If SDQ21 is present, then SDQ22 is required.
Semantic Notes:	1	SDQ23 identifies the area within the location identified in SDQ03, SDQ05, SDQ07, SDQ09, SDQ11, SDQ13, SDQ15, SDQ17, SDQ19, and SDQ21.
Comments:	1	SDQ02 is used only if different than previously defined in the transaction set.
	2	SDQ23 may be used to identify areas within a store, e.g., front room, back room, selling outpost, end aisle display, etc. The value is agreed to by trading partners or industry conventions.
Notes:		*Use this 2/SDQ/190 segment when known quantities of the line item are to be delivered to multiple locations on the same date, and the locations can be identified by a CAGE code, a DUNs number, a DoDAAC or a MAPAC.*

Data Element Summary

	Ref. Des.	Data Element	Name		Attributes
Must Use	SDQ01	355	**Unit or Basis for Measurement Code**	**M**	**ID 2/2**
			Code specifying the units in which a value is being expressed, or manner in which a measurement has been taken		
			1. Use any code.		
			2. A conversion table may be required to convert agency codes to codes used by ASC X12.		
			Refer to 003040 Data Element Dictionary for acceptable code values.		
	SDQ02	66	**Identification Code Qualifier**	**O**	**ID 1/2**
			Code designating the system/method of code structure used for Identification Code (67)		
			1	D-U-N-S Number, Dun & Bradstreet	
				Use of the DUNs number is preferred over any other coded number to identify a named party.	
			10	Department of Defense Activity Address Code (DODAAC)	
				Use to indicate either a Department of Defense Activity Address Code or a Civilian Agency Activity Address Code.	
			33	Commercial and Government Entity (CAGE)	
				Use to indicate vendors with CAGE codes.	
			A2	Military Assistance Program Address Code (MAPAC)	
				Contained in the Military Assistance Program Address Directory (MAPAD); represents the location of an entity	
				Use to indicate a MAPAC address.	
Must Use	SDQ03	67	**Identification Code**	**M**	**AN 2/17**
			Code identifying a party or other code		
Must Use	SDQ04	380	**Quantity**	**M**	**R 1/15**
			Numeric value of quantity		
	SDQ05	67	**Identification Code**	**O**	**AN 2/17**
			Code identifying a party or other code		

SDQ06	380	**Quantity**	X	R 1/15
		Numeric value of quantity		
SDQ07	67	**Identification Code**	O	AN 2/17
		Code identifying a party or other code		
SDQ08	380	**Quantity**	X	R 1/15
		Numeric value of quantity		
SDQ09	67	**Identification Code**	O	AN 2/17
		Code identifying a party or other code		
SDQ10	380	**Quantity**	X	R 1/15
		Numeric value of quantity		
SDQ11	67	**Identification Code**	O	AN 2/17
		Code identifying a party or other code		
SDQ12	380	**Quantity**	X	R 1/15
		Numeric value of quantity		
SDQ13	67	**Identification Code**	O	AN 2/17
		Code identifying a party or other code		
SDQ14	380	**Quantity**	X	R 1/15
		Numeric value of quantity		
SDQ15	67	**Identification Code**	O	AN 2/17
		Code identifying a party or other code		
SDQ16	380	**Quantity**	X	R 1/15
		Numeric value of quantity		
SDQ17	67	**Identification Code**	O	AN 2/17
		Code identifying a party or other code		
SDQ18	380	**Quantity**	X	R 1/15
		Numeric value of quantity		
SDQ19	67	**Identification Code**	O	AN 2/17
		Code identifying a party or other code		
SDQ20	380	**Quantity**	X	R 1/15
		Numeric value of quantity		
SDQ21	67	**Identification Code**	O	AN 2/17
		Code identifying a party or other code		
SDQ22	380	**Quantity**	X	R 1/15
		Numeric value of quantity		
SDQ23	310	**Location Identifier**	O	AN 1/30
		Code which identifies a specific location		

Segment:	**DTM** Date/Time Reference
Position:	210
Loop:	PO1 Mandatory
Level:	Detail
Usage:	Optional
Max Use:	10
Purpose:	To specify pertinent dates and times
Syntax Notes:	1 At least one of DTM02 DTM03 or DTM06 is required.
	2 If either DTM06 or DTM07 is present, then the other is required.
Semantic Notes:	
Comments:	

Notes:
1. Use this 2/DTM/210 segment to specify a required delivery date when it is expressed as an actual date. If the required delivery schedule is expressed as a set time period after the occurrence of some event, use the 2/LDT/220 segment.

2 Use this 2/DTM/210 segment to specify dates that apply to a line item. Use the 1/DTM/150 segment to specify date that apply to all of the line items.

Data Element Summary

	Ref. Des.	Data Element	Name	Attributes
Must Use	DTM01	374	**Date/Time Qualifier**	M ID 3/3

Code specifying type of date or time, or both date and time

002	Delivery Requested	

Use when an unpriced order is issued. The date cited in DTM02 is assumed to be the estimated date when delivery is desired.

037	Ship Not Before
063	Do Not Deliver After
064	Do Not Deliver Before
065	1st Schedule Delivery
066	1st Schedule Ship
077	Requested for Delivery (Week of)

When this code is used, cite the beginning date of the week.

| 106 | Required By |

Use to indicate delivery is due exactly on the specified date.

| 150 | Service Period Start |

Use to specify the performance commencement date for a line item that is ordering a service.

| 151 | Service Period End |

Use to specify the performance completion date for a line item that is ordering a service.

| 174 | Month Ending |

When this code is used, cite the last date of the month.

| 275 | Approved |

Date report was approved by contractor representative

Use to indicate the approval date of a Contract Data Requirements List (CDRL).

| 368 | Submittal |

Date an item was submitted to a customer

When the 2/REF/100 segment cites code TN in REF01, use to specify the date of the referenced transaction set.

| 405 | Production |

Used to identify dates and times that operations or processes were performed

Use to indicate the preparation date of a Contract Data Requirements List (CDRL).

| 600 | As Of |

Use to indicate the "as of" date for the submission of data.

| 601 | First Submission |

Use to indicate the date of the first submission of a data item specified by Contract Data Requirements List (CDRL).

| 602 | Subsequent Submission |

Use to indicate the date(s) of a subsequent submission(s) of a data item specified by a Contract Data Requirements List (CDRL).

| 994 | Quote |

The date on which a (price) quote was rendered

When REF01 is code PR, use to indicate the date of the bid, quote, or proposal.

996   Required Delivery

A date on which or before, ordered goods or services must be delivered

Use to indicate that delivery is required on or before the specified date.

DTM02	373	**Date**		X	DT 6/6

Date (YYMMDD)

DTM03	337	**Time**		X	TM 4/8

Time expressed in 24-hour clock time as follows: HHMM, or HHMMSS, or HHMMSSD, or HHMMSSDD, where H = hours (00-23), M = minutes (00-59), S = integer seconds (00-59) and DD = decimal seconds; decimal seconds are expressed as follows: D = tenths (0-9) and DD = hundredths (00-99)

DTM04	623	**Time Code**		O	ID 2/2

Code identifying the time. In accordance with International Standards Organization standard 8601, time can be specified by a + or - and an indication in hours in relation to Universal Time Coordinate (UTC) time; since + is a restricted character, + and - are substituted by P and M in the codes that follow

Refer to 003040 Data Element Dictionary for acceptable code values.

Not Used **DTM05**	624	**Century**		O	N0 2/2

The first two characters in the designation of the year (CCYY)

DTM06	1250	**Date Time Period Format Qualifier**		X	ID 2/3

Code indicating the date format, time format, or date and time format

Use only when the date cannot be expressed in YYMMDD format. In that case, use any code and carry the date and/or time in DTM07.

Refer to 003040 Data Element Dictionary for acceptable code values.

DTM07	1251	**Date Time Period**		X	AN 1/35

Expression of a date, a time, or range of dates, times or dates and times

When delivery is specified as a range of time for a given date, e.g., use code RTM in DTM06 to qualify a range of times for a delivery on March 30, 1994 between 1:00 PM and 4:00 PM local time. Use DTM01/02 to convey the March 30, 1994 date.

Segment:	**LDT** Lead Time
Position:	220
Loop:	PO1 Mandatory
Level:	Detail
Usage:	Optional
Max Use:	12
Purpose:	To specify lead time for availability of products and services
Syntax Notes:	
Semantic Notes:	1 LDT04 is the effective date of lead time information.
Comments:	1 LDT02 is the quantity of unit of time periods.
Notes:	*1. Use this 2/LDT/220 segment when the delivery schedule is expressed as a set time period after the occurrence of some event and varies by line item. If the delivery schedule applies to all of the items, use the 1/LDT/160 segment.*
	2. A request has been submitted to ASC X12 to move this segment to a new location and create a loop that includes the QTY and MSG segments and an embedded LM/LQ loop. This loop will provide the capability of specifying multiple delivery schedules (e.g., commence delivery X days after receipt of the order, deliver a specified quantity for a given time period, change the quantity and/or time period for the delivery, etc.) for an individual line item and also provide the frequency of delivery for a data item on a Contract Data Requirements List. If approved this loop will be available for use in ASC X12 Version/Release 3050. Until then, the LDT segment can only specify a single delivery schedule for a specified quantity which must be carried as a separate SUBCLIN.

Part 3

Data Element Summary

	Ref. Des.	Data Element	Name		Attributes	
Must Use	LDT01	345	Lead Time Code		M	ID 2/2

Code indicating the time range

A request has been submitted to ASC X12 to add the following codes: From Date of Latest Delivery to Final Delivery, From Date of Previous Delivery to Subsequent Delivery, From Date of Award to Date of Latest Delivery, From Date of Award to Date of Earliest Delivery, From Date of Award to Date of Completion, and From Date of Award to Date of Delivery. We expect these codes to be available in ASC X12 Version/Release 3050.

AA	From date of PO receipt to sample ready
AD	From date of sample approval to first product shipment
AE	From date of PO receipt to shipment
AF	From date of PO receipt to delivery
AH	From Date of Receipt of First Article to First Article Approval
AI	From Date of a Specified Event to Delivery

Use to indicate that the consignee or other contact must be notified within the time period cited to schedule a shipment. When used, cite the contact communications number in the 1/PER/060 segment.

AZ	From Date of Receipt of Item to Date of Approval of Item

	Ref. Des.	Data Element	Name		Attributes	
Must Use	LDT02	380	Quantity		M	R 1/15

Numeric value of quantity

	Ref. Des.	Data Element	Name		Attributes	
Must Use	LDT03	344	Unit of Time Period or Interval		M	ID 2/2

Code indicating the time period or interval

CY	Calendar Year
DA	Calendar Days
KK	Maximum Calendar Days

Use to indicate a flexible time period, e.g., X number of days or less.

MO	Month
QY	Quarter of a Year
SA	Semiannual
WK	Weeks

	Ref. Des.	Data Element	Name		Attributes	
	LDT04	373	Date		O	DT 6/6

Date (YYMMDD)

Segment:	**SCH** Line Item Schedule
Position:	230
Loop:	PO1　　Mandatory
Level:	Detail
Usage:	Optional
Max Use:	200
Purpose:	To specify the data for scheduling a specific line-item
Syntax Notes:	1　　If SCH03 is present, then SCH04 is required.
	2　　If SCH09 is present, then SCH08 is required.
Semantic Notes:	1　　SCH12 is the schedule identification.
Comments:	1　　SCH05 specifies the interpretation to be used for SCH06 and SCH07.
Notes:	*1. Use this 2/SCH/230 segment to describe a partial delivery when it can be specified as an actual date.*
	2. If the ship-to addresses differ by line item, use the 2/SCH/405 segment.

Data Element Summary

	Ref. Des.	Data Element	Name		Attributes
Must Use	SCH01	380	**Quantity**	M	R 1/15
			Numeric value of quantity		
Must Use	SCH02	355	**Unit or Basis for Measurement Code**	M	ID 2/2
			Code specifying the units in which a value is being expressed, or manner in which a measurement has been taken		
			1. Use any code.		
			2. A conversion table may be required to convert agency codes to codes used by ASC X12.		
			Refer to 003040 Data Element Dictionary for acceptable code values.		
Not Used	SCH03	98	**Entity Identifier Code**	O	ID 2/2
			Code identifying an organizational entity, a physical location, or an individual		
			Refer to 003040 Data Element Dictionary for acceptable code values.		
Not Used	SCH04	93	**Name**	X	AN 1/35
			Free-form name		
Must Use	SCH05	374	**Date/Time Qualifier**	M	ID 3/3
			Code specifying type of date or time, or both date and time		

	002	Delivery Requested
		Use when an unpriced order is issued. The date cited in DTM02 is assumed to be the estimated date when delivery is desired.
	037	Ship Not Before
	063	Do Not Deliver After
	064	Do Not Deliver Before
	065	1st Schedule Delivery
	066	1st Schedule Ship
	077	Requested for Delivery (Week of)
		When this code is used, cite the beginning date of the week.
	106	Required By
		Use to indicate delivery is due exactly on the specified date.
	174	Month Ending
		When this code is used, cite the last date of the month.
	996	Required Delivery
		A date on which or before, ordered goods or services must be delivered
		Use to indicate that delivery is required on or before the specified date.

	Ref. Des.	Data Element	Name		Attributes
Must Use	SCH06	373	**Date**	M	DT 6/6
			Date (YYMMDD)		
Not Used	SCH07	337	**Time**	O	TM 4/8
			Time expressed in 24-hour clock time as follows: HHMM, or HHMMSS, or HHMMSSD, or HHMMSSDD, where H = hours (00-23), M = minutes (00-59), S = integer seconds (00-59) and DD = decimal seconds; decimal seconds are expressed as follows: D = tenths (0-9) and DD = hundredths (00-99)		
	SCH08	374	**Date/Time Qualifier**	X	ID 3/3
			Code specifying type of date or time, or both date and time		

	002	Delivery Requested
		Use when an unpriced order is issued. The date cited in DTM02 is assumed to be the estimated date when delivery is desired.
	063	Do Not Deliver After
	064	Do Not Deliver Before
	065	1st Schedule Delivery
	066	1st Schedule Ship

	077	Requested for Delivery (Week of)	
		When this code is used, cite the beginning date of the week.	
	106	Required By	
		Use to indicate delivery is due exactly on the specified date.	
	174	Month Ending	
		When this code is used, cite the last date of the month.	
	996	Required Delivery	
		A date on which or before, ordered goods or services must be delivered	
		Use to indicate that delivery is required on or before the specified date.	

	Ref. Des.	Data Element	Name		Attributes
	SCH09	373	Date	O	DT 6/6

Date (YYMMDD)

Not Used	SCH10	337	Time	O	TM 4/8

Time expressed in 24-hour clock time as follows: HHMM, or HHMMSS, or HHMMSSD, or HHMMSSDD, where H = hours (00-23), M = minutes (00-59), S = integer seconds (00-59) and DD = decimal seconds; decimal seconds are expressed as follows: D = tenths (0-9) and DD = hundredths (00-99)

Not Used	SCH11	326	Request Reference Number	O	AN 1/45

Reference number or RFQ number to use to identify a particular transaction set and query (additional reference number or description which can be used with contract number)

Not Used	SCH12	350	Assigned Identification	O	AN 1/11

Alphanumeric characters assigned for differentiation within a transaction set

Segment:	**TD5** Carrier Details (Routing Sequence/Transit Time)
Position:	250
Loop:	PO1 Mandatory
Level:	Detail
Usage:	Optional
Max Use:	12
Purpose:	To specify the carrier and sequence of routing and provide transit time information
Syntax Notes:	1 At least one of TD502 TD504 TD505 TD506 or TD512 is required.
	2 If TD502 is present, then TD503 is required.
	3 If TD507 is present, then TD508 is required.
	4 If TD510 is present, then TD511 is required.
Semantic Notes:	
Comments:	1 When specifying a routing sequence to be used for the shipment movement in lieu of specifying each carrier within the movement, use TD502 to identify the party responsible for defining the routing sequence, and use TD503 to identify the actual routing sequence, specified by the party identified in TD502.
Notes:	*1. Use this 2/TD5/250 segment to specify the transportation method that is applicable to a line item. Use the 1/TD5/240 segment if the transportation method applies to all of the items.*
	2. Use the 2/TD5/430 segment when the transportation method applies to a line item and is dependent upon the citing of a named party.

Data Element Summary

	Ref. Des.	Data Element	Name	Attributes	
Not Used	TD501	133	Routing Sequence Code	O	ID 1/2

Code describing the relationship of a carrier to a specific shipment movement

Refer to 003040 Data Element Dictionary for acceptable code values.

	TD502	66	Identification Code Qualifier	X	ID 1/2

Code designating the system/method of code structure used for Identification Code (67)

	10	Department of Defense Activity Address Code (DODAAC)

When TD504 is code PL, use code 10 to identify the number in TD503 as the DoDAAC of the pipeline.

| | TD503 | 67 | **Identification Code** | X | AN 2/17 |

Code identifying a party or other code

| | TD504 | 91 | **Transportation Method/Type Code** | X | ID 1/2 |

Code specifying the method or type of transportation for the shipment

1. Use any code.

2. A conversion table may be required to convert agency codes to codes used by ASC X12.

3. Use code D - Parcel Post to indicate the U.S. Postal Service and not a private carrier.

        D   Parcel Post

Use to indicate the U.S. Postal Service and not a private carrier.

| Not Used | TD505 | 387 | **Routing** | X | AN 1/35 |

Free-form description of the routing or requested routing for shipment, or the originating carrier's identity

| Not Used | TD506 | 368 | **Shipment/Order Status Code** | X | ID 2/2 |

Code indicating the status of an order or shipment or the disposition of any difference between the quantity ordered and the quantity shipped for a line item or transaction

Refer to 003040 Data Element Dictionary for acceptable code values.

| Not Used | TD507 | 309 | **Location Qualifier** | O | ID 1/2 |

Code identifying type of location

Refer to 003040 Data Element Dictionary for acceptable code values.

| Not Used | TD508 | 310 | **Location Identifier** | X | AN 1/30 |

Code which identifies a specific location

| Not Used | TD509 | 731 | **Transit Direction Code** | O | ID 2/2 |

The point of origin and point of direction

Refer to 003040 Data Element Dictionary for acceptable code values.

| Not Used | TD510 | 732 | **Transit Time Direction Qualifier** | O | ID 2/2 |

Code specifying the value of time used to measure the transit time

Refer to 003040 Data Element Dictionary for acceptable code values.

| Not Used | TD511 | 733 | **Transit Time** | X | R 1/4 |

The numeric amount of transit time

| Not Used | TD512 | 284 | **Service Level Code** | X | ID 2/2 |

Code defining service

Refer to 003040 Data Element Dictionary for acceptable code values.

Segment:	**TD4** Carrier Details (Special Handling or Hazardous Materials or Both)
Position:	270
Loop:	PO1 Mandatory
Level:	Detail
Usage:	Optional
Max Use:	5
Purpose:	To specify transportation special handling requirements, or hazardous materials information, or both
Syntax Notes:	1 At least one of TD401 TD402 or TD404 is required.
	2 If TD402 is present, then TD403 is required.
Semantic Notes:	
Comments:	
Notes:	*Use this 2/TD4/270 segment to provide hazardous material information that varies by line items. If the hazardous material information applies to all the line items, use the 1/TD4/260 segment.*

Data Element Summary

Ref. Des.	Data Element	Name		Attributes	
TD401	152	**Special Handling Code**		X	ID 2/3
		Code specifying special transportation handling instructions			
		HM	Endorsed as Hazardous Material		
		NC	Notify Consignee Before Delivery		
TD402	208	**Hazardous Material Code Qualifier**		X	ID 1/1
		Code which qualifies the Hazardous Material Class Code (209)			

> *A request for the following codes has been submitted to ASC X12: Storage Compatibility Group and Hazard Class or Division. We expect these codes to be available in ASC X12 Version/Release 3050.*

		D	Hazardous Materials ID, DOT		
TD403	209	**Hazardous Material Class Code**		X	AN 2/4
		Code specifying the kind of hazard for a material			
TD404	352	**Description**		X	AN 1/80
		A free-form description to clarify the related data elements and their content			

> *Use is discouraged.*

Segment:	**MAN** Marks and Numbers
Position:	280
Loop:	PO1 Mandatory
Level:	Detail
Usage:	Optional
Max Use:	10
Purpose:	To indicate identifying marks and numbers for shipping containers
Syntax Notes:	
Semantic Notes:	1 When both MAN02 and MAN03 are used, MAN02 is the starting number of a sequential range and MAN03 is the ending number of that range.
	2 When both MAN05 and MAN06 are used, MAN05 is the starting number of a sequential range, and MAN06 is the ending number of that range.
Comments:	
Notes:	*1. Use this 2/MAN/280 segment to provide marks and numbers that vary by line item. If the marks and numbers apply to all of the line items, use the 1/MAN/270 segment.*
	2. Use to identify such data as MILSTRIP/FEDSTRIP number, Transportation Control number, Project Priority number, and consignee related codes.

Data Element Summary

	Ref. Des.	Data Element	Name		Attributes	
Must Use	MAN01	88	**Marks and Numbers Qualifier**		M	ID 1/2
			Code specifying the application or source of Marks and Numbers (87)			
			L	Line Item Only		
Must Use	MAN02	87	**Marks and Numbers**		M	AN 1/45
			Marks and numbers used to identify a shipment or parts of a shipment			
	MAN03	87	**Marks and Numbers**		O	AN 1/45
			Marks and numbers used to identify a shipment or parts of a shipment			
	MAN04	88	**Marks and Numbers Qualifier**		O	ID 1/2
			Code specifying the application or source of Marks and Numbers (87)			
			L	Line Item Only		
	MAN05	87	**Marks and Numbers**		O	AN 1/45
			Marks and numbers used to identify a shipment or parts of a shipment			

MAN06 87   **Marks and Numbers**   O   AN 1/45
                   Marks and numbers used to identify a shipment or parts of a shipment

Segment:	**AMT** Monetary Amount
Position:	290
Loop:	PO1 Mandatory
Level:	Detail
Usage:	Optional
Max Use:	1
Purpose:	To indicate the total monetary amount
Syntax Notes:	
Semantic Notes:	
Comments:	
Notes:	*Use this segment to specify the total amount of the line item.*

Data Element Summary

	Ref. Des.	Data Element	Name		Attributes
Must Use	AMT01	522	**Amount Qualifier Code**		M ID 1/2
			Code to qualify amount		
			1	Line Item Total	
Must Use	AMT02	782	**Monetary Amount**		M R 1/15
			Monetary amount		

Segment:	**PKG** Marking, Packaging, Loading
Position:	300
Loop:	PKG Optional
Level:	Detail
Usage:	Optional
Max Use:	1
Purpose:	To describe marking, packaging, loading, and unloading requirements
Syntax Notes:	1 At least one of PKG04 PKG05 or PKG06 is required.
	2 If PKG04 is present, then PKG01 is required.
	3 If PKG05 is present, then PKG01 is required.
Semantic Notes:	1 PKG04 should be used for industry-specific packaging description codes.
Comments:	1 Use the MEA (Measurements) Segment to define dimensions, tolerances, weights, counts, physical restrictions, etc.
	2 If PKG01 = "F", then PKG05 is used. If PKG01 = "S", then PKG04 is used. If PKG01 = "X", then both PKG04 and PKG05 are used.
	3 Use PKG03 to indicate the organization that publishes the code list being referred to.
	4 Special marking or tagging data can be given in PKG05 (description).
Notes:	*1. Use this 2/PKG/300 segment if the packaging information applies to a line item. If the packaging information applies to all the line items, use the 1/PKG/220 segment.*
	2. A request has been submitted to ASC X12 to add MIL-STD 2073-2C codes to ASC X12 standards. If approved, those codes will be available for use in ASC X12 Version/Release 3050 and they will be carried in PKG02/03/04. Until those codes are available, packaging information can be transmitted as a MIL-STD 2073-2C code string (as is currently done in a paper instrument) in PKG05. If additional packaging information is required to be provided to prospective bidders the N9 loop (code K7) can be used.
	3. Do not use when standard commercial packaging is acceptable.

Part 3

Data Element Summary

Ref. Des.	Data Element	Name		Attributes	
PKG01	349	**Item Description Type**		X	ID 1/1
		Code indicating the format of a description			
		F	Free-form		
			Use when the packaging information is provided in free-form text.		
		S	Structured (From Industry Code List)		
			Use when the packaging information is provided as a MIL-STD 2073-2C code string.		
		X	Semi-structured (Code and Text)		
			Use when the packaging information is provided as both free-form text and a MIL-STD 2073-2C code string.		
PKG02	753	**Packaging Characteristic Code**		O	ID 1/5
		Code specifying the marking, packaging, loading and related characteristics being described			
		A request has been submitted to ASC X12 to add MIL-STD 2073-2C packaging characteristic codes, e.g., CD - Cleaning/Drying Procedures, CT - Cushioning Thickness, etc. We expect those codes to be available in ASC X12 Version/Release 3050. In the meantime, use code 65 when providing MIL-STD 2073-2C code string in PKG05.			
		65	Core Characteristics		
			Use to indicate MIL-STD 2073-2C packaging codes. Cite the code string in PKG05.		
PKG03	559	**Agency Qualifier Code**		O	ID 2/2
		Code identifying the agency assigning the code values			
		DD	Department of Defense		
			Responsible for Military Specification		
		GS	General Services Administration (GSA)		
			Responsible for Federal Specification		
		ZZ	Mutually Defined		
			Use to indicate an activity other than DoD or GSA. Data maintenance has been submitted to ASC X12. If approved a code for Federal Government will be available in ASC X12 Version/Release 3060.		
Not Used	**PKG04**	754	**Packaging Description Code**	X	AN 1/7
		A code from an industry code list which provides specific data about the marking, packaging or loading and unloading of a product			
	PKG05	352	**Description**	X	AN 1/80
		A free-form description to clarify the related data elements and their content			
		Use to identify a string of MIL-STD 2073-2C packaging codes or to provide packaging information in free-form text. The MIL-STD 2073-2C code string uses a positional and sequential system. Coded data must appear in the sequence and the number of positions specified in Appendix F of MIL-STD 2073-1. Zeros shall be inserted in the code string for data that is not being provided. A comma (,) will be used as a delimiter between the data in the code string. Use of this data element is discouraged.			
Not Used	**PKG06**	400	**Unit Load Option Code**	X	ID 2/2
		Code identifying loading or unloading a shipment			
		Refer to 003040 Data Element Dictionary for acceptable code values.			

Segment:	**N9** Reference Number				
Position:	330				
Loop:	N9 Optional				
Level:	Detail				
Usage:	Optional				
Max Use:	1				
Purpose:	To transmit identifying numbers and descriptive information as specified by the reference number qualifier				
Syntax Notes:	1 At least one of N902 or N903 is required.				
	2 If N906 is present, then N905 is required.				
Semantic Notes:	1 N906 reflects the time zone which the time reflects.				
Comments:					

Notes: *1. Use the 2/N9/330 loop to specify clauses, special instructions, or other references which are applicable to a line item.*

2. When an alternate section is relevant for a cited clause, concatenate the alpha/numeric alternate cite with the clause number in N902.

Data Element Summary

	Ref. Des.	Data Element	Name	Attributes	
Must Use	N901	128	**Reference Number Qualifier**	M	ID 2/2

Code qualifying the Reference Number.

A request has been submitted to ASC X12 to add codes for Circular number, which will be used to specify an OMB Circular number, Special Instruction, and Federal Information Resources Management Regulation. We expect these codes to be available for use in ASC X12 Version/Release 3050.

73   Statement of Work (SOW)

Description of a product or service to be procured under a contract; statement of requirements

CJ   Clause Number

Use to indicate a purchasing activity generated clause or special provision not found in the FAR, DFARS, Agency acquisition regulation supplement, or FIRMR. Identify the source of the clause in N903.

DD   Document Identification Code

Use to indicate a Department of Labor wage determination.

DF   Defense Federal Acquisition Regulations (DFAR)

Use to indicate a clause found in the DFARS.

DX   Department/Agency Number

Use to indicate an agency clause and specify the agency in N903.

FA   Federal Acquisition Regulations (FAR)

GS   General Services Administration Regulations (GSAR)

K7   Paragraph Number

Use to identify information for contractors, e.g., packaging information. Cite an applicable number in N902 and provide the information in the following MSG segment. The numbering system can be based on the uniform contract format, e.g., H-1 for special requirements, or any other numbering system the originator desires. The 2/REF/100 segment can then be used to cite the reference when it is applicable to a line item.

KT   Request for Quotation Reference

A discrete number assigned for identification purposes to a request for quotation

Use to indicate another type of reference number applicable to the solicitation. This number is not the RFQ number (which is found in BQT02). Indicate the source of the reference in N903 and provide, if necessary, the text of the item in the following MSG segment.

	KY		Site Specific Procedures, Terms, and Conditions		

A set of procedures, terms, and conditions, applicable to a category of procurement emanating from a specific location, which will be incorporated into all procurement actions in that category by referencing its unique number rather than by incorporating the lengthy details it represents

| | KZ | | Master Solicitation Procedures, Terms, and Conditions | | |

A set of standard procedures, terms, and conditions, applicable to a category of procurement, which will be incorporated into all procurement actions in that category by referencing its unique number rather than by incorporating the lengthy details it represents

Use, if applicable, to indicate the master solicitation that contains applicable terms and conditions.

| | VB | | Department of Veterans Affairs Acquisition Regulations (VAAR) | | |
| | ZZ | | Mutually Defined | | |

Use to identify any other reference that cannot use a specific qualifier code. Indicate in N903 the source of the reference and use the following MSG segment for text, if necessary.

	N902	127	**Reference Number**	X	AN 1/30

Reference number or identification number as defined for a particular Transaction Set, or as specified by the Reference Number Qualifier.

	N903	369	**Free-form Description**	X	AN 1/45

Free-form descriptive text

Use is discouraged.

	N904	373	**Date**	O	DT 6/6

Date (YYMMDD)

Use to indicate the date of a clause, wage determination, or other reference. When the date is used it will be in YYMMDD format so a clause date should always end with the numeric 01 indicating the first day of the month. This rule is necessary to comply with ASC X12 syntax.

Not Used	N905	337	**Time**	X	TM 4/8

Time expressed in 24-hour clock time as follows: HHMM, or HHMMSS, or HHMMSSD, or HHMMSSDD, where H = hours (00-23), M = minutes (00-59), S = integer seconds (00-59) and DD = decimal seconds; decimal seconds are expressed as follows: D = tenths (0-9) and DD = hundredths (00-99)

Not Used	N906	623	**Time Code**	O	ID 2/2

Code identifying the time. In accordance with International Standards Organization standard 8601, time can be specified by a + or - and an indication in hours in relation to Universal Time Coordinate (UTC) time; since + is a restricted character, + and - are substituted by P and M in the codes that follow

Refer to 003040 Data Element Dictionary for acceptable code values.

Segment:	**MSG** Message Text
Position:	340
Loop:	N9 Optional
Level:	Detail
Usage:	Optional
Max Use:	1000
Purpose:	To provide a free form format that would allow the transmission of text information.
Syntax Notes:	
Semantic Notes:	
Comments:	1 MSG02 is not related to the specific characteristics of a printer, but identifies top of page, advance a line, etc.
Notes:	*1. Use this segment to carry the title and full text, if required, a special instruction, or other information associated with the number cited in N902.*
	2. Use of this segment is discouraged.

Data Element Summary

	Ref. Des.	Data Element	Name		Attributes
Must Use	MSG01	933	**Free-Form Message Text**	M	AN 1/264
			Free-form message text		
Not Used	MSG02	934	**Printer Carriage Control Code**	O	ID 2/2
			A field to be used for the control of the line feed of the receiving printer		
			Refer to 003040 Data Element Dictionary for acceptable code values.		

Segment:	**N1** Name
Position:	350
Loop:	N1 Optional
Level:	Detail
Usage:	Optional
Max Use:	1
Purpose:	To identify a party by type of organization, name, and code
Syntax Notes:	1 At least one of N102 or N103 is required.
	2 If either N103 or N104 is present, then the other is required.
Semantic Notes:	
Comments:	1 This segment, used alone, provides the most efficient method of providing organizational identification. To obtain this efficiency the "ID Code" (N104) must provide a key to the table maintained by the transaction processing party.
	2 N105 and N106 further define the type of entity in N101.
Notes:	*1. Whenever possible, address information should be transmitted using code values contained in a combination of the N101, N103/04 data elements. Use N102 and the N2-N4 segments only when it is necessary to transmit the full address. For example, if a vendor can be identified by a DUNs number, it is not necessary to transmit the vendor's full address since the relationship between the DUNs number and the vendor's address can be established by accessing a data base in which the information is stored, having been put there at the time the vendor electronically registered as a federal government trading partner.*
	2. Use the 2/N1/340 loop to identify organizations or people that vary by line item. If the organizations or people apply to all of the line items, use the 1/N1/310 loop.

Data Element Summary

	Ref. Des.	Data Element	Name		Attributes
Must Use	N101	98	**Entity Identifier Code**	M	ID 2/2
			Code identifying an organizational entity, a physical location, or an individual		
			A request has been submitted to ASC X12 to add additional codes for Contracting Officer Representative Party Authorized to Definitize Contract Action, Government Furnished Property FOB Point, Party to Receive Proposal, and Transportation Office. We expect these codes will be available for use in ASC X12 Version/Release 3050.		
		28	Subcontractor		
		31	Postal Mailing Address		
			Use only when an actual mailing address is required, and is different from the address provided for any other qualifier code. Do not use if another qualifier code can be used to pass this address. When used, cite the name of the party in N102 and N2 segment, if necessary.		
		61	Performed At		
			The facility where work was performed		
			Use to indicate a preliminary inspection location for a first article. A request has been submitted to ASC X12 to add a code for Preliminary Inspection Location. We expect this code will be available for use in ASC X12 Version/Release 3050. In the meantime, use this code.		
		88	Approver		

	Manufacturer's representative approving claim for payment
	Use to indicate the party approving a Contract Data Requirements List (CDRL).
AE	Additional Delivery Address
	Use to indicate a shipment in-place location.
BT	Bill-to-Party
	Use to indicate the party who will provide reimbursement for the payment of a contractor's invoice. This is an internal government billed party and not the party the contractor bills. Use is discouraged. Use only when the vendor receiving the order or other party receiving the order or a copy of the order, needs to receive this information.
BY	Buying Party (Purchaser)
	Use to indicate the purchasing office or activity.
CP	Party to Receive Cert. of Compliance
	Use to indicate the party to receive a Certificate of Conformance.
DZ	Delivery Zone
	Area where the product was delivered
	Use to indicate a geographic area to which deliveries are to be made under an indefinite delivery or requirements contract. Specify the zone in N104 (1, 2, 3, etc.) and identify the state or countries in the zone in N405/06. A separate SUBCLIN must be established for each item that will be delivered to a specific zone.
IC	Intermediate Consignee
	Use to indicate a freight forwarder.
KE	Place of Performance
KX	Free on Board Point
	Use to indicate the FOB point when it has to be described by a specific address rather than as a code value indicating either origin or destination.
KY	Technical Office
	Use to indicate the technical office that has cognizance over the technical portion of the order, if different than the office originating the order. Do not use unless it is intended for the vendor to deal directly with the cited party.
L1	Inspection Location
	Place where the item was viewed or inspected
	Use to indicate the inspection location when it has to be described as a specific address rather than a location such as origin or destination.
MF	Manufacturer of Goods
MP	Manufacturing Plant
	Use to indicate the manufacturing facility, if different from the contractor or contractor's mailing address.
OB	Ordered By
OH	Other Departments
	Use to indicate the Hazardous Materials Office. A request has been submitted to ASC X12 to add a code for this location. If approved it will be available for use in ASC X12 Version/Release 3050. Until that time, use this code.
OI	Outside Inspection Agency
	Use to indicate the inspecting activity is other than the Contract Administration Office.
P1	Preparer
	The firm, organization, or individual who determines the tax liability from information supplied by the taxpayer
	Use to indicate the preparer of a Contract Data Requirements List (CDRL).
PO	Party to Receive Invoice for Goods or Services

Use to indicate where the invoice should be mailed.

PZ   Party to Receive Equipment

Name a party to receive the transfer of equipment

Use to indicate the requesting agency/activity. A request has been submitted to ASC X12 to add a code for Requestor. We expect this code will be available for use in ASC X12 Version/Release 3060. In the meantime, use this code.

RC   Receiving Location

Use to indicate a location where the material will be both inspected and accepted. A request has been submitted to ASC X12 to add a code for Inspection and Acceptance. We expect this code to be available for use in ASC X12 Version/Release 3050. Until that time, use this code.

SK   Secondary Location Address (SLA)

Identifies a physical address location in which a telecommunications circuit terminates; this address is in addition to a main service address

Use to indicate a preliminary inspection location for a first article. A request has been submitted to ASC X12 to add a code for Preliminary Inspection Location. We expect this code will be available for use in ASC X12 Version/Release 3050. In the meantime, use this code.

ST   Ship To

Use to indicate the address to which an item must be shipped. If the ship-to address is an FPO or APO, identify the FPO or APO in the N4 segment using N401 and N403.

SV   Service Performance Site

When services are contracted for, this describes the organization for whom or location address at which those services will be performed

Use to indicate the location where a service is to be performed.

X2   Party to Perform Packaging

A party responsible for packaging an item after it has been produced

Z7   Mark-for Party

The party for whom the needed material is intended

ZZ   Mutually Defined

Use to identify the acceptance location when it cannot be described using a point such as origin or destination. Data maintenance has been submitted to ASC X12 asking for a code for Acceptance Point. If approved, the code will be available in ASC X12 Version/Release 3050.

N102   93   **Name**   X   AN 1/35

Free-form name

N103   66   **Identification Code Qualifier**   X   ID 1/2

Code designating the system/method of code structure used for Identification Code (67)

1. Use, when applicable, to identify the named party.

2. A request has been submitted to ASC X12 to add a code for Contractor Establishment Code. We expect this code to be available for use in the ASC X12 Version/Release 3050.

3. While Federal EDI will use the DUNS number, other numbers may be required for a period of transition in order to cross-reference existing data bases with new procurement actions.

1   D-U-N-S Number, Dun & Bradstreet

Use of the DUNs number is preferred over any other coded number to identify a named party.

10   Department of Defense Activity Address Code (DODAAC)

Use to indicate either a Department of Defense Activity Address Code or a Civilian Agency Activity Address Code.

33   Commercial and Government Entity (CAGE)

Use to indicate vendors with CAGE codes.

A2   Military Assistance Program Address Code (MAPAC)

			Contained in the Military Assistance Program Address Directory (MAPAD); represents the location of an entity		
			Use to indicate a MAPAC address.		
		FA	Facility Identification		
			Use to indicate a vendor facility that cannot be identified by either a CAGE code or a DUNS number.		
		ZN	Zone		
			Use to identify a delivery zone when N101 is code DZ. Specify the zone in N104, e.g., 1, 2, 3, etc.		
	N104	67	**Identification Code**	X	AN 2/17
			Code identifying a party or other code		
Not Used	N105	706	**Entity Relationship Code**	O	ID 2/2
			Code describing entity relationship		
			Refer to 003040 Data Element Dictionary for acceptable code values.		
Not Used	N106	98	**Entity Identifier Code**	O	ID 2/2
			Code identifying an organizational entity, a physical location, or an individual		
			Refer to 003040 Data Element Dictionary for acceptable code values.		

Segment:	**N2** Additional Name Information
Position:	360
Loop:	N1 Optional
Level:	Detail
Usage:	Optional
Max Use:	2
Purpose:	To specify additional names or those longer than 35 characters in length
Syntax Notes:	
Semantic Notes:	
Comments:	
Notes:	*This segment is not necessary when the cited party can be identified by a code value in N101/03/04.*

Data Element Summary

	Ref. Des.	Data Element	Name	Attributes	
Must Use	N201	93	**Name**	M	AN 1/35
			Free-form name		
	N202	93	**Name**	O	AN 1/35
			Free-form name		

Segment:	**N3** Address Information
Position:	370
Loop:	N1 Optional
Level:	Detail
Usage:	Optional
Max Use:	2
Purpose:	To specify the location of the named party
Syntax Notes:	
Semantic Notes:	
Comments:	
Notes:	*This segment is not necessary when the cited party can be identified by a code value in N101/03/04.*

Data Element Summary

	Ref. Des.	Data Element	Name		Attributes	
Must Use	N301	166	**Address Information**		M	AN 1/35
			Address information			
	N302	166	**Address Information**		O	AN 1/35
			Address information			

Segment:	**N4** Geographic Location
Position:	380
Loop:	N1 Optional
Level:	Detail
Usage:	Optional
Max Use:	1
Purpose:	To specify the geographic place of the named party
Syntax Notes:	1 If N406 is present, then N405 is required.
Semantic Notes:	
Comments:	1 A combination of either N401 through N404, or N405 and N406 may be adequate to specify a location.
	2 N402 is required only if city name (N401) is in the USA or Canada.
Notes:	*1. This segment is not necessary when the cited party can be identified by a code value in N101/03/04.*
	2. When identifying an APO/FPO, N401 carries the APO/FPO city name and N403 carries the ZIP code of the city.
	3. A request has been submitted to ASC X12 to increase the maximum use of this segment to greater than 1 to accommodate specifying multiple states or countries in a delivery zone. We expect this maximum use to be available in ASC X12 Version/Release 3050.

Data Element Summary

Ref. Des.	Data Element	Name		Attributes	
N401	19	**City Name**		O	AN 2/30
		Free-form text for city name			
N402	156	**State or Province Code**		O	ID 2/2
		Code (Standard State/Province) as defined by appropriate government agency			
N403	116	**Postal Code**		O	ID 3/9
		Code defining international postal zone code excluding punctuation and blanks (zip code for United States)			
N404	26	**Country Code**		O	ID 2/3
		Code identifying the country			
		A conversion table may be required to convert agency codes to codes used by ASC X12.			
N405	309	**Location Qualifier**		X	ID 1/2
		Code identifying type of location			
		CC	Country		
			When N101 is code DZ, if applicable, use to indicate a country in the delivery zone.		
		SP	State/Province		
			When N101 is code DZ, if applicable, use to indicate a state or province in the delivery zone.		
N406	310	**Location Identifier**		O	AN 1/30
		Code which identifies a specific location			

Segment:	**REF** Reference Numbers	
Position:	390	
Loop:	N1 Optional	
Level:	Detail	
Usage:	Optional	
Max Use:	12	
Purpose:	To specify identifying numbers.	
Syntax Notes:	1 At least one of REF02 or REF03 is required.	
Semantic Notes:		
Comments:		
Notes:	*Use this segment to specify reference numbers associated with a delivery, i.e., when N101 is code ST.*	

Data Element Summary

	Ref. Des.	Data Element	Name		Attributes
Must Use	REF01	128	**Reference Number Qualifier**	M	ID 2/2
			Code qualifying the Reference Number.		
			AX Government Accounting Class Reference Number (ACRN)		
			IL Internal Order Number		
			Use to indicate the requisition (MILSTRIP) document number.		
			TG Transportation Control Number (TCN)		
	REF02	127	**Reference Number**	X	AN 1/30
			Reference number or identification number as defined for a particular Transaction Set, or as specified by the Reference Number Qualifier.		
Not Used	REF03	352	**Description**	X	AN 1/80
			A free-form description to clarify the related data elements and their content		

Segment:	**PER** Administrative Communications Contact	
Position:	400	
Loop:	N1 Optional	
Level:	Detail	
Usage:	Optional	
Max Use:	3	
Purpose:	To identify a person or office to whom administrative communications should be directed	
Syntax Notes:	1 If either PER03 or PER04 is present, then the other is required.	
	2 If either PER05 or PER06 is present, then the other is required.	
Semantic Notes:		
Comments:		
Notes:	*Use this segment to specify the accepting official either at origin (N101 is code C4) or at destination (N101 is code ST).*	

Data Element Summary

	Ref. Des.	Data Element	Name		Attributes
Must Use	PER01	366	**Contact Function Code**	M	ID 2/2
			Code identifying the major duty or responsibility of the person or group named		
			CN General Contact		
			When N101 is code ST, use to indicate the accepting official at destination.		
			RP Responsible Person		
			When N101 is code C4, use to indicate the accepting official at origin.		
	PER02	93	**Name**	O	AN 1/35
			Free-form name		

Cite the last name first, followed by the first name. Do not truncate the last name if the whole name is longer than 35 characters. Instead, truncate or use the initial of the first name.

PER03	365	**Communication Number Qualifier**	X	ID 2/2

Code identifying the type of communication number

AU	Defense Switched Network
	Department of Defense telecommunications system and successor of the Automatic Voice Network (AUTOVON)
EM	Electronic Mail
FX	Facsimile
IT	International Telephone
TE	Telephone

Use to indicate commercial telephone number of the individual cited in PER02.

PER04	364	**Communication Number**	X	AN 1/80

Complete communications number including country or area code when applicable

When PER03 is code TE, include the area code.

PER05	365	**Communication Number Qualifier**	X	ID 2/2

Code identifying the type of communication number

Use to specify a second communication number for the party cited PER02. For example, if PER03/04 cites the commercial telephone number, then PER05/06 can be used to cite an electronic mail number.

AU	Defense Switched Network
	Department of Defense telecommunications system and successor of the Automatic Voice Network (AUTOVON)
EM	Electronic Mail
EX	Telephone Extension

Use only if PER03 is used citing either code AU or TE.

FX	Facsimile
IT	International Telephone
TE	Telephone

PER06	364	**Communication Number**	X	AN 1/80

Complete communications number including country or area code when applicable

Segment:	**SCH** Line Item Schedule
Position:	415
Loop:	N1 Optional
Level:	Detail
Usage:	Optional
Max Use:	200
Purpose:	To specify the data for scheduling a specific line-item
Syntax Notes:	1 If SCH03 is present, then SCH04 is required.
	2 If SCH09 is present, then SCH08 is required.
Semantic Notes:	1 SCH12 is the schedule identification.
Comments:	1 SCH05 specifies the interpretation to be used for SCH06 and SCH07.
Notes:	*Use the 2/SCH/405 segment to describe a partial delivery when it can be specified as an actual date and the ship-to address differs by line item. If a single ship-to address was identified in the 1/N1/310 loop, use the 2/SCH/230 segment.*

Part

Data Element Summary

	Ref. Des.	Data Element	Name		Attributes
Must Use	SCH01	380	**Quantity**	M	R 1/15

Numeric value of quantity

	Ref. Des.	Data Element	Name		Attributes
Must Use	SCH02	355	**Unit or Basis for Measurement Code**	M	ID 2/2

Code specifying the units in which a value is being expressed, or manner in which a measurement has been taken

1. Use any code.

2. A conversion table may be required to convert agency codes to codes used by ASC X12.

Refer to 003040 Data Element Dictionary for acceptable code values.

	Ref. Des.	Data Element	Name		Attributes
Not Used	SCH03	98	**Entity Identifier Code**	O	ID 2/2

Code identifying an organizational entity, a physical location, or an individual

Refer to 003040 Data Element Dictionary for acceptable code values.

	Ref. Des.	Data Element	Name		Attributes
Not Used	SCH04	93	**Name**	X	AN 1/35

Free-form name

	Ref. Des.	Data Element	Name		Attributes
Must Use	SCH05	374	**Date/Time Qualifier**	M	ID 3/3

Code specifying type of date or time, or both date and time

002	Delivery Requested

Use when an unpriced order is issued. Assumed to be an estimated date.

037	Ship Not Before
063	Do Not Deliver After
064	Do Not Deliver Before
065	1st Schedule Delivery
066	1st Schedule Ship
077	Requested for Delivery (Week of)

When this code is used, cite the beginning date of the week.

106	Required By

Use to indicate delivery is due exactly on the specified date.

174	Month Ending

When this code is used, cite the last date of the month.

996	Required Delivery

A date on which or before, ordered goods or services must be delivered

Use to indicate that delivery is required on or before the specified date.

	Ref. Des.	Data Element	Name		Attributes
Must Use	SCH06	373	**Date**	M	DT 6/6

Date (YYMMDD)

	Ref. Des.	Data Element	Name		Attributes
Not Used	SCH07	337	**Time**	O	TM 4/8

Time expressed in 24-hour clock time as follows: HHMM, or HHMMSS, or HHMMSSD, or HHMMSSDD, where H = hours (00-23), M = minutes (00-59), S = integer seconds (00-59) and DD = decimal seconds; decimal seconds are expressed as follows: D = tenths (0-9) and DD = hundredths (00-99)

	Ref. Des.	Data Element	Name		Attributes
	SCH08	374	**Date/Time Qualifier**	X	ID 3/3

Code specifying type of date or time, or both date and time

002	Delivery Requested

Use when an unpriced order is issued. Assumed to be an estimated date.

077	Requested for Delivery (Week of)

When this code is used, cite the beginning date of the week.

106	Required By

Use to indicate delivery is due exactly on the specified date.

174	Month Ending

When this code is used, cite the last date of the month.

996   Required Delivery

A date on which or before, ordered goods or services must be delivered

Use to indicate that delivery is required on or before the specified date.

	SCH09	373	**Date**	O	DT 6/6

Date (YYMMDD)

Not Used	SCH10	337	**Time**	O	TM 4/8

Time expressed in 24-hour clock time as follows: HHMM, or HHMMSS, or HHMMSSD, or HHMMSSDD, where H = hours (00-23), M = minutes (00-59), S = integer seconds (00-59) and DD = decimal seconds; decimal seconds are expressed as follows: D = tenths (0-9) and DD = hundredths (00-99)

	SCH11	326	**Request Reference Number**	O	AN 1/45

Reference number or RFQ number to use to identify a particular transaction set and query (additional reference number or description which can be used with contract number)

Use, as applicable, to cross-reference to cited line item, for example, to an RFQ or requisition number.

Not Used	SCH12	350	**Assigned Identification**	O	AN 1/11

Alphanumeric characters assigned for differentiation within a transaction set

---

Segment:	**TD5** Carrier Details (Routing Sequence/Transit Time)
Position:	430
Loop:	N1 Optional
Level:	Detail
Usage:	Optional
Max Use:	12
Purpose:	To specify the carrier and sequence of routing and provide transit time information
Syntax Notes:	1 At least one of TD502 TD504 TD505 TD506 or TD512 is required.
	2 If TD502 is present, then TD503 is required.
	3 If TD507 is present, then TD508 is required.
	4 If TD510 is present, then TD511 is required.
Semantic Notes:	
Comments:	1 When specifying a routing sequence to be used for the shipment movement in lieu of specifying each carrier within the movement, use TD502 to identify the party responsible for defining the routing sequence, and use TD503 to identify the actual routing sequence, specified by the party identified in TD502.
Notes:	*Use the 2/TD5/430 segment when the transportation method is applicable to a named entity for a line item. If the transportation method is not dependent on the citing of a named party but varies by line item, use the 2/TD5/250 segment.*

Data Element Summary

	Ref. Des.	Data Element	Name		Attributes
Not Used	TD501	133	**Routing Sequence Code**	O	ID 1/2

Code describing the relationship of a carrier to a specific shipment movement

Refer to 003040 Data Element Dictionary for acceptable code values.

	TD502	66	**Identification Code Qualifier**	X	ID 1/2

Code designating the system/method of code structure used for Identification Code (67)

10   Department of Defense Activity Address Code (DODAAC)

When TD504 is code PL, use code 10 to indicate the number in TD503 is the DoDAAC of the pipeline.

	TD503	67	**Identification Code**	X	AN 2/17

Code identifying a party or other code

	TD504	91	**Transportation Method/Type Code**	X	ID 1/2

Part 3

Code specifying the method or type of transportation for the shipment

1. Use any code.

2. A conversion table may be required to convert agency codes to codes used by ASC X12.

3. Use code D to indicate the U.S. Postal Service and not a private carrier.

D	Parcel Post	
	Use to indicate the U.S. Postal Service and not a private carrier.	

Not Used	TD505	387	**Routing**	X	AN 1/35

Free-form description of the routing or requested routing for shipment, or the originating carrier's identity

Not Used	TD506	368	**Shipment/Order Status Code**	X	ID 2/2

Code indicating the status of an order or shipment or the disposition of any difference between the quantity ordered and the quantity shipped for a line item or transaction

Refer to 003040 Data Element Dictionary for acceptable code values.

Not Used	TD507	309	**Location Qualifier**	O	ID 1/2

Code identifying type of location

Refer to 003040 Data Element Dictionary for acceptable code values.

Not Used	TD508	310	**Location Identifier**	X	AN 1/30

Code which identifies a specific location

Not Used	TD509	731	**Transit Direction Code**	O	ID 2/2

The point of origin and point of direction

Refer to 003040 Data Element Dictionary for acceptable code values.

Not Used	TD510	732	**Transit Time Direction Qualifier**	O	ID 2/2

Code specifying the value of time used to measure the transit time

Refer to 003040 Data Element Dictionary for acceptable code values.

Not Used	TD511	733	**Transit Time**	X	R 1/4

The numeric amount of transit time

Not Used	TD512	284	**Service Level Code**	X	ID 2/2

Code defining service

Refer to 003040 Data Element Dictionary for acceptable code values.

Segment:	**CTT** Transaction Totals
Position:	010
Loop:	
Level:	Summary
Usage:	Mandatory
Max Use:	1
Purpose:	To transmit a hash total for a specific element in the transaction set
Syntax Notes:	1 If CTT03 is present, then CTT04 is required.
	2 If CTT05 is present, then CTT06 is required.
Semantic Notes:	
Comments:	1 This segment is intended to provide hash totals to validate transaction completeness and correctness.

Data Element Summary

	Ref. Des.	Data Element	Name	Attributes	
Must Use	CTT01	354	**Number of Line Items**	M	N0 1/6
			Total number of line items in the transaction set		
			Enter the total number of PO1 segments contained in this transaction set.		
	CTT02	347	**Hash Total**	O	R 1/10

Sum of values of the specified data element. All values in the data element will be summed without regard to decimal points (explicit or implicit) or signs. Truncation will occur on the left most digits if the sum is greater than the maximum size of the hash total of the data element.

Example:

-.0018 First occurrence of value being hashed. .18 Second occurrence of value being hashed. 1.8 Third occurrence of value being hashed. 18.01 Fourth occurrence of value being hashed. ------- 1855 Hash total prior to truncation. 855 Hash total after truncation to three-digit field.

CTT02 is the sum of the value of quantities ordered (PO102) for each PO1 segment. Never use to carry an operational amount.

Not Used	CTT03	81	**Weight**	O	R 1/10
			Numeric value of weight		
Not Used	CTT04	355	**Unit or Basis for Measurement Code**	X	ID 2/2
			Code specifying the units in which a value is being expressed, or manner in which a measurement has been taken		
			Refer to 003040 Data Element Dictionary for acceptable code values.		
Not Used	CTT05	183	**Volume**	O	R 1/8
			Value of volumetric measure		
Not Used	CTT06	355	**Unit or Basis for Measurement Code**	X	ID 2/2
			Code specifying the units in which a value is being expressed, or manner in which a measurement has been taken		
			Refer to 003040 Data Element Dictionary for acceptable code values.		
Not Used	CTT07	352	**Description**	O	AN 1/80
			A free-form description to clarify the related data elements and their content		

Segment:	**AMT** Monetary Amount
Position:	020
Loop:	
Level:	Summary
Usage:	Optional
Max Use:	1
Purpose:	To indicate the total monetary amount
Syntax Notes:	
Semantic Notes:	
Comments:	
Notes:	*Use this segment to provide the total amount of the order.*

Data Element Summary

	Ref. Des.	Data Element	Name	Attributes	
Must Use	AMT01	522	**Amount Qualifier Code**	M	ID 1/2
			Code to qualify amount		
			TT Total Transaction Amount		
Must Use	AMT02	782	**Monetary Amount**	M	R 1/15
			Monetary amount		

Segment:	**SE** Transaction Set Trailer	
Position:	030	
Loop:		
Level:	Summary	
Usage:	Mandatory	
Max Use:	1	
Purpose:	To indicate the end of the transaction set and provide the count of the transmitted segments (including the beginning (ST) and ending (SE) segments).	
Syntax Notes:		
Semantic Notes:		
Comments:	1	SE is the last segment of each transaction set.

Data Element Summary

	Ref. Des.	Data Element	Name		Attributes
Must Use	SE01	96	**Number of Included Segments**	M	N0 1/10
			Total number of segments included in a transaction set including ST and SE segments		
Must Use	SE02	329	**Transaction Set Control Number**	M	AN 4/9
			Identifying control number that must be unique within the transaction set functional group assigned by the originator for a transaction set		
			Enter the same number cited in ST02.		

Glossary of EDI Terms

ACH—Automated Clearing House.

ANSI—American National Standards Institute.

ANSI ASC X12—The Accredited Standards Committee X12 includes members from government and industry in North America who create EDI draft standards for submission to ANSI. A move to merge ANSI ASC X12 with EDIFACT began in 1997. Also known as ANSI X12 or ASC X12.

ANSI standard—A specification document that is issued by the ANSI. Prior to release, designated industry committees use public consensus and review procedures for approval. Each standard is reviewed by the issuing committee within five years for update.

Application acknowledgement—A transaction set designed to respond to an EDI transaction set that has been received and processed. The purchase order acknowledgement is an example of an application acknowledgement. It is used to respond to the purchase order, presenting such things as whether the receiver can fulfill the order and if it can be done in time.

Application advice—A transaction set that documents errors in the content of any transaction set beyond the normal syntax checks.

ASC—Accredited Standards Committee.

Authentication—Permits the receiver of an electronic transmission to verify the sender and the integrity of the content of the transmission; typically makes use of an electronic key or algorithm that is shared by the trading partners. This is sometimes referred to as an *electronic signature*.

CCITT—Consultative Committee on International Telegraphy and Telephony.

Ciphertext—The encrypted output of a cryptograph algorithm. Ciphertext serves as the input to the decryption process.

Clear text—Original, unencrypted data. Used as input to the encryption process or can be the output of the decryption process.

Compliance checking—A validation process that is used to ensure that a transmission complies with ANSI X12 or EDIFACT syntax rules.

Component—A component, sometimes referred to as a *subelement*, is a subdivision of an element. Components are rarely used in ASC X12 transaction sets. However, EDIFACT transaction sets frequently make use of components.

Cross Reference File (xrf)—A file that you can create to list all segments and elements within a transaction set. It also includes segment numbers, offsets (column positions), element lengths, and data type information.

Data element—The basic unit of information in the EDI standards containing a value that represents an individual fact. It may be a single-character code, a plaintext description, or a numeric value. Examples of a data element are: price, product code, and product attribute such as size or color.

Data element separator—A unique character preceding each data element that is used to delimit data elements within a data segment.

Data element type—A data element may be one of six types: numeric, decimal, identifier, string, data, or time.

Data Interchange Standards Association—The Secretariat and administrative arm of ANSI X12.

Data segment—A well-defined string of alternating data elements and data element separators. This is similar to a line item on a business form.

Decryption—A process of transforming ciphertext into clear text for security or privacy reasons.

Delimiters—These consist of two levels of separators and a terminator. The delimiters are an integral part of the transferred data stream. Delimiters are specified in the interchange header and may not be used in a data element value elsewhere in the interchange. From highest to lowest level, the separators and terminators are segment terminators, data element separators, and subelement separators.

Direct transmission—The exchange of data from the computer of the sending party directly to the computer of the receiving party. A third-party value-added service is not used in a direct transmission code.

DISA—See Data Interchange Standards Association.

EC—See Electronic commerce.

EDI—Electronic Data Interchange. A format in which business data is represented using national or international standards. See also ANSI ASC X12 and EDIFACT.

EDIA—Electronic Data Interchange Association. A nonprofit, public interest organization designed to develop, foster, and maintain a program of action to achieve coordination of data and information systems by the standardization of descriptions and codes for intracompany computer-to-computer EDI for business transactions.

EDIFACT—Electronic Data Interchange For Administration, Commerce, and Trade. "UN" was added to EDIFACT to indicate messages are approved as United Nations international standards for EDI. Thirty-seven countries are currently implementing UN/EDIFACT. A move to merge ANSI X12 with EDIFACT began in 1997.

EDI mail—EDI standard documents, such as purchase orders, invoices, and functional acknowledgements, that are sent to and received from trading partners.

EDI translation—The conversion of application data to and from an EDI standard format.

EDI translator—The computer software used to perform the conversion of application data to and from an EDI standard format.

EFT—Electronic Funds Transfer.

Electronic commerce—Transacting business via electronic means. This includes all forms of electronic media such as fax, e-mail, and EDI. Electronic commerce is not restricted to EDI only.

Electronic envelope—Catch-all term for the electronic address, communications transport protocols, and control information. It is the electronic analogy of a paper envelope, i.e., a communications package.

Electronic mailbox—The place where EDI transmission is stored for pickup or delivery within third-party service provider's system. Trading partners can also maintain mailboxes within their own domain.

Element—The smallest entity found within an EDI transaction set. Elements comprise segments. You can think of a segment as a record and an element as a field within the record.

E-mail—Electronic mail. Text messages sent from one person to another person, on the same or different computer systems. Systems at the same building or site may be connected together with a LAN, while systems at different sites are generally connected by a WAN.

Encryption—A process of transforming clear text into ciphertext for security or privacy reasons.

Facsimile (or FAX) machine—A scanner/printer combination that transmits text and graphics over telephone lines. It uses CCITT Group 3 data compression techniques. Small paper documents can be transmitted over long distances very quickly. However, the information is not parsed into structured data elements as in EDI.

Functional acknowledgement (FA)—A message or transaction set transmitted by the recipient of an EDI transaction back to the sender. The FA indicates receipt and syntactical acceptance of the transmitted data (as specified in the governing EDI standard). The FA allows the receiving party to report back problems encountered by their syntax checker as data is interpreted. Note that an FA is not intended to serve as an acknowledgement of the accuracy of the data within the transaction set.

Functional group—A group of one or more messages or transaction sets bounded by a functional group header segment and a functional group trailer segment. It is a collection of electronic document information for the same business application.

GENCOD—French retail industry standard.

Industry convention—A subset of EDI standards used by a specific industry.

Industry guideline—Used to establish governing EDI conventions within different industries, thereby providing useful information on how to interpret and apply the governing EDI standards.

ISO—International Organization for Standardization.

JIT—Just in time (inventory).

LAN—Local Area Network. LANs are usually restricted to a building. See also Router and WAN.

Mapping—The process of identifying which segments and data elements are used within a transaction set. Trading partners must agree on the format of a transaction set by using transaction set guidelines similar to those contained in Appendix A.

Message—In the U.S., a message is the entire data stream including the outer envelope. Outside the U.S., a message is the equivalent of a transaction set in the U.S.

ODETTE—European automotive industry standard.

PAEB—The Pan American EDIFACT Board is separate from ANSI X12, and it serves as the coordinating body on EDI for national standards organizations of North, Central, and South America.

Parse—The separation and/or conversion of data from one format to another to make it usable in another application. For example, the data found in the segments and interior elements of an EDI transaction set may be parsed into database records and fields for subsequent processing by an external computer application.

Proprietary format—A data format specific to a company, industry, or other limited group. Proprietary formats do not comply with EDI standards.

Router—The bridge between two or more LANs. a LAN and a WAN, or a LAN/WAN to Internet Service.

Scheduler—Trading Partner Desktop and Trading Partner Workgroup includes a scheduler feature that automatically runs one or more task lists at a predetermined time. (See Task list.)

Security—The process of monitoring access to a system and its information for the purpose of denying unauthorized use and to protect data from unauthorized disclosure. See Encryption.

SGML—Standard Generalized Markup Language, ISO standard 8879.

SPEC 2000—Airline industry standard for spare parts.

Subelement—See Component.

Syntax—The grammar or rules that define the structure of EDI standards.

Task list—Trading Partner Desktop and Trading Partner Workgroup has a Task List feature which is used to build a list of processing tasks in a list. Like a program script, each task is run as encountered. Task lists can be arranged in hierarchical order so that system- and network-level task lists call trading partner-level task lists.

TDCC—Transportation Data Coordinating Committee.

TPA—Trading Partner Agreement.

TRADACOMS—United Kingdom retail industry standard.

Trading partner—The sending and/or receiving party involved in the exchange of EDI transmissions.

Transaction set—In the U.S., a transaction set uses standard syntax to define business information. It must include a transaction set header segment, one or more data segments in a predetermined order, and a transaction set trailer segment.

Outside the U.S., transaction sets generally comply with EDIFACT standards. EDIFACT transaction sets also use header segments, interior data segments, and trailer segments. Just as in the U.S., these are the electronic equivalent of a business document or form.

Translation—The process of accepting and converting a nonstandard document into an EDI standard document format.

UCS—Uniform Communications Standard for the grocery industry.

UN/EDIFACT—See EDIFACT.

UPC—Universal Product Code.

VAN—Value-added network. These are usually third-party service organizations.

VDA—German automotive industry standard.

VICS—Voluntary Interindustry Communication Standard for the retail industry.

WAN—Wide Area Network. A WAN is usually used to connect LANs through routers.

WINS—Warehouse Information Network Standard.

X12—See ANSI ASC X12.

Index

I don't have time for learning curves.

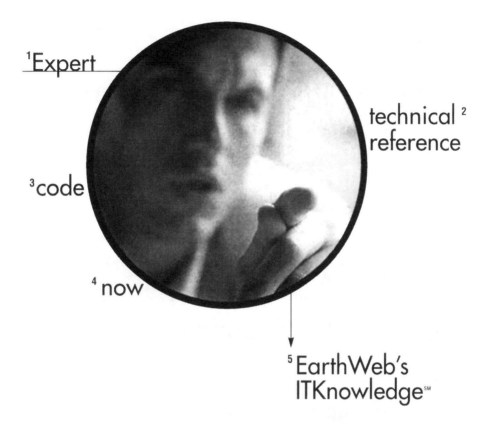

[1]Expert

technical [2]
reference

[3]code

[4] now

[5] EarthWeb's
ITKnowledge^{SM}

They rely on you to be the **❶** expert on tough development challenges. There's no time for learning curves, so you go online for **❷** technical references from the experts who wrote the books. Find answers fast simply by clicking on our search engine. Access hundreds of online books, tutorials and even source **❸** code samples **❹** now. Go to **❺** EarthWeb's ITKnowledge, get immediate answers, and get down to it.

Get your FREE ITKnowledge trial subscription today at itkgo.com.
Use code number 026.

EARTHWEB
Go further *faster*

About the CD

The companion CD includes a working version of Trading Partner Desktop EDI software from Mercator Software. The program has all necessary files, including asynchronous communications programs and transaction sets, that are required to operate with the hands-on activities contained in this book. You can install and use the program for a 60-day period. The Trading Partner Desktop should autorun. When the Setup screen appears, click the icon to the left of Trading Partner and follow the prompts. The License Key is a211cd56.

A Samples folder is also included on the CD. This folder contains the files that are referred to in Part 2 of this book. It also contains a spare copy of the Fieldlst.exe utility that is used to create cross reference (xrf) files from database map (dbm) files. This process is described in detail in Chapter 10. Use Windows Explorer to access this folder.

NOTE: The Trading Partner Desktop software included on the CD that is supplied with this book is provided to you in accordance with the terms of an agreement between Mercator Software, Inc. (MSI) and Wordware Publishing, Inc. MSI is not responsible for technical support or for any failures of the software. You should only contact MSI if you wish to discuss the purchase of the production version of either the Trading Partner Desktop or Trading Partner Workgroup software.

WARNING: Opening the CD package makes this book nonreturnable.

CD/Source Code Usage License Agreement

Please read the following CD/Source Code usage license agreement before opening the CD and using the contents therein:

1. By opening the accompanying software package, you are indicating that you have read and agree to be bound by all terms and conditions of this CD/Source Code usage license agreement.

2. The compilation of code and utilities contained on the CD and in the book are copyrighted and protected by both U.S. copyright law and international copyright treaties, and is owned by Wordware Publishing, Inc. Individual source code, example programs, help files, freeware, shareware, utilities, and evaluation packages, including their copyrights, are owned by the respective authors.

3. No part of the enclosed CD or this book, including all source code, help files, shareware, freeware, utilities, example programs, or evaluation programs, may be made available on a public forum (such as a World Wide Web page, FTP site, bulletin board, or Internet news group) without the express written permission of Wordware Publishing, Inc. or the author of the respective source code, help files, shareware, freeware, utilities, example programs, or evaluation programs.

4. You may not decompile, reverse engineer, disassemble, create a derivative work, or otherwise use the enclosed programs, help files, freeware, shareware, utilities, or evaluation programs except as stated in this agreement.

5. The software, contained on the CD and/or as source code in this book, is sold without warranty of any kind. Wordware Publishing, Inc. and the authors specifically disclaim all other warranties, express or implied, including but not limited to implied warranties of merchantability and fitness for a particular purpose with respect to defects in the disk, the program, source code, sample files, help files, freeware, shareware, utilities, and evaluation programs contained therein, and/or the techniques described in the book and implemented in the example programs. In no event shall Wordware Publishing, Inc., its dealers, its distributors, or the authors be liable or held responsible for any loss of profit or any other alleged or actual private or commercial damage, including but not limited to special, incidental, consequential, or other damages.

6. One (1) copy of the CD or any source code therein may be created for backup purposes. The CD and all accompanying source code, sample files, help files, freeware, shareware, utilities, and evaluation programs may be copied to your hard drive. With the exception of freeware and shareware programs, at no time can any part of the contents of this CD reside on more than one computer at one time. The contents of the CD can be copied to another computer, as long as the contents of the CD contained on the original computer are deleted.

7. You may not include any part of the CD contents, including all source code, example programs, shareware, freeware, help files, utilities, or evaluation programs in any compilation of source code, utilities, help files, example programs, freeware, shareware, or evaluation programs on any media, including but not limited to CD, disk, or Internet distribution, without the express written permission of Wordware Publishing, Inc. or the owner of the individual source code, utilities, help files, example programs, freeware, shareware, or evaluation programs.

8. You may use the source code, techniques, and example programs in your own commercial or private applications unless otherwise noted by additional usage agreements as found on the CD.